P9-AQM-887

GOD AND THE SUPERNATURAL

GOD AND THE SUPERNATURAL

A CATHOLIC STATEMENT OF THE CHRISTIAN FAITH

By

M. C. D'ARCY, S.J.
FR. CUTHBERT, O.F.M.Cap.
CHRISTOPHER DAWSON
C. C. MARTINDALE, S.J.
E. I. WATKIN

Abridged Edition

SHEED AND WARD
NEW YORK · 1954

FIRST PUBLISHED 1920
ABRIDGED EDITION 1936
REPRINTED 1954
BY SHEED AND WARD LTD.
33 MAIDEN LANE,
LONDON, W.C.2
AND
SHEED AND WARD INC.
840 BROADWAY
NEW YORK 3

IMPRIMATUR
✠ JOSEPH BUTT
WESTMONASTERII, DIE 10A JULII, 1936

MANUFACTURED IN THE UNITED STATES OF AMERICA

CONTENTS

PREFACE TO ABRIDGED EDITION

IN presenting to the public a new edition of *God and the Supernatural*, it may be well to state that apart from the omission of two essays, which substantially reduces the bulk of the book, omissions due to changed circumstances, and a few literary corrections, the text remains the same as in the first edition.

One omission is that of the Introductory essay contributed by Fr. Ronald A. Knox, in which he analysed the religious situation existing in England in 1920 when the book was first published. That situation has in many respects changed during the past fifteen years; consequently the essay can no longer claim to give an accurate survey of religious thought in England to-day. For this reason the author requested that his essay should now be withdrawn. The essay on the Person of Christ has also been withdrawn. The essay was written with a view to certain opinions current at the time the book was first published. The writer the more readily withdraws the essay, since he has more fully, and to his mind more satisfactorily, written on this mystery of the Catholic Faith in his more recent book, *In Christ*.

For the same reason that they are now out of date, certain illustrative passages in the other essays have either been deleted or rewritten. The allusions in these passages were to contemporary events or opinions which have since ceased to have vital interest to the public mind. The Synopsis of the essays have given place to an index much fuller than that to the first edition, for which the Editor thanks Miss D. C. Borton.

EDITOR'S PREFACE TO THE FIRST EDITION

THE question is sometimes asked, "Is Christianity a failure?" The answer to such a question will largely depend upon a man's temperament or mental outlook: as often as not, upon his ignorance more than upon his knowledge.

Before we can say whether Christianity has succeeded or failed, we must know what Christ and His Church set out to accomplish; before we can say whether the Christian creed is still vital or practically dead, we must know what that creed is.

The great mass of the English-speaking race, if asked to define positively what Christianity stands for in the world, would find it difficult to give a clear, unambiguous answer. The word "Christianity" has come to mean so much and so little. When it means much it is commonly a strongly felt but vaguely understood sentiment; whilst intellectually it may stand for almost anything according to the theory or opinion of the individual.

But mostly it means so little: a fashion of speech with no definite idea behind it; a form of worship hardly, if at all, understood.

And yet the ordinary English-speaking citizen is not irreligious—still less anti-religious—in sentiment. Creedless and irresponsive to "the churches" he may be, but he is seldom lacking in religious sensibility of some sort.

But a religion without a creed, though it may seem sufficient when life runs smoothly, does not suffice in a crisis when a man is brought face to face with the mystery and difficulty of life. Then for practical purposes it will be a religion with a creed or no religion at all. Lacking an accepted, authoritative creed, the religiously inclined will seek to make a creed for themselves.

The writers of this book are not concerned to discuss why it is that Christianity has come to mean so little to the mass of our people. They have merely faced the fact that Christianity as a substantive and intelligent Faith has been lost and is practically unknown to the people at large; and in the following pages they have made an attempt to set forth the fundamental doctrines of the Christian Faith as those are held by the members of that Church which claims, and has ever claimed, to be the depository of the Faith of Christ. They, therefore, expound no new creed, but the historic creed of the Catholic Church.

Both as a Creed and as a Church, Catholicism for long has been the unknown quantity in the religious experience of the English-speaking world; and because unknown outside the Catholic body itself, it has been misrepresented and generally ignored. And yet, if the present writers are right in their judgment, many who to-day speak of Christianity as a failure and are casting about for a religious creed, will find in the Catholic Faith the "unknown God" whom in their spiritual restlessness they are seeking.

This book is written in no controversial spirit: the writers have merely endeavoured to set forth the doctrine of the Faith they hold, in language intelligible to the ordinary educated reader.

They have not written for the professed theologian: their book is not meant for the theological schools. For this reason they have, as far as possible, avoided the technical language of Catholic theology. They know by experience how frequently the technical terminology familiar to the theologian, is not only unintelligible to the lay reader, but is apt to be positively misunderstood and to convey utterly erroneous notions of the doctrine expounded.

Where the writers necessarily join issue with current religious theories or opinions, they do so with a deep appreciation of the earnestness and sincerity which commonly lie behind even the "heresies" as they regard them.

Though written by different writers this book, we trust, will be found to have a vital and organic unity: it is not a collection of disparate essays. The writers have been left free to develop their different theses and to express themselves according to their individualities; but, besides the fact that they hold the same Faith, they have been guided by a fundamental common purpose and a common sympathetic outlook on the world around them.

How far they have achieved their purpose of making the Faith they hold intelligible to the seeker after truth, is a question others must answer. The defects of the book are theirs: whatever of vital value there is in it belongs to the Faith itself.

FR. CUTHBERT, O.F.M.Cap.

I

THE SUPERNATURAL

BY

C. C. MARTINDALE, S.J.

ALL very great things are presumably very simple; and about simple things it is hard ever to say much. Now under the whole of Catholic faith and practice lies a great, yet very simple, notion and doctrine of the Supernatural. Much, in both creed and code, is scarcely more than its departmental expression: its relation to the Natural, and its way of working once it is brought into any such relation. It is at once clear, therefore, how much vaster in its sweep the notion itself needs must be, how far more huge the fact, than its various applications and functionings.

Hence it is obvious that no book, which purports to set forth Catholic doctrine in a coherent and really intelligible way, can do without a chapter, placed quite at the beginning, which shall explain that notion without which so much of the rest were meaningless. It is true that at the end, and after seeing the thing at work, we shall have a much richer idea of what it is; but some sort of idea we must force ourselves to gain at the very outset, lest the essence of what follows be looked for where it is not.

But the very vast may well be the very simple; and many words may have to seek their excuse simply from the confusion which surrounds the idea we believe to be the true one, or because it has grown so unfamiliar to the majority of our countrymen that only by a very serious effort, and by being stated in many different ways, can it even be grasped at all by our unaccustomed brains.

I

In the English temperament there is a curious alliance of shyness and of enterprise. It is English to be a pioneer; by the "white man's burden" we mean our own, manfully shouldered in an India or an Egypt. We regret "spacious days" by-gone, when we had more of a chance to disregard red-tape entanglements, laws of sea and land; we still cherish a liking for raids. Our enthusiastic appropriation of the Americanism "stunt" meant that we had found a word to suit an instinct; we even concoct imaginary goals, and set up an infinity of artificial hindrances, that we may play a Game; and we play it, they say, all the better once it looks to be a losing one.

Yet until latterly, at any rate, we adored custom, if not always law, provided they were our own customs. Three-quarters of the Englishman's rudeness when "abroad" was sheer panic lest he should make a fool of himself among customs he knew nothing of, and therefore did not like. In obstinate self-defence he carried his determination to have bacon and eggs for breakfast into the oddest places, and he always thought French a silly language.

Still, there is a different and more lovable side to our national coyness: we have developed a very real sense of truth and honour, which makes a halo round what concerns property, and a sentiment which idealizes the home. Again, we go out, grumblingly I know, and endure extreme hardship when somehow our sense of duty, or just docility, dictate it. But it *is* "duty," rather than the "hope" or desire of the "glory," which the fine and popular song suggests as the motive and aim of England.

All this shows that it is essential for our race to live in a materialistic mist with rays of the ideal confusedly penetrating it. We cannot do without either. We undoubtedly have the "business," but we are miserable without some sort of "dream." "A dream cometh through the multitude of the business." When we pursue the dream we go the longest way about it and rejoice in "muddling" through. But the point is, we *must* have both. Therefore it is ours to like to have ideas, but to hate isolating them and looking them squarely in the face; even a fact we don't care to examine too curiously. We, in our land of pale-tinted skies, and grey-green landscapes, and unclear horizons, have a love for unproved origins, hazy outlines, and half-ambiguous ends. In practice we constantly reconcile contradictions. See the development of our Empire! It "makes for righteousness," so we most reasonably believe; but by a zigzag course, and from starting-points preferably forgotten. See our Constitution, unsystematic, singular resultant of inter-corrective forces, a bewilderment for the logical "Roman"!

This practical attitude is ours in regard to all that is pre-eminently called the Transcendent. We disregard, distrust, and even brutally deny it; and yet all the while are at its mercy. We proclaim our affection for "hard facts," and succumb, each of us, to our little private superstitions. In America, where "business" is fiercer, the revenge of the Transcendent has been more violent: materialist millionaires have been the softest of sentimentalists, and politicians the most academic of idealists.

You need not go to music halls to see how sentimental Englishmen really are. In religion it is much the same. Since the Reformation, most of the *intellectualism* has been exiled from the national religion; much too of the ascetic moral will. Sentiment, which was always there, has tended to be left, and alone left, in our religions of personal experience, direct "communion" with our God, and of individual conscience. "Sometimes," a lady once said to me, "I feel that Jesus Christ *must* be God, and then I feel He *can't* be." From childhood, religion associates itself with tender sentiment—that is, until its vetoes awaken a resentful mood, and even then there are reactions. Quite grown-up men feel good, or regretful that they are bad, or vaguely hopeful to be better, in response to the spinal tremor due to the deep notes of an organ.

Not that we are sneering, assuredly, at sentiment. Most of its up-gushes, it is true, denote an escape, for the while, into the unreal and foster a sweet lie within the soul, and make us pretend we believe in their misconstruing of the world and of ourselves; but sentiment, as such, may be, and should be, a normal and quite reputable reaction of alive humanity to certain challenges.

But we go further. I fancy that the best ghost or fairy-tales come from Germany and England. And it is we and Germany who come in second—a bad second, I confess, after America—in the race for the Transcendent, as expressed in all sorts of occultisms, spiritualism, Christian Science or New Thought. Not that we are altogether vulgar. Blake was the supreme revelation, I suppose, of a real and by no means rare factor in our temperament. Christian Science has added little save the relatively new attempt to philosophize the northern mystical impetus. In our old-fashioned Christianity the strange dogma of "conversion" sufficed to account for individualist up-rushes of religious sentiment, crystallizing at times into forms of really new behaviour and even sects. But, I am bound to say, the charm and dignity of that old Evangelicism has evaporated from the spiritualisms of to-day. They cease to interest, once they try to state their philosophy, so second-rate are they, and so indicative of our incapacity, to which I alluded, for clear ideas; and we regret this manipulation of ancient and venerable notions by fingers so far from expert.

But looking at our country, and at America, quite generally, who can fail to notice that at no period in their history, and now less than ever, when business and science so preoccupy us, when we are so resolute that creeds and Churches are done with, has the revenge of the Transcendent so violently declared itself; the instinct for something not to be confined within the limits of getting, or even of knowing. Popular, noisy, fantastic, this phenomenon often is; or again, draped in the robes of science or of philosophy. Every bookstall, every Sunday paper, the lifts and placarded corridors of Tubes, announce that it is there; the frequenters of those lecture-halls and readers of that literature clearly enough proclaim that no mere re-ordering of the beggarly elements of this world, no *mere* "reconstruction," will be enough for them. Morbid as we believe this symptom to be, altogether out of proportion to a true balance of a man's psychic powers, we have said enough to show that a doctrine of the Supernatural is not in itself alien to part of the total make-up of our compatriots; and we are accustomed, I think rightly, to surmise that any strong instinct ought, in some way or other, to be satisfied. *Mere* repression, as the doctrines of psycho-analysis no less than ancient common sense most irrefutably make clear, is apt to be dangerous. Happy may a man deem himself should he discover a doctrine, even if not demonstrably true, which both takes account of the instinct we have described, and does not overstimulate it; which disentangles or states its meaning clearly, and in practice guides and governs it. It can still do all that, even if it turn out to be essentially superior in origin, work or aim, to any human instinct whatsoever.

I begin, therefore, by saying that the Catholic Church emphatically states that there exists an order of existence which is to be called supernatural, quite as truly as there obviously exists a way of being which we call "natural" and to which we are accustomed; and that the two are meant to be brought into relation with one another. The Church is not so optimistic as to suggest that all these cravings after and dabblings with the "preternatural" or at least preternormal, are right; but she is by no means so disdainfully pessimistic as to say they need be wholly wrong.[1] Precisely because she so thoroughly understands and caters for the Natural, she is prepared to explain it to itself and guide it towards what it so much desires and so restlessly gropes after, the Supernatural.

[1] Spiritualism, e.g., she does not say to be wholly wrong, though as practised by Spiritualists it is wrong.

II

I wish, therefore, to state as clearly as possible what the Catholic doctrine of the Supernatural is, avoiding, as far as I can, the technical formulæ of theology, or else explaining them succinctly.

(i)

I must first say that it is a perfectly definite doctrine with an exact meaning, and you must forget all connotations you may have given to the word. It does not only mean what outstrips the ordinary powers of human nature. There is no vague association here with the mysterious or even the miraculous; still less with the magical, the visionary, or the ghostly.

Our doctrine has to do with the free gift, offered by God to man, and by man freely appropriated, of a way of *being*—not of acting, or thinking, or feeling, save by consequence[1]—higher than what is co-natural to him. To keep this constantly in the memory, I will write the word hyphened—"super-natural"—throughout the remainder of this chapter.

A super-human life, therefore, is given to and can be appropriated by Humanity.

For Catholic dogma implies that life, in the full sense, is not the common property of all that exists; while of some things that exist it is not a property at all. Thus, a stone cannot in any true sense be said to *live*: a flower indeed "lives," and it can "die"; but its life is more circumscribed in kind than, say, a lion's. Catholic philosophy does not tolerate, and we think never will, the claim of any scientist who says that *all* matter lives (as some are forced to maintain, to support their hypothesis that no *break* can have taken place in evolution, and that whatever we observe in the very highest must have been in germ in quite the lowest); matter as such, we consider, has not been discovered, and cannot successfully be surmised even *ever* to "come to life," as they say, automatically; nor does our normal philosophy allow that under pressure of any "cosmic evolution" the life of a plant can evolve or be developed by any culture, into the life of the animal. The border-line may indeed be difficult, in this case or that, to designate; but we certainly maintain that all things are definitely on this side or that of *a* line which

[1] Or under the transient influence of "actual grace" in those not yet living supernaturally.

demarcates the living from the non-living, and even the highest and most seemingly independent form of plant life from the most undifferentiated form of animal life, and that the gulf, how narrow soever, is unfathomable and unbridged.

We do, however, quite definitely assert that a break exists between any form or condition of matter, and intelligent life. We would far rather admit that *all* life was intelligent, and that with such life all that existed was endowed—contrary as this would be to observation and experiment—than allow that any kind of life, recognized as non-intelligent, that is, non-spiritual, could be evolved or developed into the life of intelligence and free-will as possessed by man. Indeed, the average man will roundly assert that his *kind* of life does differ from the *kind* of life which the plant or the animal possesses; and we assert that any "scientific" hypothesis which proclaims the opposite *is* but hypothesis, unproved by any evidence, and philosophically demonstrably false. We declare that the power, say, of recollection, the fact of self-consciousness, reflection, and the phenomenon of choice, none of which we admit to be disproved by any discovery or invalidated by any theory whatsoever, do indeed *essentially* differentiate human life from any lower form.

If more, again, be needed as commentary on this, it will be found where a later chapter speaks of the nature of man. Only it must be remembered that all this belongs strictly or at any rate primarily, to philosophy, and not theology. We hold that neither contradicts the other, but we acknowledge that if a man be possessed of what we maintain to be false philosophical beliefs, he will be likely to hold our theology to be false; or, if he says he holds it as "true," he will be using the word "true" in a different sense from ours, and mean "symbolically" true, perhaps, or else pragmatically, that is, that it will work, that it has its value, while as to its essential truth or falseness he will not pronounce.

He must, however, remember that any attack on Catholic theology is waste of powder and shot, if the assailant's underlying philosophical principles are at variance with those held by the Catholic theologian. Readers, then, of this book will be constantly reminded of our philosophical principles, though it is not directly written upon philosophy.

Now I will state a minimum. No one can possibly assert that there *can* be no higher form of life than the human. In fact no dogmatic arrogance, surely, would declare that human life *exhausts the possi-*

bilities of Life. As well might the rose assert there *can* be no lion; or the lion, no man. It is no doubt true that human thought, unaided, cannot affirm that there *is* any such super-human life, save that of God Himself.[1] But while reason might surmise that there could be a super-human kind of life; and while human imagination has at all times played with the thought that there may be; the great intuitives or mystics have cried loudly that there is. And with them, in this proclamation at least, the Catholic Church is in accord, though for reasons other than theirs.

She dogmatically declares that there *is* a super-human life, and that it is God's free will to raise thereto such members of the human race as freely co-operate with His design, so that they, remaining men, are yet "super-natural" men; for this life is not one that *belongs* to beings of a higher order, so that men cease to be men and become that sort of being; nor yet, are men made by it into a sort of being altogether different. They remain men, but super-naturalized men.

And I will here recall once more the scope of this book, which is, not to prove that the doctrine of the Church is true, but clearly to set out what it is. Yet, later in this volume, indications will be given as to *why* the Church considers she is justified in teaching at all, and why she holds that her teaching is necessarily true. Nowhere, in the Catholic system, is there any question of blind unmotived faith, and I would beg readers, for the time, to keep out of their minds all that they may mean, personally, by the word faith, and all such phrases as "taking things on faith," or any idea that they are being asked to take some leap into any sort of dark. We are here asking you to listen to *what* we say, and not *why* we say it, save in a secondary way.

The Church then says that there is offered to man the chance of living by a super-human life. It is not merely a lofty and moral life, not an unselfish life only, not just a devout, sinless, prayerful life: it is nothing into which, by any process of purification and inspiration, human life can be raised or developed within its natural functionings and out of its natural resources or possibilities; it is the fruit of no culture nor of admonition or stimulus even from God directed to co-natural plane or elements of man's existence. It is not then a life that can be merited by any human effort such as the

[1] That human thought not only can conceive of the "possibility" of God, but ought to assert that as a matter of demonstrated fact, He does exist, is set forth below. See Essay III.

happiness which is his who at last perfectly achieves success in any field where his human energies find play; still less is it a life *owed* to humanity, as though it were needed by or suited to its proportionate perfection, as a full equipment, say, of limb, and sense-organs, or an adequate brain, may be said to be owed to and normally might be claimed by anyone who is meant to be fully a man. But it is a life directly imposed by God totally transcending the elements which compose human nature and what, left to themselves, they could use; just as to move freely about transcends what a flower can do; or to work out a mathematical problem, what a dog can do. Yet it is wholly in harmony with human nature, somewhat as mind totally and in its nature transcends brain, and yet is able, and in a sense needs, to work with the brain for its organ. It is, even, a more complete interweaving of more disparate elements than that of the spiritual significance of a sonata by Beethoven with the sounds as struck upon a piano, or even, as received in my brain and ear.

(ii)

It is taught that this super-human life, though not owed to human nature, is none the less intended by God for human nature; and was in fact given by Him to man at the beginning of human history. This is the meaning of our formula, "Adam was created in grace." For Grace (*gratia*) means "free gift," and the free gift in question is, precisely, this super-natural life. But the gift was given, not absolutely, but conditionally; and owing to the non-fulfilment of the condition, on which they held it, by our first parents, they in fact lost it and were reduced to their co-natural condition merely. They were to keep the gift if they obeyed a moral obligation laid upon them; they disobeyed, and lost it. This, strictly, is the meaning of the dogma of the Fall. It does *not* mean, degeneration from any high state of natural civilization; nor, again, that any wound was directly inflicted upon human nature as such; still less that human nature is now corrupt and vile and capable only of sin. But though nature suffered in many ways the counter-shock of the deprivation of super-natural grace, the Fall, as such, does not concern just nature, but occurred on the super-natural plane: our knowledge of this is entirely a matter of revelation, and anthropology has nothing whatever to say about it, for or against. All that this doctrine immediately states is, that human nature, ever since it has existed, was capable of recognizing and therefore of obeying or disobeying a moral injunction: it disobeyed; and a super-natural consequence attended upon the disobedience. I do not enlarge upon the indirect consequences of this "sin" in the natural life of man, nor discuss any *details* concerning the central super-natural event.

Besides this, the Church teaches that Adam was regarded as no isolated individual, but as Head of the human race, and as summing it up in himself; and that, accordingly, "in Adam all died"; by virtue of our social solidarity with him, we too were deprived of the super-natural life he forfeited. Since, of course, all this will be properly treated of below, I need not here indicate how on the one hand this doctrine of social solidarity, proper to the entire human race, so that no man stands or falls by himself, is thoroughly in harmony with modern social ideals and aspirations; but I will just recall that no *injustice* was done to unborn generations by their birth *without* a gift which was utterly not *owed* to them. This is doubly true when we recall the complementary doctrine of *Original Sin*—which, again, is no positive taint or corruption inherent in our nature, but a negative fact, the deprivation of an un-owed super-human gift intended by God for us—namely, *Ultimate Redemption*. It is clear that, since we could never have earned, or ourselves by our own powers have gained, that super-human asset, so neither can we, by our own powers, regain it. But as we should have had it but lost it, owing to our social solidarity with one who possessed it but lost it, so we shall repossess it by our incorporation with a Second Adam who possesses it and will not lose it. A new Head for a new Race was forthwith promised; one who should Himself contain that Life and should, to all incorporate with Him, impart it. This was the Son of God made man, Jesus Christ, who not only had the Life as a gift, but had it, and better than it, as His co-natural way of being. "As in Adam all died, even so in Christ shall all be made alive." Incorporate with Adam, we lived by his life and died in his death. Incorporate with Christ, we share, and better than of old, in that super-human life which springs from His own nature, and *is* this nature, in so far as the human can be, by God's operation, mated with the Divine. *Felix culpa, quæ tantum atque talem meruit Redemptorem.* True, just as in the first instance, Grace was not forced on Adam, and the Fall was free; so neither will the Ultimate Redemption be forced upon us; we must freely choose it, though, it will be seen, to that very choice God *helps* us. But "to as many as receive Him, to them gives He power to become Children of God," who heretofore were children of men merely; and the new society, thus formed of all who are organically united with the Second and better Adam, forms that super-humanized race, or body, which is called the Church.[1]

Such is the past history of the Super-natural Life in the world, and such, so to say, its actual primary product: social incorporation with Christ, the Church.

(iii)

Its implications, however, can be further defined. To all forms of life a form of consciousness belongs, higher in kind as the life itself is in kind higher, so that a man is aware of his friend in a way in which a dog is not of his master. So, to this super-human life belongs a super-human way of consciousness; and since all forms of consciousness may be described in terms of union with their object, so, too, this super-human consciousness involves a super-human form of union with its object, God. And to that of which a man is conscious, he can unite himself, again, by will, or separate himself therefrom; and he loves it or hates it. And in proportion as he loves it, he grows like it, and an assimilation, and even a quasi-identification, comes about. So, when a man truly loves a woman who deserves that love, not only he all but automatically eliminates from himself all that offends her—for that tends to separate them, and so he hates it, and springs away from it; but also, he thereby grows most beautifully like that which in her he sees to be so beautiful, and which, indeed, will have revealed in himself as hateful, and henceforth impossible, much that he may so far have tolerated in his own loveless life. Now it is certain that even natural consciousness and reason can in their measure be aware of God, and enable the will to unite itself to Him who, it is seen, is infinitely preferable to all else; and thereby a gradual assimilation of human nature to that which is its source and goal can, without any over-stepping of its bounds, be achieved. But if the Super-natural Life, as I have described it, be a fact, it follows that there goes along with it not only a super-natural consciousness of God, but a super-natural adhesion of the will to Him by love directly infused by Him, and a super-natural union of the whole soul with Him, its super-natural assimilation to Him, and participation in Him. But this conscious-

[1] See Essay VIII.

ness, at present, is imperfect; it is in a sense inhibited; but the substance of that which shall issue into it is there; it may be said, that though they who live by this life are not yet in heaven, heaven is most assuredly even now in them. Even of knowledge infused by faith St. Paul says that we know God now but dimly, as in a mirror; through natural objects, that is, and through the medium of ideas to which they give rise: "analogically," as they say; truly, yet inadequately; with an inadequacy not only of amount, as though just by progression in that sort of knowledge we should achieve that to which we are destined, but with an inadequacy due to that of the *knowing instrument*. But, when the super-natural consummation is effected, we shall "know," he declares, "even as we are known," and see God "face to face." And this is what St. John means when he writes that "we are called 'sons of God'—and so indeed we *are*"; the future contains only the fixation and full manifestation of a present fact. And this, St. Peter means, when he holds out to us "participation in a divine substance." This is the doctrine of Grace and Glory.

I do not, of course, assert that all men necessarily, or in fact, receive this gift; nor that all who do, retain it. But at the root of Catholic doctrine is this affirmation, that God desires to raise all human creatures, capable of true human life, to a super-human way of living, and so of knowing, loving, and being united to and like, Himself. I here say nothing of the process of vocation to this life; nothing of the machinery, so to speak, by which it is conveyed to us, appropriated by us, or developed in us. It is the Catholic dogma as such that I have meant to set uncompromisingly forth, that there may be no mistake about the background of our whole system, or of what is implied at each step in it.

III

(i)

There is, perhaps, no dogma of which the declaration and development, in Scripture and in history, can be more clearly traced than this; nor one of which the consequences, even social and political, are more wide or deep.

It is by no means absent from the Synoptic Gospels; in St. Paul and St. John it is stated with a firmness and lucidity which reveal it as for ever the irreformable possession of the Christian Creed and consciousness. No closeness of human union is more perfect than that of marriage, as both Gospels and Epistles portray it—a union wherein "twain become one flesh" and are "joined by God," and such, that by no man can they ever be put asunder; yet that union is by St. Paul presented as but the true image of the union between Christ and His Church, wherein with the human is wedded the Divine. And again there is the allegory of head and body, Christ the head, we the limbs, organically one whole, one life in all, each unintelligible, fragmentary, without the rest. And there is that, again, of the edifice—that house which is Christ and we, founded, walled, roomed, roofed, but all one house of many parts, *membra domus*, as the Latin so well puts it. And above all, it is in that doctrine of the *Plenitude* of Christ, the Pleroma, whereby He is insufficient without us, and we impossible without Him, so that we, growing into Him, one by one through the long centuries and the many millions made incorporate, accomplish gradually that Mystic Christ who has to be "formed" in the individual and the world. Those who fail to appreciate St. Paul's realism in all things, fail to appreciate his mysticism. Imperial was St. Paul's outlook on the world he lived in; and in his doctrine all that is most vast and most detailed, most ultimate and most immediate, most human and most spiritual, is joined. Anything short of this, is a calumny upon him; not to see this in him, is never to have his vision.

St. John says of his Gospel: "These things were written that you might believe that Jesus Christ is the Son of God, and that believing you might have Life in His name; for He is come that we 'might have Life, and have it more abundantly.' He, the Word made Flesh, has in Him, *is*, all that the Father has and is, and 'of His Fulness we have all received.'" Through St. John's magnificent Prologue, where in a splendour almost too dazzling to be as yet intelligible, and requiring to be re-read as Epilogue, we pass into the palace as through some portico where, in rich heraldic symbolism, are emblazoned the King's pedigree and achievements. Yet even so, there remain the outer Courts in which the Baptist is seen preaching, pointing away from himself, handing over his disciples to the Greater than he; the supremely best of the great religious Past indicating an utterly far Better in the future; it is the transition from John to Jesus; from John, misunderstood by the learned and devout of his own period, to Jesus, whom Jerusalem and Rome alike, each in her sphere, will, they too, misunderstand and reject the New even as they wrought the ending of the Old. From the following chapters we learn more fully what Christ revealed. A man is born of his parents into his co-natural kingdom, the earth: to live in the super-natural kingdom of the Heavens, he must be born anew, and from above, of water and the Spirit. And yet the New Life is no inert thing "in" man as jewel in a casket. Christ gives a Living Water, which becomes in the soul a Fountain, leaping up into Eternal Life, immortal and life-giving, overflowing, making glad refreshment for God's City, the Spirit in man and converting other men. And through substantial union with Christ is the Life imparted, and not otherwise: He restores the paralytic "to life"; but "greater things than this shall you see." Souls, dead and buried, prisoned within their poor co-natural limits, break forth and live, having received His Life whose Life is the Father's. "I," says Jesus, in an amazing identification, "I am the Resurrection and the Life." He who "believes on," "hears," "comes to," "sees," *appropriates* Jesus, lives by His Life and, save by self-willed separation, need never "die." On its proportionate food, the new Life is fed: the divine Life, by a Food itself divine,—Christ's Bread; Christ's Flesh and Blood; he who eats and drinks of that, identifies himself with *that*, "hath Eternal Life." One bread of many grains; one Body of a thousand living cells, having one unifying life throughout them; the One Vine, whereof Jesus is stem, and we the branches, one sap springing throughout the whole.

It is this doctrine which is repeatedly set forth symbolically in the Apocalypse: the mysterious white emblem given to the conqueror-Christian, bearing the soul's new name known only to him who receives it and to Him who gives it, indicative of the new shared Self of Christ and Christian: Christ's own "new name," now not alone Eternal Son of God, but First-born of the Sons of Men: and above all the secret communion of Lover and Beloved, behind the closed door of senses and of thought, through which the knocking Christ has been allowed to enter and to pass into the innermost of the soul, and there reside.

The doctrine of the outpouring and inhabitation of the Spirit, continues to affirm the reality of the super-natural Life; and the great Greek Fathers more magnificently than any others made use of it and hymned the "deification" of the Christian Soul, and in language which we—grown timorous almost, more careful, to say the least, by reason of misapplication and misstatement of our faith—would shrink to use, exclaim that God became man, that men on their side might become Gods. Augustine, though into him the treasures of the Old World so richly poured that he shifted the centre of gravity from East to West, made the Church talk Latin instead of her old Greek, and dominated thought at least until Aquinas; altered too the angle of men's vision with regard to Grace. Partly from temperamental tendency and personal history, partly because of the Pelagian too great glorification of nature, he made a different perspective, and saw human helplessness and sin more vividly, perhaps, than did the optimistic Greeks and Orientals. He watched Grace in its function of healing a sick humanity rather than as raising that humanity, already good, to a freedom and well-being so transcendent that its poor past, and even its present, might almost be forgotten in the blaze of its ultimate glory. But the essential optimism of the doctrine reappeared in full force in the creative atmosphere of the Middle Ages, when the whole world was to popular feeling as well as in theology "sacramentalized"; when (as in the writings of the Victorines) the true life and self of things was sought not so much in what the senses or even the intellect could show or map out, but in that for which they stood, to which they pointed; and which humanity might gain by the use of what was seen or understood.

And in different ways, tilting the balance of emphasis now towards intellect, now towards will, men like Aquinas and Bonaventura described the journey of the soul to God.

Since that time, of course, Catholic thought has been too systematized for any of its contents to be lost: disproportion, even, of statement has been rare and due to the exigencies of the moment and to controversial pressure, and has not proved permanent.

Though, say, in the seventeenth century and after, a too "static" quality seemed to be imparted to this section of theology which deals with the doctrine of Life; yet it can be shown that precisely this doctrine—beyond, we may surmise, all others—is singularly in harmony with what is good in the dynamic and vitalistic preferences of our own age.

But in no better way can the living belief of the Church be summed up and canonized, than in those prayers which it is the duty of her priests daily to recite in Mass and often in their Breviary, and which are constantly upon the lips of those whose privilege it is to sing Office in monastic choirs. Many of these are prayers of the old Roman rite, and throughout the ages misnamed dark the religious mentality of hundreds of thousands was shaped, or kept its shape, owing to these incomparable prayers. Only in the sublime Latin language can their austere beauty be appreciated: but I will translate one prayer which the priest says when at Mass he blesses the cup of mingled wine and water which is to be consecrated into the blood of Christ:—

O God, who didst wonderfully establish the dignity of Human Nature, and didst still more wonderfully recreate it, grant that by the mystery of this Water and this Wine, we may be made fellow-participators in His Divinity who in our humanity did not disdain to share.

In that is summed up the doctrine we have described.

Before concluding this chapter I wish, at the risk of fatiguing readers by constant repetition, to recall that I have so far tried to make an outline map, so to say, and no more, of the Catholic country; singling out this particular doctrine for description, as a man from an observation-post may observe a territory as *construed*, so to say, by its hills and streams, or again, by its roads and hedges, disregarding villages or farms. Not only these, but the implications of the doctrine itself, its necessary role in all that concerns, say, sin or the future life, the Sacraments, the fellowship of men and the communion of the Saints, the whole system of the Church, and the organic principles of human society on quite the widest scale, will be, as far as is needed, worked out in later chapters.

I earnestly beg readers to read this section patiently and carefully; to read, next, the rest of the book; finally, to re-read this chapter. Then, please God, its meaning will be a hundred times more rich though already, I hope, it is intelligible as a scheme and outline.

Once more, then: God intends to give to all men who will accept it, the free gift of a super-human life, with eternal consequences to themselves both if it be appropriated, and if it be rejected.

All Catholic dogma is made meaningless if this essential element be not grasped.

I will go further, and say that without it our chance of understanding history in the past, and even the psychological problem presented by the race to-day, is practically lost. And again, that all ambitions of social reform, all schemes for the world's salvation, are, if they exclude God's super-natural *vocation*-of humanity, so essentially inadequate as to be doomed to failure.

(ii)

At the beginning of this chapter I said that the national temperament was such as to welcome and even to demand some escape from the limits of the obvious, from all that can be weighed or measured, and that is on the hither side of the human horizon. Nor is the race so purely practical as to rest content with the attempt to solve such problems as the housing of the workman, the reduction to discipline of some native tribe, or even the verification of some soaring hypothesis of science. We seem always to insist upon some Temple, if not Cathedral, nor find adequate solace in grandiose town-halls, dignified police stations, or elegant and hygienic lavatories. Excellent are all these things; but they excel precisely on a plane which we are for ever trying to transcend. And it was also said that seldom so clearly as to-day, though seldom so unguidedly, has this spiritual impetus revealed itself. Some sort of super-human life is clamoured for. Men stretch out their hands in passionate yearning for a further shore: *Tendebantque manus ripæ ulterioris amore.*

Therefore while the dogmatic materialist, and even the dogmatic rationalist may show themselves the hottest enemies of the Catholic doctrine of the super-natural, they would seem to be few and not destined to success. Temperament, especially national temperament, is of all things the hardest, M. Bergson has reminded us, to modify. It is, paradoxically, if this be not remembered, the would-be friends of *some such* doctrine as ours is, who prove our most confusing foes.

One class of these, indeed, is manifestly seeking for the thing which we preach, and yet is most out of sympathy with our actual preaching.

It is composed partly of those who, in their spirit of moderation and correctness, and their devotion to a "godly righteous and sober life," feel rather shocked by the uncompromising Catholic declaration that no sort of "natural life," however good, is the proper ideal for a Christian to possess; but that we must take into account something so frankly super-human that it seems to (or indeed does) "reach out into the infinite." Are there not here, they feel, all manner of risks: excess, fanaticisms, wild renunciations, condemnations of life's good things as bad, visioned Utopias which as often as not, take the heart out of all effort to improve this world's injustices? How often we have heard sheer luxury described in terms of thankful reverence for God's good gifts, and self-sacrifice resented for its rebuke to self-indulgence, under guise of a quite pious reprobation of the "exaggerated." Even here, our snobbish coyness! The "charming eccentric Lord Arthur" may work in the slums to his heart's content, and to the admiration of all who are not asked to imitate him. But the commoner's son is "neglecting obvious duties" if he doesn't hunt the dollar. I have even heard the virtues of the Fathers of the Desert decried as "not quite respectable"; and a professional cleric sighed that St. John of the Cross was "violent," and could not have been "comfortable to live with." To the suggestion that the scourge of small cords could scarcely have been called gentle, nor was it comfortable to be asked to "follow" one who "had not where to lay His head," and to carry a cross up Calvary, it was retorted that the Temple scourging was exceptional, not characteristic; in fact, no very valuable part of Christ's example, and almost to be regretted, and probably didn't happen just like that, and was perhaps symbolical. And as for Calvary and crosses, ordinary life—the Rectory, the Common Room, the claims of social status, supplied plenty of the latter; and anyhow, Calvary was a crisis, and abnormal. The injunction to "be perfect as your Father in Heaven is perfect," was interpreted as recommending to mankind "perfection in man's sphere," or "on man's plane" (though even that begged the question: who shall define the perfection possible to mankind, or into what new spheres the soul may not be capable of breaking, into what "silent seas" it be not *called* to sail?). In short, it was the very paganism Aristotle struggled to transcend; the θνητὰ θνητῷ, "mortal life to mortal man"; not the ἀθανατίζεσθαι ἐφ' ὅσον ἐνδέχεται the injunction to "play the immortal" as far as possible. There are, and always will be limits: that is true. The vague, we shall see in a moment, is here the shapeless merely; Greek "perfection" was undoubtedly a science of right "limits"; but even the best Greek sculpture went perilously near that cult of the unduly finite which is theirs who so insist on the observance of "good form" in their religion.

Another group, far more sympathetic in manner, yet not less hostile substantially, to the Catholic doctrine, is composed of those who loudly sing the praises of and inculcate a "super-natural" life, meaning by that a life of heroic altruism. By these, "natural" life is conceived, falsely, as purely self-seeking, and not (as it is) social, co-operative, so that the individual can quite well sink and forget himself in the interests of the many without in the least transcending the limits of his nature; for so, in fact, he does most richly "realize" himself. Or again, they identify it with some progressive purification of the instincts, as though, again, human life were by nature downward in tendency and calculated to seek the grosser and the worse. That is not so either. We may, and constantly do, aspire to self-improvement and emancipation from the drag of sense and the prison of current ideas without at all having the right to regard ourselves as "super-natural." In short, for such speakers the Super-natural is but the Natural raised to some very high power, a fact to be crudely expressed in the formula h^n, not $h + s$, where h is humanity, s, super-humanity; though, indeed, I should myself prefer, if we are to play with symbols, the formula $h \times s$. For in Catholic doctrine, the Super-natural is not merely *added* to the Natural, as hat to head, but conspires with it into an exquisite new unity, almost as though (to keep to crude and raw examples) the body were unable, from intrinsic force, to grow a skin, and were then endowed, by exterior assistance, organically with one. The point of this example is wholly in the *unity* created (the body exacts a skin, as nature does not super-nature; and the skin is chemically of the same sort as the rest of the living creature); I mean this, that the super-naturalized man is not two persons, nor yet, precisely, a different *sort* of person, but *himself*, living his *own* life, yet in vital union with an essentially higher one. In short, it is true that the Kingdom of God is to be "within us"; yet it is from heaven that the New Jerusalem descends and from God's Throne; and while the New Life is, as from its very definition it must be, our own life and ourselves, yet from no mere intensification of our natural life can it result. I will confess to finding an intense delight in this inter-penetration and organic unification of two different sorts of lives, and I resent the frightful impoverishment of our doctrine due to inability to distinguish between such *sorts* of lives, and our tendency to imagine that by watering the rose sufficiently, it will begin to walk; or, that by multiplying the convolutions of its brain, the ape will think; or, that by practice of refinement and the virtues, nature will melt upwards, somehow, into super-nature. But what when we discover those who far outstrip what the Catholic faith affirms? These are the Theosophists, to whom this much of credit must be given, that their minds are not shut to the notion of super-natural life as such, though when they seek to philosophize about it, even to rationalize it, even to describe it in terms of imagination, they come to the heavy grief of the materialist. Yet were they to restrain themselves to the doctrine that the life of sense and of thought, and even the natural life of worship and belief, are not everything, but that a loftier mode of being exists, or can exist, which does not *replace* the natural life of man; nor even just co-exist side by side with it, but that it interpenetrates it vitally, not even as water interpenetrates sponge, nor as air, the lungs, but more as soul indwells the body, wholly (because spiritually) in every part of it—were this their doctrine, and no more than this, we had been ready friends. But when they say that all humanity has a right to this, and indeed possesses it by virtue of its innermost universal and indeed radically divine nature, we believe them to be wholly wrong, and to ruin alike the natural origin and the supernatural destiny and the mingled history of the soul, and to head straight for all sorts of pantheisms, cosmic monisms, and confusions of all most fatal sorts. And when they describe in singular detail all kinds of levels within the superhuman life, depth within depth of it, and paint strange pictures of the manner of the soul's existence upon each, or in each, and even the scenery and foods of those Astral and Devachanic planes, and all the rest, we well recognize how terribly necessary is, and always has been, the austere discipline of the Church which vetoes all such extravagances. The history of Gnosticism, of which Theosophy is the contemporary manifestation, is of high value, not only as revealing certain permanent psychic and spiritual tendencies in humankind, but, since the existence of the Catholic Church, as emphasizing certain enduring qualities in Catholicism. On the whole, Gnosticisms have revealed much, doubtless, that is ugly and arrogant; have produced a spiritually proud elite, secure in its unshared knowledge of "deep things"; have provided the spectacle of the habitual ill-balance of that very elite and of illuminists generally, so that the sun-scorched wings of these soaring souls go trailing, soon enough, in the mud; have issued in loftiest intuition and sublime utterance alternating with fantastic perversions of the wits, putrefactions of the moral sense, abracadabras and all charlatanism. But alongside of all this is the far more pathetically human spectacle of the desire of man, cheated because undisciplined, unguided, and ungoverned; lost in mist or morass, because with the stimulus has come no check.

It is our belief that the Catholic Church, and she only, has from the outset supplied both a stimulus and a check which, in conjunction, are unparalleled. The East, on the whole, offered an impulse which should carry man into the transcendent; Greek thought, on the whole, reminded the intellect of its limitations; the Catholic dogma harmonizes both, and the Catholic *ascesis* copes adequately with both. Hence at the outset you may see how unique is the effect of this dogma of the Super-natural upon human nature. It never for a moment permits us to forget that it *is* human nature, and will always remain so; yet it inspires it to seek for a way of being which essentially transcends that, and unites it more than does any flight of human intellect or imagination, more than does any effort of natural desire, with God. In view of this, human history, once governed by Catholic belief, can never, in the individual or the mass, be static. It is movement and endeavour inevitably. It "reaches from end to end," strongly. It "builds the New Jerusalem"; it carries the world right up to the Source of Life and therewith it unites it; and yet, it corrects and heals Society itself, inasmuch as it shows how, and how alone men are equal and must be free; independent, and yet interlocked in brotherhood: for, equal are they now in vocation and in destined dignity; they must be judged in the light of what they can be and shall be; and peremptorily we declare that all human conditions which interfere with the free attainment of that end are essentially unjust; and thus it creates that which the "world" has never done, a true democracy. Yet, such is the mercifulness of this dogma, that it is seen how, owing to the inner freedom of man's responsive will, and the freedom of God's grace, even unjust conditions cannot ultimately defeat, in any mechanical way, the the triumph and happiness, as of Society, so of the individual.

Thus, already Catholic dogma, and it alone, is perceived as harmonizing the whole of existing human life, and adding infinitely to its scope and meaning and value.

II

THE IDEA OF GOD

BY

M. C. D'ARCY, S.J.

I

THE Catholic doctrine of God is a compound of assurance and humility. The assurance is conveyed in St. Paul's words to the Athenians: "What ye worship in ignorance this set I forth to you." His words fell on the wayside. The Athenians, "who had received most sparks of the Logos but were unable to reach perfection even with that,"[1] regarded him as a plagiarist and a charlatan. And yet after-events justified him. For it will readily be admitted now that Christianity did bring the world to its feet, and summed up and surpassed the contemporary ideals in religion and philosophy. But when Catholicism comes forward to-day with these same words on its lips, the claim may seem fantastic folly in face of the development in thought and experience of the last nineteen hundred years. What sufficed in a bygone age cannot suffice now, and the cry "plagiarist" or "charlatan" is repeated. Nevertheless, the Church must still echo the same words with the same assurance, at the peril of denying its very existence. And the reason is simple. The Church speaks in the name of God. What it sets forth cannot be made and unmade by man. Human reasoning, sound as it may be, is still human, while Revelation is the Logos of God, the Eternal speaking in time.

The position implies an almost paradoxical theory of reason. Intellect of itself is flawless; it is the faculty of truth. To deny this is to commit intellectual suicide; in fact the denial can only be verbal, for in the very denial a belief in the truth of one statement at least is implicit. To go behind Knowledge in order to criticize it is an impossible feat, for our criticism is an intellectual act; we might as well turn out the light in order to study our appearance in the dark. Obvious as these statements may appear, they are required in order to dissociate the Catholic doctrine from any form of Agnosticism, whether it take the form of Sentimentality or Mysticism or the Kantian severance of the pure and practical reason. The sharp

[1] St. Clement of Alexandria, *Cohort.*, 7. "Plagiarist and charlatan" is an attempt to express the meaning of the *slang* Athenian word "σπερμολόγος."

distinctions made between Appearance and Reality, biological theories of the growth of mind and of the provisional value of dogmas, are wittingly or unwittingly subversive of all truth. There must be some unassailable standpoint in thinking, and the glimpses seen from such high ground must be in the right direction even when they are baffled by the horizon.

Catholic theology, then, does not disparage reason: it is not agnostic. But none the less it does not stake all on the findings of the intellect. This is because reason in us is clogged by the nature in which it is implanted. We are spectators of what is, not of a mere masque or phantasmagoria, but of the view spread out before our eyes, the heights, the great table-lands, cannot be taken in by dwellers in the valley. We cut up life into sections, and with difficulty piece them together; we have to allow for prejudice in our estimates and for unknown factors. We might compare the mind to a shell. In an oyster the shell shuts off the world, but in man the shell is translucent; all things flood in: the self can englobe all reality, though that reality must dwindle in size so as to be accommodated within the microcosm. For the analogy to be complete, the shell should become an appetite and activity—no mere intermediary—and its power would be limited not by itself but by the nature of the self.

The story of the Universe is another Person's, and we are part of the story, its characterization, not its author. Our aim is to live that story, not necessarily to think it out, since philosophy is only a reflection on life. We do not know even the secret of ourselves; we may understand other *things*, but animal life we have to interpret, and other persons are not mere intelligibles, creations of logic; they escape us in thought; for to grasp them fully we should have to become them. Still less, then, can men comprehend God. To quote a well-known saying, our object is not so much to get heaven into our heads as our heads into heaven. Hence the best effort of man is but a shooting at a mark beyond his range, and grace and Revelation are needed to strengthen the hand and make the mark clearer. Revelation is God's own explanation, the "stronger vessel, the divine word, on which we may take our journey through life more safely and securely."[1]

Revelation is, of course, not a *Deus ex machina*, God's Apologia, making all that was obscure clear, and giving a compendious chart of the Divine Nature. The common misgiving that it disinherits

[1] Plato, "Phædo," 85 D.

reason to give honour to some higher occult faculty is baseless. Revelation is a response to an overwhelming practical need. Man's lot would be pitiable, if with his frail intellect and unsteady desires he had to fulfil God's designs in his short and never-to-be-repeated life, without any help from on high. Intellect at its best has failed to comprehend life. Platonism with its strange mixture of harshness and sublimity was left incomplete by its author; Neo-Platonism, despite the genius of Plotinus, lost itself in magic or cold abstractions. The rarefied air on such heights drove men back to the cities of the plain, to the joys of the senses or to the sadness of a Dion Chrysostom: "Children crying in the night, and with no language but a cry." An answer was needed, and it came. If that answer was authentic and God's own word, then Revelation is the central fact of human history and the space of nineteen centuries cannot leave it behind. What, then, have those centuries contributed? It has become a prevailing idea in the Liberalist schools of theology that the meaning of that revelation has grown with time. And by this they mean that God had to use the inadequate and even misleading diction and ideas of the age to make known a truth. Criticism under the guidance of the Holy Spirit will gradually unearth the truths behind the formulæ, purge them of error and state them anew in accordance with the developed consciousness of man. Not all dogmas will survive this process. To justify its method, Liberal Christianity relies chiefly on the assumption that evolution must be applied in religion just as much as in biology or geology. The assumption rests on a misconception both of religion and the Incarnation. For in natural religion (never merely natural, since God sowed the seed and is the Husbandman) we have the expression of man's contact with the divine. There man meets his destiny—what precisely makes his soul greater than the world: a theme greater far, in fact, than any story of cosmic evolution. Swayed by desire, now high, now low, at times he defiles, at times he guesses beyond, the truths discovered by his reason. But these truths of religion stand fast, unalterable like mountain heights reaching on to the clouds. There is a "cloud of unknowing" between human thought and God, and neither the world nor the soul could give up their secret till in the fullness of time (an expression so fatal to evolutionary theology) the Word of God descended from the impenetrable heavens and became flesh. But be it observed—Revelation, surpassing, as it did, human expectation and desire, did not contradict what natural religion had established.[1] The vanishing splendours of human thought were made manifest in a visible Person. "The great Angel-blending Light shrinking His blaze to shine in a poor shepherd's eye." The nineteen centuries of Christianity have been all too short to study that word of life—so infinite are its contents. Hence one age has marvelled at the majesty, another at the love of the self-same reality; devotions, religious orders have sprung up in different centuries, according as one trait or another of the Incarnation has appealed to them. Time has brought an increasing appreciation of these values whole and entire from the beginning. By tradition, that dispensation of Providence, Christian has helped Christian, each contributing his quota to his fellows and descendants. And as science and philosophy have developed, they have lit up afresh the truths of God. For these latter are seen in new relations, and better understood. The more the Church pondered over the Incarnation, the clearer became the necessity of the Immaculate Conception.

Such being the nature of Revelation and development, the error of new theologies lies precisely in this that they are new. They fall under the definition of heresy, in contrast to Christianity which, in St. Augustine's words, is "tam antiqua sed tam nova"—so old and yet so fresh; they resemble a man tired with the strain of keeping to the point, who digresses into "judgments that cannot consist in the narrow point and centre of Virtue without a reel or stagger to the circumference." We cannot leave behind what has once been true, for progress is an advance into truth, a deeper appreciation and love of what is familiar, be it a birthright, or a gift such as Revelation.

Dogmas relating to God's nature are not fashions sufficient for the day, to be forgotten to-morrow. Often enough they issued clear and decisive at the end of an acrid dispute, as a declaration of the unswerving tradition and chartered liberty of Christendom. Progress cannot destroy their integrity, and orthodoxy can never be out of

[1] For an excellent criticism of the idea of Progress *vide* Gilbert Murray's *Religio Grammatica.* Intertwined with religion are morality and the various other activities of human life. Consequently we should expect the rise and fall of religious ideals in history, even as we meet knavish and noble ambitions among our contemporaries. Furthermore, as the present is mounted on the shoulders of the past, it can see former mistakes and learn from them. This is the element of truth in the evolution of religion. But men did not grow a sense of the divine as they grow a new skin. "The passionate thought" present vaguely, and in general, to consciousness, directed the soul towards its object, as the poet broods and picks out what he seeks, before the poem has taken clear shape in his mind. The history of the world is unintelligible, unless from the beginning there existed a real enterprise, a quest for the Holy Grail, dimly discerned by the pure of heart and longed for by all humanity.

date; for, to borrow a striking image, the Church is like a charioteer driving down the ages at breakneck speed. swerving now to the right, now to the left, always erect and undismayed.

II

With the facts of Revelation and the stimulus of a new hope, reason can move unerringly; and it is a doctrine of Catholicism that God can be known by human reason. "For the invisible things of Him from the creation of the world are clearly seen, being understood by the things that are made, His eternal power also and divinity." How the certainty of God's existence passes from a notional to a real assent will depend to a great degree on the apperceptions of each individual. Catholic theology is mainly concerned with proving to any plaintiff that God's existence is not a matter of conjecture. Not all men need these proofs, which are abstract and cold; for their heart has already burned within them at the sound of His voice. Some could as soon doubt of their own existence as of God's. Usually, however, we pass through certain stages. At first, externalized and merely receptive, we pay little attention to God. Then comes the ambition to do or be something, and we begin to be ourselves in our actions; but the enormous gulf between our own yearnings and the achievements brings about a crisis. We choose God or renounce Him. He becomes "the one thing necessary"; or else we turn our backs, and accept a dreamy or worldly or embittered existence as a substitute.

This process, however, is throughout concerned with the value of the idea of God, not with the question of His existence. To deny Him we have to deny what is admittedly there as a notion, and this is very significant. God is not a discovery or property of any particular age, no more than is the idea of parentage or goodness. May it not be, then, that just as the idea of parentage and goodness arose because men were aware in some manner of parents and good people, so, too, the presence of a certain reality instinctively filled man with awe and created the special attribute "Divine" as alone appropriate to that object? Knowledge is of reality. Whenever we directly or indirectly apprehend an object, be it ourselves, a body, or spirit, we affirm categorically in the same act its independent existence. Is, then, the idea of God on the same plane as the ideas we cannot doubt such as the idea of the self or substance or spirit? Speculation here must move very warily, for it is easy to slip. For instance, the knowledge of God is not intuitive, an apprehension as indubitable and direct as that of the principle of contradiction or the perception of colour. Common experience and the limited nature of the human mind make this obvious. Ontologism, too, which would deduce all our other ideas from the idea of God, may describe the condition of the angels, but man starts with his senses. St. Anselm, in what is called the Ontological argument, is far more plausible. God is the most perfect Being conceivable, but a Being with existence is more perfect than a being without, therefore God must exist. This argument, however attractive, generally leaves us with a sense of dissatisfaction. God is the most perfect Being conceivable. Yes! but the word "God" does not stand for the bare limit in the ascending scale of thought. If it did, St. Anselm's argument would thoroughly deserve the criticism often directed against it, that the argument involves an illicit transition from the ideal to the real order. But the notion of God, of a Being, namely, with sacred and peculiar prerogatives, something distinct and expressed in language by a distinct attribute "Divine" is throughout presupposed. When we speak of "the idea of God" the word "idea" is used, not as a conjecture or an individual's surmise of the nature of God, but as an expression of the object—just as we speak of the conception of duty or of will. The preposition "of" is used for equivalence, as in the phrase City *of* London. If this be true, the objection based on the distinction of an ideal and real order is overcome.

But other objections can easily be raised; for many of our ideas do not imply existence, and in truth, for a full discussion of this word "idea," a long philosophical analysis would be needed. Yet, briefly, if this idea that we possess of the Divine[1] does not demand some divine object, then the idea must be either a mere ideal or chimera or invention. Without hesitation we can dismiss the chimera or fairy tale. Despite the many accretions to the simplest connotations of the word Divine, and the infinite variety of cults, there is one meaning discoverable underneath the debris. Otherwise, comparative religion would have no meaning, and besides one could argue equally well against any real notion, be it matter or morality. Certain

[1] As St. Thomas Aquinas says, we cannot know that a thing exists, without also knowing to some slight degree what it is. But in the text I am speaking of the most elementary idea of God—just what language implies in the use of the word Divine, and what religion, to be a religion at all, has for its object. It is an attempt to go behind ordinary arguments which are as much concerned with God's nature as with His existence. I shall speak farther on of the nature of God in the Catholic conception.

anthropologists pretend to understand the manufacture of religion out of taboo and magic. But the stream cannot rise higher than its source and if the conception of God arises purely from sexual aberrations or midnight alarums or the childish fascination for dolls, then God should be still as repulsive or creepy or dollish. Mr. Chesterton has given us a more picturesque and rational explanation: "Primitive man went out with his head full of Gods and heroes, because that is the chief use of having a head. Then he saw the sun in some glorious crisis of dominance of noon or the distress of nightfall and he said, 'that is how the face of God would shine when he had slain the dragon.' " Anthropology is useful in explaining the development or decadence of an idea already there. The idea of God flickers and grows bright according as the atmosphere, environment, and tradition are favourable or not; but the validity of the conception is something quite different from the process of development.

That the idea of God is not a mere abstraction will be evident if we compare this idea with the idea of goodness. This latter is an ideal, an abstraction, as wide as being itself, and embodied in varying degrees of perfection in individual things. The idea of God is singular; in no sense a universal, a whole, nor the unity of a system. The emotions of religion—after all the best witness as the emotions take their complexion from the object—clearly mark the difference; for men fall down in adoration before a Being who is no mere system or form, but a Creator ten thousand times greater than the world; and sacrifice, a constituent of almost all worship, implies the recognition of God as the sovereign lord of the universe. When, then, we consider how irreducible this idea is, how different from invention and unrealized ideal, may we not conclude that it is born of reality in as true a sense as the ideas of body and spirit and concrete good? We do not live in a world of our own making; we are spectators and discoverers of the unique and independent objects around and about us, of dead matter and living spirit, of time and eternity, and of the freshness that breathes deep-down things—the brooding of the Holy Spirit.

Of the manner in which we learn by knowledge, Catholic philosophy makes two main divisions; what is called intuition or immediate apprehension, and inference. It is to this latter that our knowledge of the existence of God is assigned.[1] Inference, however, may

[1] The Vatican Council was, however, particularly careful not to insert the word "inference" when declaring that God could be known by reason (*Acta*,

sound uninviting, for it is associated with the discovery of something quite unknown before as when a scientist arrives at an unheard-of cause or a new planet by a long train of reasoning. God is not a new discovery. He is known through His creation: "The heavens declare the glory of the Lord." As an illustration of how this may be, and of the intimacy of God with His creatures, the knowledge of our own selves supplies a suggestive, though faulty, analogy. We have no intuition in this life into the substance of ourselves, as Hume correctly argued. Nevertheless, this knowledge is not a conclusion suddenly sprung upon us, for we are aware of ourselves in and through our operations. Again, we see anger in another's countenance—the soul manifesting itself up to a point in the body. Now we know God in and through His works. They express Him finitely and in an infinitesimal way. But the analogy of the soul fails in this that God is not essentially connected with creation. His nature is not spent in giving. God's works are not God, though they would vanish if He were not with them. If we pursue the only right method and look into the peculiarity of our idea of Him, we shall find that God is not as the soul to its parts. He occupies a unique place in thought, that of the Creator to creation—a relation unique and understood to be incomparable. But we undervalue the powers of the soul if we deny it any possible contact in thought with the Infinite, with what is most real. If the finite depends for its very existence on a creator and sustainer, it is to be expected that it would have some dim knowledge of that fact. When we speak of the Infinite, the Eternal, we mean something positive, even though we are aware that such names are mere shadows of the reality of the Divine nature. The world is, therefore we perceive it. Persons are real and distinct from inanimate things, and consequently we apprehend them as different, and feel a different emotion in their presence from what we feel before a log. So, too, it is because there are good and moral acts that we observe them and are stirred to a specific emotion. It is because nature is beautiful that the onlooker is mastered by a wordless æsthetic emotion, and it is because there is Some One walking in His own creation that men fall down and adore, overcome by

col. 76, 132). Not even "innate ideas" were condemned—little as they have to recommend them. St. Thomas, somewhat embarrassed by certain opinions of St. Augustine (*Contra Gentiles*, III, 47), leaves the question an open one. "There is a certain general and confused idea of God, which is present in all men, whether it be that God is known by Himself like other principles of demonstration" or, as he prefers himself, we reach God by inference. Cf. Article "Dieu." *Dict. de Theologie Cath.*, II, col. 256.

the sense of reverence and awe. They have felt the mysterious character of nature, its secret, the other side to its being.[1] The emotions of awe and reverence and the act of adoration could not arise in emptiness.[2] They are a response; they are elicited by something outside man. Reverence in the deepest sense can be paid only to an object all holy, and worship is due to a God alone. We are in touch with the Divine:—

> Does the fish soar to find the ocean?
> The eagle plunge to find the air?
> That we ask of the stars in motion
> If they have rumour of Thee there.

It would almost appear, then, that Atheism is an impossible position to take up. Yet the fact remains that there are Atheists. This difficulty can be met by the equally certain fact that we can deny what we are certain of. Mill denied that two and two must make four. An idealist denies material reality (and often free will and personality), but in his unreflective consciousness he is continually accepting it. And Atheism is often the result of reflection—a philosophical attitude. If it is not that, it is the outcome of a lack of interest, and the difficulty of keeping in touch with a super-sensual world.[3] We can forget God just as we can lose interest in other people and forget that they have souls; more easily, indeed, because the idea to begin with is dim, and may, alas! so easily be clouded over. Or again, prejudice may obscure the obvious; objections raised against the existence of a good God may produce a doubt. It is when the reflective consciousness has thrown down the gauntlet and

[1] Cf. *Confessions of St. Augustine*, Bk. IX, c. 25, and Bk. X, c. 9. "The authentic voice of nature says, 'We made not ourselves, but He made us that abideth for ever.'"

[2] This argument is almost the reverse of the Modernist's. He proceeds from desire and need to posit God as existing—like a spider, as Bacon said, spinning its world out of its own bowels. It is subjectivist. But reverence is of an object; it is a rational emotion. The object we reverence we instantly pay homage to. It is impossible to pay homage to what one desires because there is no certainty of its existence.

[3] The tendency to confuse the nature of God with creatures would follow almost as a corollary, if what I have said of the mode of our apprehension of Him be correct. We associate Him with special places—Dodona or Mecca—with special objects, sun and moon and sky—with what is highest in ourselves; the Anima Mundi—the Goddess of Reason. It is not that a pagan always worships a stock or stone as a stock or stone; but he has not in his consciousness clearly the relation between the stone and God, owing to the fact that God is seen through His creation.

challenged the believer to support his belief by proof that the standard arguments for the existence of God must be brought out. They take an unbeliever on his own ground, and proceeding from common assumptions such as cause and effect, movement or contingency, design in the universe, the dictates of conscience, prove that there must exist a First Cause, a Self-sufficient Being, who can be no other than the God we worship in religion.[1]

These arguments do not conclude to a God unknown before; they justify the conception when it is regarded as illusory and connect it up with other truths of our understanding. They establish certain attributes of God, tell us something about the Divine, which before perhaps we confused in our mind with other things.

Other less formal but cogent means of bringing man to confess God consist in pressing the questions of the "why" and "whither" of man's life, emphasizing the futility of life without God—what a painful nightmare it would be, ever vanishing into nothingness, existing for a moment and passing away save for the memory of it by fits and starts as past; calling to mind justice so often left unredressed, the balance on the side of wrong; the secrets of the inner life of souls so wonderful when revealed, but unknown, unnoticed in millions of lives. If the world is not a story with a plot, then to an earnest man it is a place of mockery, or topsyturvydom, and we should have to reverse all our estimates of greatness and point the finger of scorn at a Socrates or a Plato, a St. Augustine or St. Francis of Assisi, for searching for a phantom or nonentity, wasting the better part of their lives in a useless pursuit.[2]

[1] These particular arguments demand such a careful elaboration—with every step worked precisely—that it is impossible in an essay such as this is to set them down one by one. But briefly, the Cosmological Argument relies on the principle of causality—that everything which has begun must be attributed to a cause fully capable of producing it, and secondly on a fact that something has begun. Then straightway one arrives by the principle of sufficient reason at an absolute cause, for no contingent being will have sufficient reason in itself for its existence. After this conclusion, one must show that this absolute cause is distinct from the universe and that it is not blind. This argument from the contingency of nature is especially forcible because it appeals to what we realize—our own incompleteness; and we shall see the argument sometimes used in a spiritual way, when the religious mind prays to God to complete his incompleteness (*v.* R. Browning's "Wanting is What?"). It may be objected the word contingency begs the conclusion, and I am prepared to admit this if the objector will also admit that there was no need to draw out the argument to such a length, for in knowing contingent being, he knew the absolute cause to some extent, though indirectly.

[2] Cf. Mr. Balfour's concluding words in *Theism and Humanism*: "He is Himself the condition of scientific knowledge. If he be excluded from the causal series which produces beliefs, the cognitive series which justifies them is

III

The difficulties really begin when we consider the nature of God, for here the writing on the wall is deciphered variously. St. Thomas Aquinas held that we know that God exists and we know what He is, but in a very dim and confused manner. Catholic doctrine is a *via media* between Agnosticism and extreme Rationalism. It cannot take up the illogical position of a Herbert Spencer, acknowledge a God, and then dismiss Him as unknowable; nor, again, can it see eye to eye with those who claim to be as familiar with God as with their next-door neighbour. In proceeding thus it is logical. God is not a man in the moon or a shadow roaming the world. We know Him in and through His works and presence, and this is a form of knowledge, however inadequate. But to repeat, if God be really God, we cannot hope to understand Him. He would not be God if we could. "A horse would call the god a horse: an ox, a god ox-shaped."[1] This is the *cul de sac* of anthropomorphism. St. Paul knew better: "O the depth of the riches of the wisdom and of the knowledge of God! How incomprehensible are His judgments and how unsearchable His ways! For who hath known the mind of the Lord? Or who hath been His counsellor?" It is the lesson of Job and of all real religion.

I have said that the conception of the Divine is accompanied with the emotions of reverence and awe and the desire to worship. These latter, if analysed, imply that the object of adoration must be the complete owner of life, "the Sovereign Lord of all things." As owner God cannot be less than personal. Inanimate nature—so much inferior except in size to ourselves—calls for no reverence in itself. We must make it a shrine or superstitiously endow it with personal powers, before we can worship there. But may not God be more than personal? To answer this requires a digression, but as modern thought inclines to the answer "yes," it will be convenient to stay a moment over the meaning of the word. A person is

corrupted at the root; and as it is only in a theistic setting that beauty can retain its deepest meaning, and live its brightest lustre, so these great truths of æsthetics and ethics are but half-truths, isolated and imperfect, unless we add to them yet a third. We must hold that reason and the works of reason have their source in God: that from Him they draw their inspiration: and that if they repudiate their origin, by this very act they proclaim their own insufficiency."

[1] Xenophanes of Kolophon. Æschylus, *Agamemnon*, II, 155–90, admirably expresses man's thought of God: "Zeus, whoe'er he be—if it be gracious to him to be invoked by such a title, by that do I address him," etc.

individual—that is to say, indivisible and incommunicable, but the peculiar character of an individual human being in distinction from an atom lies in this, that he is the owner of himself and responsible to himself. His nature issues into self-consciousness; he is the principle of his own actions, and the self he moulds is sacred; sacred—because it is a spirit: in other words a nature to which the words "good" and "true" are strictly applicable. But it is created in the image of God. As such it belongs to God; and human beings, though owners, are, as conscience reveals, more properly stewards. We use the word personality, in ordinary language, especially to describe the self in so far as it is moulded by ourselves. Now God is individual and incommunicable in His essence, and He is the complete owner of Himself, not a steward. His actions, therefore, as being entirely His own, good with goodness itself, are also most personal. We, to our sorrow, know ourselves to be only semi-personal. We cling to that privilege because we feel obscurely that by so doing we are likening ourselves to what is the perfection of being.

To return, awe and worship are directed to a Being who is not only personal, but all-holy, to whom wrong must be intrinsically hateful. Lastly, this Divine Being who inspires awe must be authoritative and ineffable. That is why all real religion, as was said above, involves submission and obedience. "To see God is to die." Only the initiated can approach the mysteries; and mysticism is in full accord with this attitude in its highest utterances, in its insistence on negatives in speaking of God. For God is so infinite that words fashioned for human ends split into fragments when used of Him. The mystic enchanted with the reality, feels no description can answer to experience.

Here, then, we are face to face with a real difficulty. If God be ineffable and infinite, how can a finite mind understand Him? Are we cut off from all relation with this self-subsistent, incommunicable God? "For who can speak of God without a solecism or think thereof without an ecstasy?" Surely we must stain God with our own finiteness if we speak of Him at all; or God, if He communicate with us, must, like a Midas, gild us with His own divinity. Catholicism here parts company with most philosophies; they either, as Kant did, acknowledge an abyss between the finite and infinite which cannot be bridged, or they fall into Pantheism; and Pantheism lowers God to a human level or waives aside human imperfections, making us and the world fragments or parts of the Divine. But

Catholic philosophy holds obstinately to God's prerogatives, and yet will not rob man of one jot or tittle of either his finiteness or independence—and still bridges the gulf.

There are two questions which must be separated here. The first is how can we assert anything of God, since He is so completely different from us finite beings; and the second is, what is the relation between God and the world, between the infinite and the finite? The answer to both lies really in developing the meaning of the terms so that the relation gradually emerges, and in what has been called the doctrine of analogy.

We adore, not the unity of a system, not a mere thought, not something below the stature of a human person, but a holy, sovereign Being, Lord of Nature and Life. We know ourselves as independent beings who nevertheless are finite and not belonging to ourselves. Everything we meet and understand has the mark of finiteness upon it, yet we distinguish lesser and greater perfection. We meet and imagine beautiful and good persons and things; we observe a hierarchy in goodness and perfection. Some of these attributes which belong to the world around us, though dwelling in mean habitations of earth or flesh or spirit, are in their nature pure and ideal—forms, as Plato would have said, patterns of which we can see but fleeting images. But there is a Being whom we know to exist, and who by His very nature must possess all that is perfect. We know, too, that He is the cause and source and life of all things, and therefore we have a right to translate the perfections immanent in the effect to the cause. But here the peculiarity of the transference becomes apparent, for the cause and the effect differ radically, as the infinite from the finite. It is difficult to express this properly, because no image is exact. God is in a sense what Plato called "beyond being," because being is understood by us only in limited specific natures. And this brings out one aspect. If a smith made a clock-work toy, as Hephæstus wrought golden wheels that ran blithely of their own accord, and that toy could observe its maker, it might argue, "I can move, that is my distinctive perfection; my maker, then, must move too." But if it were wise it would not assume that the movement was of the same nature in both. Now God is the ground of our being. There is a unity, thin and evanescent as it may appear. By putting this unity and disparity together we have what is known as the doctrine of analogy—that a perfection in God will be analogous to that perfection as it exists in a human being.

Wisdom and goodness and power as attributed to God are not misnomers; only there is no common measure between His wisdom and ours; He is more than generically distinct from us; He *is* Goodness, Wisdom, Truth. Nay, these attributes are identical in Him, for He has only one name, God; and all the ideals of thought or desire are contained singly and undispersed in Him. So far from God passing into an abstraction, a gaunt and empty figure, He is above description because the riches of His essence are beyond "our benumbed conceiving." We can put together the scattered fragments of His Glory, but we cannot see them inextricably one, interpenetrating each other and identical in the Divine Nature. Around us are the traces of the divine profusion. And just as "all men's Babylons strive but to impart the grandeurs of his Babylonian heart," so the perfection of God, like an over-full cup, has run over and poured out into the world. "But in the depths of the Eternal Light in one sole volume is contained whate'er the universal world contains. There is the universal mould of all this globe."[1] But man, not gifted with the sight of God in this life, must choose what he thinks most glorious, and invoke God by such titles; telling of His Omnipotent Will, His Omniscience, His Love; cataloguing the one single Word with negative labels: immensity, immutability, infinity—having to rest content with such faint and far-off praise.

IV

God, then, is not utterly inscrutable, and the second question must now be answered. How is He related to the Universe? An easy answer at all times has been through Pantheism. Religion takes for granted a unity; mysticism at times uses the vocabulary of identification, and the reflective consciousness is ever tempted to make life into a logical system, with one principle to which all others can be reduced. Parmenides is the outstanding advocate of crude Pantheism in ancient times: what is, is; the universe is a plenum. In Plotinus, the Higher Pantheism insinuates itself, though no formula can do justice to the richness and majesty of his doctrine. There is the One, sometimes called God; it is the principle of being, though itself beyond being. Three layers—photospheres—are formed by radiation from this One: Mind, Soul, and Nature. These three are the manifestations. They are the radiance of the One coming into being, the descent and breaking up of unity into multiplicity. Some

[1] Dante, "Paradiso," canto xxxiii.

of the sayings of the mediæval writers and mystics are just as Pantheistic in tendency. In Scotus Erigena "God is the totality of all things which are and are not, which can and cannot be. . . . All discords are resolved when they are considered as part of the universal harmony." And through the centuries this view has persisted, Spinoza producing a great geometry of life, Hegel a great Panlogism. At the present day the Pantheist is usually an Idealist as well. The life of the world is mind; matter and mind cannot co-exist in their hostile camps in the One; so matter must go. Mr. Bradley and Professor Bosanquet and others, see life as a great coherent system of mind. All subjects are but provisional subjects; they are really adjectives, predicates of Reality. "Our minds, if they could be visualized, although they repeat in each an analogous nature, would not look like self-contained shapes, each repeating the other side by side, like our bodies set in a row; they would look like bits of machines or organs of organisms, fragmentary and incomprehensible till the whole were supplied to which they respectively belonged." And again: "I cannot believe that the supreme end of the Absolute is to give rise to beings such as I experience myself to be. . . . If I possessed myself entirely, I should be the Absolute, and I should not be what I experience existentially as myself."[1] This form of Pantheism, then, is whole-hearted; the finite world is but the provisional scrutiny of the Infinite; and I quote this view because it has been prevalent in this country and abroad, and is the impulse behind certain theories of State reform, eugenics, and religion. And it is worthy of note also because it shows that in the subtleties of the reflective consciousness the true idea of God has to all intents and purposes disappeared. The name of God is first surreptitiously, then more confidently, introduced as synonymous with universal mind, the system of the whole, and the world becomes the expression of the very nature of God. This is to spoil a profound truth by exaggeration. Catholics believe in divine immanence but deny that God is exhausted in His creatures—that He Himself is identical with the largesses He has scattered broadcast over the world. But perhaps the peculiar danger of the doctrine of immanence is its accord with the pride of man, notably to-day. For it encourages that intoxicated form of democracy which finds in the voice of the people the ultimate justification, taking literally the *vox populi* to

[1] Professor Bosanquet in a Symposium of the Aristotelian Society: "On Finite Individuals."

be the *vox Dei.* Such a this-world view, to use Baron von Hügel's phrase, closes the shutters down on the after-world and the Divine. An earthly millennium is substituted for Heaven, and an earthly city built without pinnacle or spire or temple.

The exaltation of human worth has, however, the seeds of mortality within it. The picture of man beating his breast and imploring a Redeemer is far truer to life than a Siegfried or Superman. The insignificance of human life, the daily tragedy, make the "Ye are as Gods" gospel taste like wormwood. The recent good tidings of a finite God coming to rescue us is nevertheless a deceit. This is no solution. His coming is but a stage entry of the hero to capture the applause of a hysterical audience. In Bernard Shaw, the Finite God is not even that; He is to be the object of *our* pity, of *our* help. *Mr. Brittling Sees it Through* raised hopes that Mr. Wells was becoming a Christian. The Finite God seemed a very human makeshift for the Son of Man. But "God, the Invisible King," leaves the impression that the writer is rapidly forgetting the meaning of religion. In that book, "God is a person not all-wise nor all-powerful nor omnipresent . . . He strives to exist in every soul . . . He is in time." . . . "He is not the Life-Force," though, notice, this life-force "is aware of itself not as a whole but diffusedly as individual self-consciousness." "God is the immortal part of mankind." "He began and will never end." "He is boundless." "He is thought, love, and courage." "We find God within" for "modern religion bases all on experience." "He comes into countless lives," and "the believer owes all his being and every moment of his life to God." "He is courage—He is a person." "In the dawning of mankind He had an awakening, and as mankind grows He grows." "He is a Being of the minds and in the minds of men." "He is the undying human memory, the increasing human will." "He is synthetic reality." Later, he asks: "Why should not the soul of the species, many-faceted, indeed, be nevertheless a soul like our own," to wit, God? Much is made of his purpose; it is "the attainment of clear knowledge as a means to more knowledge, and of knowledge as a means to power." Above all, his purpose is the conquest of death. The remainder of the book is spent in a more detailed examination of this purpose: how men should respond and not be damned: how barristers should behave: the status of women and the organization of the religion. He makes as interesting a picture as he can, but I feel we should be as disappointed if we met his God as Henry VIII was with Anne of Cleeves. With God, as religion and theology understand Him, Mr. Wells will have nothing to do. Of the Veiled Being, "whether it is simple or complex or Divine, we know nothing; to us it is no more than the limit of understanding, the unknown beyond." Now, frankly, this separation of thought and experience, this Nominalism, won't bear examination. Again, some of the quotations given run badly together. God is not omnipresent; He is a person, yet He is in countless lives at the same time. The Life-Force is aware of itself in man's self-consciousness, yet God is the thought and the courage of mankind. He is a being of the minds of men, yet He is another person coming in. His purpose is clearer knowledge—of what? Progress without content or direction is sadly indefinite. But I would leave all this aside, for it is the ideal at the back of Mr. Wells's mind which rivets one's attention. Mr. Wells, though a scientist, or, perhaps, because he is a scientist, is very interested in Men—spelt with a capital M. Unfortunately, mankind doesn't sound very inspiring, and it is a hard thing to worship, so he takes the characteristics he likes best among men; their courage, their personality—and with a stroke of the pen he creates a God of the species (a tribal God? but perhaps a little more primitive)—a youth who is ever looking forward, who will cheer us on, be our captain, attack with his dispensary the Jabberwocky death (as science of course progresses, and mankind, *alias* God, prospers). With a little pseudo-science about fourth dimensions and the spirit world, he bolsters up his puppet; a new Religion descends from above, and so everybody is to be wiser and more religious for ever after.

This God of Mr. Wells has lost the faint likeness to the Son of Man. It has feet of clay, is earthy. No doubt the finite God of William James furnished the materials for Mr. Wells. "Monotheism itself has always viewed God as but one helper *primus inter pares* in the midst of all the shapers of the great world's fate." It must not be forgotten that James in his writings usually had in mind his *bete noir* Pantheism with its doctrine of the Absolute, and that he rendered yeoman service in upholding a personal God. He describes God in terms "which, I think, nobody could be inclined to dispute," "as the deepest power in the universe, to be conceived under the form of a mental personality—living outside of my own, and whose existence I simply come upon and find. The Divine personality and ours are consanguineous at least in this that both have purposes for which they care, and each can hear the other's call." He prefers to think of God as finite, because it brings Him nearer; theories which play with terms such as infinite, immutable, are mere barren metaphysics. Here he is consistent with himself and with Pragmatism, which, in the words of Pierce quoted by James, claims "that our conception of the practical consequences is for us the whole of our conception of the object so far as that conception has positive significance at all." It is all-important to realize that this belief in a finite God stands or falls with the truth of Pragmatism and other theories sceptical of the value of the intellect. For the Pragmatist does not quarrel with the logic of theology, but with the reality of the terms: they are moonshine, meaningless labels. Wells follows suit in calling himself a Nominalist. If, therefore, Nominalism is false, the finite God of James and Wells falls to the ground. But even with practical value as the sole test, we have lost something by dismissing an infinite omnipotent God. Preach as much as you wish the idleness of speculation, nevertheless the mind of man will never rest in its search for the perfect, the Grail. Finite helpers can satisfy only for a time; they are within a life greater than their own, and they have no answer to the most profound questionings of the soul. The hierarchy of beauty and goodness visible in the world point beyond themselves to a consummate beauty—the Master and Interpreter of Fate. The Universe is too significant to be anonymous, and if it has a meaning and an owner, then all in it, earth and body and spirit, are protected by, and ensconced within, Infinite care.

To return to our problem, how God and finite selves are related. We have said that philosophy generally has tended to solve it by Pantheism, finding no other solution to the difficulty that, if God be not everything, then He is limited; for there will be a One which contains God and other things. The Absolutist philosophers call God the Absolute, and attempt to reduce the multiplicity of being to appearances of that One. The form of that unity differs, for in Spinoza the finite realities are attributes or modes or else illusory. For Professor Bosanquet and many other philosophers to-day the best simile seems to be that of an organism. Dr. McTaggart stands by the reality of persons; he finds God superfluous, omits Him and makes the unity what he calls a college or society of persons. Professor Pringle-Pattison in his Gifford lectures, "The Idea of God," has many excellent criticisms of both the Materialistic and Hegelian excesses. He refutes most cogently the Idealist theory of knowledge and its subtraction of finite independence. Nevertheless his own answer is not thorough and ends by being a watered-down Pantheism. He quotes with approval "Man is the true Shekinah," the visible presence, that is to say, of the Divine. "We may conceive God as an experience in which the Universe is felt and apprehended as an ultimately harmonious whole; and we must of course distinguish between such an infinite experience and the experiences of ourselves and other finite persons. But we have no right to treat either out of relation to the other." (What is this but half-hearted Idealism?) "We have no right to suppose the possibility of such an infinite experience as a solitary monad, an absolute in the old sense of the term already condemned." . . . "The true revelation of the Divine must be sought in the systematic structure of finite experience as a whole." Elsewhere he sums up: "Such a theory as I have tried to expound finds it impossible to take God and the world as two separate and independently existing facts. A deistically conceived God existing in solitary state before the world was, and to whom the finite world bears only a contingent relation, as called into existence by the word of His power, is, I have insisted, a figment of the logical imagination. God exists only as a self-communicating Life; in theological language creation is an external act or process—a process which must be ultimately understood not as the making of something out of nothing, but as a self-revelation of the Divine in and to finite spirits. . . . This, then, is the true Absolute, a term which would be inapplicable to the transcendent God of an abstract monotheism, but which is not unfitly applied to the sweep of a Life which realizes itself in and through the process of the finite world, as consummated in the Divine sonship of man."

It is not easy to form a significant and precise idea of this God. He is not apart from the life of the world, yet in other places He has the grandeur of a personal God and He is not the finite centres. They are organically[1] connected with Him. In his reply to Dr.

[1] The word "organic" is to Professor Pringle-Pattison the key to his theory. It is also, I think, the key to his failure. "Organic" is correctly used of one among certain forms of unity, which we know of in the world. As applied to other forms of unity, it may be nonsense or metaphor. It would be nonsense if applied to a set of counters, it is metaphor as applied, say, to a state. Half the mistakes of philosophy are due to calling some unity by the name of another, and not noticing the difference. Is the word organism applicable to the relation of God and the world? Surely only to the extent that the purpose of both is the same. The terms "God" and "the world" each have such a peculiar and individual meaning that the use of the word organism to express their unity becomes misleading and mischievous.

Rashdall, Professor Pringle-Pattison quotes the criticism of a reviewer that a God who is revealed in Cæsar Borgia as well as in St. Francis would be intolerable, and escapes it by distinguishing the Absolute or Nature from God; but then God is not merely immanent, not essentially connected with the universe. The consequences of such a distinction, if thought out, would bring the writer to the Catholic view that God is so perfect a Being, so simple and single that in His essence is contained perfectly what we see diluted and dispersed in specific imperfect natures. Suppose as an allegory one woke up some fine morning and discovered that an unseen hand had bestowed on all the objects of the room a singular grace and beauty, so that they drew the onlooker to them to love the unseen artist. The countryside, too, took on this radiant beauty, infinitely varied, in the hedgerows, the cornfields, the peasant folk. And then suppose that somebody came with the news that a Person had passed along whose presence had shed such love and beauty that all nature had blossomed, striving to reflect His beauty, and so return His love in its own poor and inadequate way. Should we rest content with this derived beauty, saying: "Now thou dost dismiss Thy servant, Lord, in peace, for my eyes have seen all Thy glory?" Would we not rather hasten to the presence itself, and expect and know that He contained in Himself more beauty and love than it had ever entered into our heart to conceive? Is this fountain-head an abstraction, a figment of the logical imagination? Why, necessarily, God alone can be the vessel of His own infinite perfections: no creature could contain them; it would crack and fall to pieces. It can only contain them in a finite way, analogously and in proportion to its own nature.

V

But the question may still be urged: granted that God must be transcendent as well as immanent—that He is not essentially connected with us, that the views above criticized are wrong—how is He related to us and to the world? Has Catholic theology no answer to that? Far from it. Catholicism has a long and very subtle answer which pries into the very catacombs of thought.[1] A brief answer must suffice here. The problem ultimately concerns the relation of

[1] It follows on the same lines as the argument already sketched (p. 59) called Analogy, and comes to this that creation cannot conceivably add to the reality contained in God, for it is but the reproduction on an altogether different plane of being of what is already in God. The effect has in an analogous manner what the cause has perfectly.

the One and the many, a problem as old as the hills, and it may be stated in this form: God is all reality, in the sense that if anything other than God existed, it would add nothing to God. There follows the dilemma: either creatures are not other than God, or if they have a separate existence, God is not God. Now it is to be observed that to be cogent the difficulty has to be put in this arithmetical form. Of course, the relation of God to others is not an addition sum. God is not one added to several other units. This would be mere metaphor, taken from arithmetical unity, where the units are nothing but units—seven ones or ten ones. There is no inherent difference in the numbers *qua* numbers. God is not a gigantic total. And even granting that such a summing were possible—a summing of sticks, antelopes, gum and souls—the sum total God would possess merely the perfection and imperfection of the collection. But the world is made up of things with specific natures of their own, and any unity of them all must be a specific one. In other words, the word unity has as many meanings as there are different relations; we must first find the nature of the relation before we can talk of the nature of the unity. And we shall find that the relation of God to the world and to us is a unique kind of relation which cannot be brought under any other form of relation or unity, and furthermore that it is not fully intelligible because one term of the relation is God, and of His Nature we do not know enough. All we can fully understand is what this relation cannot be. Some help may be coined by considering the hierarchy in finite unities. A heap of stones is a heap and nothing more; a mechanical whole possesses a closer unity, and *qua* unity it has a nature above the mere addition of the parts. An organism seems a still closer unity; the organism has its own nature, and yet contrives to leave greater individuality and separateness to the members. The soul unites the faculties, yet is not identical with them. They can, as Plato pointed out, be in conflict with one another, and yet the soul is one. In fact, we can argue that the higher the unity with the parts the greater is the distinction of the whole from the parts *qua* parts. It is more aloof with a nature of its own, and the greater also is the independent functioning of the parts. One could argue, then, that there is nothing unreasonable in a relation such that the unity (or here a better word is needed), though in a sense the whole, is such that it has a nature distinct and incommunicable of its own, and the parts, though dependent on the whole, have also a distinct nature of their own. This hints at what

I have said the relation of God to the finite must be, for we mean by God a Being who embraces all reality and yet is incommunicable and self-subsistent, and we do find the twin facts in ourselves that we are independent and not mere adjectives, and yet we are dependent and owe all to God; we are introduced, then, to the highest of all relations, whose nature it is impossible completely to understand. For whereas we understand one term, namely ourselves, the other, God, has its mysteries which we cannot comprehend.

We must, then, avoid pictures which set God and ourselves in a row to be numbered by the drill sergeant of our imagination. If we must have pictures, the image of a central fire lighting up circle after circle is less misleading; but for a unique relation no parallel can be given, certainly not when one term is God.

The book of God no man can write; he must lay down his pen. This is the streak of Agnosticism in Catholic theology. The Incarnation gave Life and that more abundantly, but the Son of God said: "Come to Me." He did not sit in the chair of the Doctors, and St. Thomas Aquinas gave up writing towards the end, in exchange for a better thing. When excessive speculation is imputed to Catholicism, let it be remembered that it is her adversaries who, like Ixion, embrace a cloud for a divinity, or trespass on ground consecrated to God alone. Orthodox theology is the defence of certain precious facts: God's unique personality, His creation of us through love, our independence and, at the same time, fulfilment in Him. These are the facts we live by; loyal to them we can advance into speculation, until the converging lines are lost in God.

Not altogether unjustly has speculation been accused of making a pyramid with God the vanishing-point at the top. Thought does tend to reduce a multiplicity to a unity which is a bare abstraction, pouring an infinite sea into a sand puddle. But we can correct the abstraction. The pyramid should be inverted to give the real Catholic position. God possesses all the riches which have been sorted out, concentrated in Himself. Life in Aristotle's image may be pictured as a progression from the angle to the triangle which includes it, to the square. St. Thomas regarded the material individual as the barest unity; it is nothing else save by contact, and hence it is almost nothing itself. A plant is richer and more one because it lives by absorbing the life of other things—though the other must die that it may live. An animal is higher still because it is another by sight and sense. An intellectual being has the divine prerogative that it can by mind "become all things" and so far from losing individuality thereby, it is more unified, more richly one.

With these premises Catholicism can find room for all that is best and most attractive in ancient and modern thought. Creation is not a magical formula, not the setting adrift of a world outside the control and providence of God. It is rather a restatement of the cardinal facts of life: that the world is not God; that God has not repeated Himself, if such a thing were possible, and the reverse fact that the world is contingent and has not the source of its own being within itself. Why God created this particular world, there is no partaker of the counsels of God to tell us. How God created the world must be as obscure as the question treated above of the relation of the Infinite to the finite. There are faint analogies; an artist is said to create; out of the material of his mind he produces a work, which is his without his having lost anything. A teacher instructs a pupil; he gives out information; his own knowledge is not decreased thereby, while the pupil's knowledge will not equal the knowledge of the master owing to his inferior capacity.[1] But no analogy will suffice. It is the mysterious and appropriate action of God to which there is no human parallel. We have to resort to Platonic myth to help us. Imagine a being whose very nature it is to be awake, tossing out rays of life unceasingly—all else slumbers like Endymion—in the night of forebeing, or mere possibility. *Et lux in tenebris erat.* Nature awakes, rubs its eyes, but it cannot shake off entirely the shackles of sleep, for God alone is awake by His very nature; and so they awake in Him, their imperfect natures dancing like motes in His light. His eternal watch is not thereby affected; He cannot become drowsy; the imperfection is in these creatures, these vespertilios: their nature is incapable of ceaseless vigil—"and He came and He found them sleeping, for their eyes were heavy." But if this consuming and creating activity of God be love, then creation is one great eternal[2] act of condescension—abyss

[1] Anyone interested in the further investigation of this question will find an extremely subtle treatment in the chapter on Essence and Existence in any text-book of Scholastic Philosophy.

I have called creation the appropriate act of God purposely. It may belong to the nature of perfect love; God's love, to give life and existence to the object (the essence as a possible in scholastic terminology). An artist in a sense gives birth to his idea on canvas or in marble, but it is cold and lifeless. Michelangelo standing before his Moses struck it, crying "Speak." Pygmalion by excess of love gave life to his Galatea. This myth perhaps reveals and hides the power of love in God the Creator.

[2] Eternal, because God is not in time. Time is a function of the finite.

calling to abyss; heaven to chaos; God inviting "the dingiest clot" to an *agape*, the love-feast of Himself. "Wherefore should any set thee love apart? Seeing that none but I makes much of naught." God is the Demeter of existence. And Love demands real otherness, the setting at a distance of the soul that she may run to meet the bridegroom. Even to the end these must be two, close as the union may be. And the response must not be constrained; God must hide and the soul be free to choose. Of its own accord—though the Hound of Heaven be behind and the lure before—must it climb from imperfection to fulfilment, a Psyche in search of Eros.

Philosophy cannot straighten God's purposes, His love, into a straight line. But God's love is the *motif* of the New Testament. *Ista revelatio ipsa est attractio. Nemo venit nisi Pater traxerit*; and the watchword for entrance into God's mystery is: "We must love God because He first loved us."

Creation, then, is an act of love, and the Catholic development of this thought absorbs, as I have said, all that is best in philosophy, ancient and modern; the infinitely desirable Supreme Being of Aristotle drawing all things like a lodestone; "the beauty absolute and simple which, without diminution and without increase or change, is imparted to the ever-growing and perishing beauties of all other things," which Plato divined. And passing over the long list of contributors or prophets of the Catholic idea of God, let us take only Professor Pringle-Pattison's "eternal fashion of the cosmic life"—the self-revelation of the Divine in and to finite spirits. Catholicism admits the presence of God in creation, which is a continual act, not a word once spoken or a careless wave of the hand. God is maintaining the creature in its existence; He is concurring with every act of movement, leaving us just room to be ourselves. The whole earth is full of His glory. He fills every creature with benediction. "From sky to sod, the world's unfolded blossom smells of God."[1] That remarkable priest-poet Gerard Hopkins

We delude ourselves when we think of God living before creation and suddenly saying "Fiat." "All things are unchangeably but freely willed as to the order and measure and fashion of being in Thy eternity which is Thyself, my God." —St. Augustine.

[1] Professor Aliotta has expressed very forcibly the function of nature in terms similar to Catholic theologians: "The belief in the Uniformity of Nature, and science is the belief in the coherence of Nature, scl. that the cosmos is not one of caprice but reason. And if reason is real even when external to the human subject, if the 'ought' which its norms contain be valid apart from our

saw "lovely-felicitous Providence" in the wreck of the *Deutschland*:—

I admire Thee, Master of the tides,
Of the Yore-flood, of the year's fall,
The recurb and the recovery of the gulf's sides,
The girth of it and the wharf of it and the wall;
Stanching, quenching ocean of a motionable mind;
Ground of being and granite of it; past all
Grasp God, throned behind
Death with a sovereignty that heeds but hides, bodes but abides.

Mr. Balfour distinguishes two conceptions of God, the religious and the metaphysical. "The metaphysical tends to regard Him as the logical glue which holds multiplicity together and makes it intelligible. The religious willingly turns away from such speculations about the Absolute to live and worship a spirit among spirits." He owns to never having succeeded in fusing the two conceptions, though he refrains wisely from asserting their incompatibility. Catholicism can be said to fuse them, for her refusal to admit the Hegelian Absolute or a One manifesting itself and essentially or organically connected with this world and ourselves, is based on the nature of two persons, a God who cannot split Himself up, and man who cannot lose the self conferred upon him. The living relation between the two is Love, the revelation of God first in nature and later in the Incarnation—"He has first loved us"—and man's return of love. That is why the old idea of Necessity, of the Three Fates, is brought under Love, and the logic of predestination transformed into Providence. For Providence is the tender care of a Person, a Father who feeds the fowls of the air, clothes the lilies, and knows what we have need of. But as we are persons, too, He will not compel us; omnipotence in a God is Providence and Love; we must ask, knock, seek, and find. Spiritual writers are for ever talking of the Will of God, and it is no fiction. It is the purpose, the omnipotence of God at work as expressed in His solicitude. Outside man's will is this divine presence; His territory extends right up to the citadel of man's will. Closer He is than hands and feet. All nature, all that is not the infinitesimal self, is the "shade of His

minds, are we not necessarily led to an external consciousness for which these norms may be of value? . . . Thus the Eternal speaks to the reluctant mind of the scientist through scientific appearances: he is the unconscious priest of an undying religion."

hand outstretched caressingly." Nature is sacramental, not alien from Him. Time is but God's contrivance for giving us the opportunity to know Him. Through that time gleams the skein of eternity; all that is past and gone is rescued from the tomb by belonging to the Eternal purpose. How idle and foolish beside this is the worship of mere progress, of the Nietzschian ideal of man passing to superman. Men are not mere dung to fructify the seed of the future; they cannot wait for the Colophon, for the pages of their lives are being written in the sweat of their brow. No! there is one unchanging and abiding God giving permanence to the fleeting acts of man. The right meaning of the word Progress is lost once the Catholic idea of God wanes. Extreme Evolution, the Reincarnation of Theosophy, the Becoming of Elan Vital of Bergson, the Everlasting Return of Nietzsche, err in confusing God and the Universe. God is conscious not *in* time, but of time. Progress is the time-expression of an eternal plan. The past is the life-history of human souls, of their will and contribution to their heirs. By God's design the human race is knit together in a close and mysterious membership. Adam's fall affected all his children; the Son of Man took upon Himself the sins of all. The true meaning of civilization is growth in fellowship and common life. It belongs, then, to His plan that one generation should assist another, whether in the secondary aims of bodily well-being or science, or philosophy, or in the sharing of aspiration and ideal. Discovery is of the essence of self-realization, and self-realization can only come in the full play of the separate faculties, in the disinterested pursuit of minor ends. The aims and objects of industry, art, science, and politics are not against God nor outside His reach. He is not a one beside others; love for Him does not diminish minor values, for all that is resides in Him as its source. Plato's flight to God is not the highest Catholic conception. It may be necessary, it often is necessary to leave the creature to find the Creator; but the perfect ideal is the synoptic vision of all reality as included within the divine Love, and therefore most lovable in itself. And it is this ideal which is at the back of progress and civilization, and has been raised to a still higher plane by the union of all Catholics in Christ. But of this more will be said in the essays which follow.[1]

[1] Nothing, perhaps, has so interfered with a belief in God as the problem of suffering. In this essay we do not refer to this subject, as it is discussed in Essay V of this book.

VI

By reason, then, and natural religion we can arrive at an inadequate knowledge of God. We know Him in and through His works; we are not shut off entirely from knowledge of His Nature, though there is a dark wood between our paths and His, and we can only argue by analogy to the nature of the reality on the other side. We are sure of His possessing in one simple essence in His Personality, all that is perfect—Goodness and Love. Confronted with our own finite individuality, which cannot be explained away, we legitimately lay down a special relation between ourselves and the supreme being which will manifestly be unique. This in reference to our coming to be from nothing—for we could not create ourselves, and God could not have produced from His own perfect nature an imperfect being like ourselves—is creation; in reference to our continuing in existence, growing and developing ourselves it will be conservation and concurrence. Furthermore, as God is a Person and we are persons, His purpose in creating us will be love, and love will make necessity Providence in our regard. Withdrawn from Him at first, man will gradually recognize His presence and His purpose more and more. God "having first loved us" even in the natural order, the soul must rest dissatisfied with the best this world can offer; it will make a flight to God, as Plato said. Since in the marketplace it cannot hear the still small voice, it retires to the temple and the desert. At its best this phase of human effort will reach the Form of the Good of Plato or the One of Plotinus, and in religion the worship of an Isis or a Mithras. But with meaning was Tiresias depicted as blind. The highest effort of man after God is a groping, stumbling journey, "for our minds are no more fit for what by its very nature is clearest than are the eyes of bats for the light of day." The finite cannot comprehend the Infinite. A fuller revelation than that given in the natural order had to come; Truth had to manifest itself in flesh and blood; God to become man. This advent was gratuitous; the finite could not claim it, for he was raised far above himself in some mysterious mode so as to be able finally to enjoy God as He is. How this can be we know not, for to see God face to face requires a faculty which must be divinized. God became man that man might become as God. By God's self-humiliation man has been exalted to the heavens.

From what has been said of man's natural knowledge of God, we can understand how far the doctrine of the supernatural end of man surpasses his highest dreams. Man was made for God—*fecisti nos ad Te*—but the level of his attainment cannot be above his own finite plane; he cannot see God face to face without being raised to what with all reverence may be called an equality with God. And yet man seeks God naturally[1] and with all his soul, if "haply he may find Him." What degree of attainment is possible, it is not easy to state, for we have no means of judging. Man has never been left entirely to his own resources, or lived unassisted in the natural order. Nevertheless the fitness of the natural for the supernatural would imply that the supernatural is the extension to infinity of a feeble tendency—the crowning of a beggar maid by a king. It pours, as it were, a precious ointment into man's eyes so that he can see God the object of his longing without being struck blind. A proof of the eminence of our nature is that grace does not radically transform it. A horse raised to a higher order, to the level of man, would cease to be a horse, but our intellect is in a sense "capable of God." It needs to be perfected, not changed. As an inhabitant in human beings, the mind sees all things through the medium of its owner, the person; it casts its shadow even as the body. At present we are thwarted as well by sensible images, by distraction and distension of mind. But given the soul at one with itself, the process of self-realization completed, then it would know God in knowing itself, understanding its own nature and its relation and dependence on God—how it is a "cry to God" a poem written by Him and speaking His praises. God would be the completion of incompleteness. His essence would still be dark to our eyes, owing to the shadow we cast. The soul would love Him in a finite way, as *its* fulfilment, the Truth and Life *of* itself. The distinction between this and the gift of the Beatific Vision will be apparent if we recall that in Heaven we see God as He is in Himself. The shadow is removed and there is nothing between. In that perfect communion the creature thinks no longer in terms of itself, but of another, God. In the Beatific Vision we shall be conscious of God as we are conscious of ourselves in this life. God still remains another, because our nature to absorb

[1] The word "nature" is among the vaguest terms of everyday thought. When used of man, it generally means either primitive as opposed to artificial or civilized: "man in his natural condition," scl. a savage; or perfect: a man in his highest or fullest development. This latter, the Aristotelian sense of the term, is the one used in the text. But there are other complications, owing to Original Sin, and above all, the prevenient grace of God, for man is not left entirely to his own resources. "God first loved us."

Him must be so dilated as to cease to be itself. This is the vestige of finiteness discernible even in heaven.

What Catholic theology is concerned to safeguard is the distinction, the gulf between God's nature and ours. Man's need of God has sometimes been stated as a claim on Him. This would bind God, as a government is pledged to the nation. If stress is laid on the exigencies of nature, God tends to become the mere expression of the creature's desire. For a similar reason it is impossible that the soul should have an intuition of God, using intuition in a technical sense.[1] For intuition means that a faculty whether of sense or thought has a natural object to which it is exactly proportioned, as sight to colour, and that therefore it apprehends the object whole and without any intermediary. It has a right to that object. In this sense, man cannot, it is clear, have an intuition of God; no human faculty could apprehend the Divine nature—sooner could a camel pass through the eye of a needle. And honestly we realize this in our very need. The fact that we pray to God and ask His assistance and do not demand Him shows that we instinctively appreciate the difference. This craving for God, which as a symptom of the truth of His providence and revelations, proves so suggestive, has been pressed by the Modernists into the exaggeration that it is constitutive of God. Modernism makes a distinction between the truth of fact and value, between knowledge and the religious consciousness. God must be what the feeling of the heart desires. Whether He exists or not, matters not; it suffices that religious souls have required a Redeemer and a Comforter. The universality of such a need constitutes a truth of value. At its best, this view seems to isolate one factor in religion and exclude the rest; at its worst, it verges on scepticism. Granting that we approach God through our desire for Him, still we do not burn our boats of history and philosophy. The biography of religious men show them hesitating before and pondering over facts. We start as pragmatists, but the first conclusion of Pragmatism is that Pragmatism won't do; we start desiring God, and in a twinkling we see that desire is not sufficient. But the most serious error

[1] It is sometimes said that mystics have an intuition of God in this life. Certainly in contemplation the soul may pass beyond sensible images and inference. St. Thomas Aquinas admits such an immediate apprehension. But it is not intuition proper, for God is seen still by faith and not by sight, rather in the manner I have described a little farther on in the text. The statements of mystics cannot be taken too literally, since the immediate apprehension of the essence of God would be everlasting.

in the view is the inversion of the right order of thinking and desiring.[1] Good does not exist because we desire it; just the opposite! Because there is goodness, we desire it; because God is, therefore we seek for Him. "We must love God because He has first loved us." And against the Modernist presentation of the case, it can never be repeated too often that man's groping for God cannot be a sure way; there is no intuition of the Infinite, no capacity in man which can embrace "the succinct, conjoint, and golden point" of the divine nature. All the anticipations, prophecies, types, raptures of the time before Christ were but as altars to an unknown God ignorantly worshipped—then "through the thunder came a human voice saying, 'O heart I made, a heart beats here! Thou hast no power, nor may'st conceive of mine. But love I gave thee, with myself to love; and thou must love me who have died for thee'!" "This revelation set I forth to you." After the Incarnation of the Son of God, truth is no longer travailing in the womb of man. In Him is truth; our interrogations have been answered. Nowhere better than in the Confessions of St. Augustine are the two attitudes depicted. He had hungered for God; he had known the heights of Platonic philosophy, but his anticipations were as a drop of water in the ocean compared with the unfathomable riches revealed in Christ. And I cannot end better than by quoting that famous passage which contains as in a breviary the Catholic conceptions of the world made by God, the restless craving for Him, His superabundant return. "Too late loved I Thee, O Thou Beauty of ancient days, yet ever new! Too late I loved Thee! And behold Thou wert within and I abroad, and there I searched for Thee; deformed I, plunging amid those fair forms which Thou hadst made; Thou wert with me, but I was not with Thee. Things held me far from Thee, which, unless they were in Thee, were not at all. Thou calledst and shoutedst and burstest my deafness. Thou flashedst, shinest, and scatteredst my blindness. Thou breathedst odours and I drew in breath and pant for Thee. I tasted, and hunger and thirst. Thou touchedst me and I burned for Thy peace. When I shall with my whole self cleave to Thee, I shall nowhere have sorrow or labour: and my life shall wholly live as wholly full of Thee."

[1] Modernists disparage reason because they are still under the spell of Kant's distinction of the Pure and Practical Reason. The distinction is not such a force nowadays in philosophy, but it persists in theology.

III
THE NATURE AND DESTINY OF MAN

BY
CHRISTOPHER DAWSON

I

IN her doctrine of Man the Catholic Church has always held the middle path between two opposing theories, that which makes man an animal and that which holds him to be a spirit. Catholicism has always insisted that man's nature is twofold. He is neither flesh nor spirit, but a compound of both. It is his function to be a bridge between two worlds, the world of sense and the world of spirit, each real, each good, but each essentially different. His nature is open on either side to impressions and is capable of a twofold activity, and his whole destiny depends on the proper co-ordination of the two elements in his nature: and not his destiny alone; for since he is a bridge, the lower world is in some sense dependent on him for its spiritualization and its integration in the universal order.

In the early ages of the Church the main opposition to this view of man's nature came from those, who, like the Gnostics and Manicheans, held man's nature to be purely spiritual and his connection with the body to be in itself an evil and the source of all evil.

This view, as held by the Catharists and Albigensians, was also the dominant heresy of the Middle Ages, and even to-day it has its adherents among Christian Scientists, Theosophists, and Spiritualists.

During the last four hundred years, however, spiritualism has been a steadily declining force, and the materialistic view of man has become the great rival of Catholicism. It is true that during the present age a strong wave of Spiritualism has passed once more over Western civilization, and has shown itself both in literature and art, in philosophy and religion, not to speak of such lower manifestations as magic and table-turning. Nevertheless this movement does not rest on any clear view of the relations of spirit and matter. It is in the main a reaction of sentiment against the dogmatic scientific rationalism of the nineteenth century. In literature it is represented by the mystical materialism of Maeterlinck, as well as by the orthodox traditional Catholicism of Claudel, and the vague symbolism of W. B. Yeats. It is neither a philosophy nor a religion, it is rather agnosticism becoming mystical and acquiring once more a hunger for the infinite. The resultant attitude towards religion is well expressed by one of the younger French poets, P. J. Jouve:—

J'ait dit Dieu—je dirais l'etoile
Ou le vent dans les arbres nus;
L'Univers, l'antique Raison,
Athena bleu ou Christ en Croix,

Et ce serait toujours plus vrai.

It may be that this movement is a temporary phenomenon, without any deep roots in the mind of the age, and without importance for the future; but it is also possible that it marks the beginning of a religious age and the permanent weakening of the rationalist and materialist tradition which has increasingly dominated Western civilization ever since the fifteenth century.

The change that came over Europe at that period is too complex to be ascribed to any one cause. It was the breaking up of the social and religious unity of the Middle Ages. In every direction men were conscious of new power and new knowledge, and they used their new opportunities to the full in a spirit of ruthless self-assertion which took no heed for the rights of others and no respect for authority and tradition. In this sudden and violent expansion, the genius of that age foresaw and traced out all the essential achievements of the modern as against the mediæval world. Indeed the mind of some of the great artists and humanists, above all of Leonardo da Vinci, is more modern than that of the philosophers of the eighteenth-century enlightenment, or those of the pioneers of nineteenth-century industry and science.

It is easy to understand that such an age should evolve a new view of human nature. The men of the Renaissance had turned their eyes away from the world of the spirit to the world of colour and form, of flesh and blood; they set their hopes not on the unearthly perfection of the Christian saint, but on the glory of Man—man set free to live his own life and to realize the perfection of power and beauty and knowledge that was his by right. They returned to the old Ionian conception of Nature "Physis," a single material order, which, whether it be rational or irrational, includes in itself all that is. "Nothing is more Divine or more human than anything else, but all things are alike and all Divine."

It is true that few thinkers were sufficiently consistent or sufficiently bold to expound this idea explicitly, like Giordano Bruno. Nevertheless it is implicit in the life and work of many of the men of the Renaissance. Rabelais, for example, may have been sincere in his professions of belief in God, but the true tendency of his ideas is shown when he substitutes for the spirit and the flesh, for supernatural grace and corrupt nature, the opposition of "Physis" and "Antiphysis": the joyous "Physis" of the humanist and poet, of the peasant and the soldier, of all that is real and carnal and unashamed of itself, and the hateful dark "Antiphysis" of the schoolmen and the monks, hostile to life and destructive of joy.

But it was only in the exceptional minds of an exceptional age—men like Bruno and Rabelais—that the new ideas attained to clear expression; the ordinary man, even if he lived like a humanist, still half belonged in thought and feeling to the Middle Ages. Moreover, the Christian Renaissance of the sixteenth century largely undid the work of the Pagan Renaissance, so that by the beginning of the seventeenth century the tide seemed indeed to have turned.

Nevertheless the rationalist and humanist traditions were carried on, whether by unsystematic sceptics like Montaigne or dogmatic atheists like Vanini, until in the course of the eighteenth century it came at last into its kingdom. From that time the negative work of destructive criticism and the positive construction of a rationalist and naturalist synthesis have been carried on vigorously, especially in the more favourable environment produced by the political and industrial revolutions, and the passing away of the *ancient regime*.

The naturalist conception of man has above all been influenced by the Darwinian doctrine of the Origin of Species, and by the evolutionary theories to which this gave rise. The doctrine of a continuous development through the whole of animate nature, and the gradual evolution of the human species under the influence of natural selection, seemed to show that no principle external to the material world need be invoked to account for man: he was of a piece with the rest of nature. Further, the theory of evolution was linked with the earlier liberal theories of political and social advance to form the modern doctrine of unlimited and inevitable material progress, a doctrine fundamentally unscientific and based on an irrational optimism, but which has nevertheless become a part of the mental furniture of the ordinary modern man. As yet, however, the naturalist movement has not received its definite philosophy. There has been no lack of ambitious attempts to elaborate naturalistic syntheses, but none has been final. Neither Condorcet nor Holbach, nor Bentham nor Comte nor Spencer nor Haeckel can be said to be the philosopher of the movement. Nevertheless, in their doctrine of man there is a large element common to all these philosophers. Whether they be Deists, Materialists or Agnostics they generally agree that man is a part of the material world; that in the knowledge, the control, and the enjoyment of this world he finds his true end, and that no spiritual principle can intervene in this closed order governed by uniform physical laws. Taking it as a whole, however, modern naturalism is due not so much to any philosophic theory, as to the material triumphs of modern civilization and man's conquest of nature. The realm of mystery before which man feels himself humble and weak has withdrawn its frontiers. Man can know his world without falling back on revelation; he can live his life without feeling his utter dependence on supernatural powers. He is no longer the servant of unknown forces, but a master in his own house, and he intends to make the most of his new-found powers.

The resultant attitude to life is well shown in the following extract from Professor Bateson's Presidential Address to the British Association in August, 1914.[1] "Man is just beginning to know himself for what he is—a rather long-lived animal with great powers of enjoyment if he does not deliberately forgo them. Hitherto superstition and mythical ideas of sin have predominately controlled these powers. Mysticism will not die out: for these strange fancies knowledge is no cure: but their forms may change, and mysticism, as a force for the suppression of joy, is happily losing its hold on the modern world. As in the decay of earlier religions, Ushabti dolls were substituted for human victims, so telepathy, necromancy, and other harmless toys take the place of eschatology and the inculcation of a ferocious moral code. Among the civilized races of Europe, we are witnessing an emancipation from traditional control in thought, in art, and in conduct, which is likely to have prolonged and wonderful influences. Returning to freer, or, if you will, simpler conceptions of life and death, the coming generations are determined to get more out of this world than their forefathers did."

This view of life is clearly rather practical than philosophical. It is only possible to one who looks at the surface of life; if we look at man from within, its simplicity is easily seen to be delusive.

[1] *Report of Brit. Assoc.*, 1914, p. 29.

If man limits himself to a satisfied animal existence, and asks from life only what such an existence can give, the higher values of life at once disappear. It is from that very element of the eternal and the unlimited, which the materialist seeks to deny, that the true progress of the human race has sprung. Throughout his history, man has been led, not as Buckle taught, by the rational pursuit of practical and material ends, but by belief in a transcendent reality,[1] and in the truth of moral and spiritual values. This is to a great extent true even of the values of that civilization which the disciple of naturalism accepts as his end. Even Professor Bateson himself demands of his ideal eugenist community that it shall not eliminate the Shakespeares and the Beethovens. Yet what value remains in Shakespeare's work if the doubt of Hamlet is a simple physical neurasthenia, and the despair of Lear but the reaction of a wounded animal to hostile circumstances?

Man's true excellence consists not in following the law of animal nature but in his resistance to it, and in his recognition of another law. The law of the animal world is the law of instinctive desire and brute force; there is no room in it for freedom or right or moral good. In man alone a new principle comes into play; for he recognizes that beyond the natural good of pleasure and self-fulfilment, there is a higher good which is independent of himself, a good that is unlimited, ideal, spiritual. It is true that man does not necessarily follow this good; it is easy enough for him to disregard it and to lapse into animalism, but even as he does so, he has the sense of choice, of responsibility, of something he has gained, or lost.

This contrast between man's moral consciousness and the world of sense-experience is one of the fundamental problems of existence, and it presents an obvious difficulty to the materialist or naturalist for whom this world of sense-experience makes up the whole universe. Yet some of the most thorough-going and clear-sighted of materialists from the days of Huxley onwards have accepted it resolutely with all its difficulties. In one of his essays, Mr. Bertrand Russell even makes it the foundation of his ethical theory.[2] He admits that the world shown to us by science is a world of blind force, and that man with his knowledge of good and evil is a helpless atom in a world which has no such knowledge. His origin, his growth, his

[1] i.e. transcending the world of sense-experience, not, of course, the order of nature.
[2] "The Free Man's Worship," reprinted in *Mysticism and Logic*, 1918.

hopes and fears, his loves and beliefs are but the outcome of accidental collocations of atoms, and are destined to be swallowed up again by blind material forces. Nevertheless, he rejects the conclusion that our moral ideals are worthless and that naked Power alone is to be worshipped. "If Power is bad, as it seems to be, let us reject it, from our hearts. In this lies man's true freedom: in determination to worship only the God created by our own love of the good, to respect only the heaven which inspires the insight of our last moments. In action, in desire, we must submit perpetually to the tyranny of outside forces; but in thought, in aspiration, we are free, free from the petty planet in which our bodies impotently crawl, free even, while we live, from the tyranny of death."

Thus he arrives at the paradoxical conclusion that we must love a good God Who does not exist, and refuse to serve Nature which does exist but is not good. It is not likely that a religion of this kind will ever become popular, since men will always be inclined to adapt their morality to their general conception of the universe. Rather than acquiesce in a flagrant contradiction between the real and the ideal, they will lower their ideal to the level of their conception of reality. In order to avoid Mr. Russell's dilemma, it becomes necessary for the materialist to deny the transcendence of the moral ideal, unless the difficulty is slurred over, as it is by Haeckel and so many others in an irrational and sentimental idealization of nature.

On the other hand, when once the absolute superiority of the human spirit to the rest of the material universe is admitted, it becomes intellectually, as well as practically difficult to halt at the point at which Mr. Bertrand Russell halts. For if it be once affirmed that in the human consciousness a principle, or an order of being, higher than anything that is found in the material world, has made its appearance, it is difficult to suppose that that principle can be of so transitory and limited a character as he maintains.

Even in the limited field of experience open to our minds, the power of spirit is out of all proportion to that of other forces of nature. The force of conscious reason is able to mould and direct in a thousand ways the world of unconscious matter and animal nature. Thanks to the power of reason, man is like the god of this planet. He is able to dominate his environment and to co-ordinate the forces of nature in his own service. Nor is this conscious dominion over nature the only kingdom of man's spirit. The realm of abstract thought is greater than that of action. The riches of the kingdom of the spirit are inexhaustible, and here the greatest minds are often those that feel their own limitations most keenly, as though in all their science and philosophy they are no more than children picking up shells on the shores of an illimitable sea.

There is a point at which the world of spirit comes in conscious contact with the world of matter. That point is man. It is in the highest degree unreasonable to limit the whole world of spirit to its manifestation in the human mind, and to conceive of the universe as a vast material cosmos in which a solitary fragment of spiritual being exists in the case of one reasonable and moral creature. It is surely more rational to suppose that the world of thought and of spiritual values, on the threshold of which man has the consciousness of standing, is a real world, an order no less great than the material order, and that it is in this alone that we shall find a solution to the otherwise hopeless conflict of man's spiritual aspirations and the limitations of his material existence.

At first sight this problem is only accentuated by the admission of the existence of a spiritual world. For if man is spiritual, why does he not live by the spirit? By reason he is able to control the external world but not his own nature, and though he can recognize the supreme value of the moral order, he seems incapable of making it dominate his own individual and social life. Many of his acts spring, not from reason, but from impulse, and that impulse is grounded deep in his animal nature. Indeed, the main driving force behind human life seems to be a subconscious life-instinct, in itself not essentially dissimilar from the life-instinct of the animal world. This life-impulse manifests itself in all the natural desires centreing round the struggle for existence in all that serves the life of the individual or the species on the animal plane. It finds its central and most characteristic expression in the sexual impulse, and it is on that account named "Libido" by Jung and his school of psychologists; but it extends far beyond the limits of the sexual functions, and makes itself felt even in the higher levels of human experience, which are apparently very far dissociated from the primary physical needs.[1]

II

This life of unconscious or semi-conscious instinct is, however, far from covering the whole field of human activity. Even the lowest

[1] Compare the extended use of the term *concupiscentia* by St. Augustine.

savage lives not entirely by instinct, and in civilized man the domination of other conscious and rational forces is plain enough. Reason makes it possible for man to review and judge his instincts, to foresee the consequences of his impulsive actions, and to restrain them in cases in which their fulfilment is disadvantageous to himself; for instinct is blind and may lead the individual to his ruin, as a moth is led to the candle flame. Nevertheless, as a rule, rational action is not fundamentally different, as regards its end, from instinctive action. For the most part the conscious motives that inspire the activities of the individual and the society are but a continuation of the physical life-impulse on the rational plane. A conscious self-interest, the deliberate aiming at pleasure, wealth, and power, whether in the case of the individual or of the group, takes the place of the obscure, physical impulses which dominate the life of instinct. The one may indeed conflict with the other, for success in the social competition of civilized life requires a self-suppression and a kind of asceticism which runs directly counter to physical instinct. This conscious self-seeking is in essence entirely different to animal instinct, although from a moral point of view, it is no higher. It is in fact evil in a sense in which animal instinct cannot be, for it is not, like the latter, the natural activity of a higher, spiritual force. The life of animal instinct is better than that of rational self-interest in that it is less limited; for it serves not merely the purposes of the individual, but those of the species, and more, of the whole of nature. The individual is the servant and instrument of a universal impulse.

With the rational life, however, the individual has conquered impulse in so far as it makes him the servant of obscure and unrealized purposes. He serves not a universal and ultimate purpose, but some special and secondary end, i.e. he uses impulse and material things generally for his individual pleasure and profit, and these may have no ultimate justification and serve no purpose in the general scheme of things. Now if the materialist hypothesis were true, it would naturally follow that the life-impulse, whether as unconscious instinct or as rational self-interest, would be not only the dominant power, but the only power in man. For it is inconsistent to deny the reality of the spirit as being, and to continue to maintain it as a motive force in action. There would be no room for freedom or moral responsibility, but man would be the slave of physical impulse and self-interest, and as the life-force drove, so must he go.

Actually, however, as we have seen, man has a spiritual side to his nature. He is conscious of another good besides the good of instinct and self-interest, a good which is absolute and spiritual, and he has some vague conception of a spiritual power to which he is responsible.

On the foundation of this spiritual consciousness, and in order to satisfy his spiritual needs, he builds up his systems of natural religion, systems which may be powerless to dominate the life-impulse effectually and habitually, but which are at least able to modify it and to give man the desire for a higher and freer life.

In primitive society, where man is absorbed in a struggle for bare existence with the mysterious forces of nature, religion, like the rest of life, is more or less on the plane of instinct, and is concerned with material rather than spiritual objects. But even here the spiritual consciousness exists, though it is confused by the sense of mystery which overshadows the material world, and causes primitive man to look on all material things and forces as moved by indwelling spirits. So, as man advances in civilization and in control over his life, the religion of nature becomes less important, and that of society takes the first place. The ordinary life of the people becomes rationalized and secularized, but their deeper needs remain. Although the religion of society seems to be utilitarian, a spiritual element is implicit in it. For example, if the religion of many early civilizations is directed mainly to success in war, the ultimate end of that success is not to gain material advantages for the society, so much as to exalt its god by its victory.

But it is only when civilization is mature, when society becomes self-conscious and the struggle for bare survival is slackened, that the spiritual needs of man's nature exert their full power. It is then that he begins to reason about life and the end of life, and to contrast his actual existence with the ideal life which his spirit desires. He revolts against his slavery to the law of animal instinct and selfish desire, no less than against the law of death, which seems to render vain all the achievements of the human mind. He feels himself the plaything of physical needs and physical sufferings which make his individual life a selfish struggle for survival ending in inevitable extinction. If he lives for his society as the one thing in his life which is permanent, and through which he may in a sense survive, he does but enter upon a wider cycle of the same life-process. Civic life can only satisfy when the society itself subserves a spiritual end. There is nothing in social life as such which is more spiritual than individual life. Animalism can dominate the former as easily as the latter, even more easily. The group purpose is as well served when the human pack tears to pieces its weak or maimed member, as when it throws itself with self-regardless courage at the throat of the common enemy.

It is, in fact, when we look at the history of mankind in the mass that the evils of human existence are most apparent. We see empires built on oppression and the blood of the poor, by degrees melting into ruin, and being replaced by some equally bloodthirsty but more barbarous power which goes at last to meet the same fate. Nor does civilization bring freedom; for the spectacle of a civilized society dominated, not by one unconscious natural instinct, but by a conscious lust for pleasure or power or wealth, is even more horrible than the other. What wonder if some men have always turned away from the cruelty and greed and lust which seems to dominate the struggle for existence, and have refused life itself, if it is only to be purchased on such terms?

This is the fundamental problem which has pressed on the human race for thousands of years and which is as living now as it was in the days of the Buddha. The last generation, indeed, believed that Science had solved this problem like so many others. It was their boast that:

> Science has pierced man's cloudy common sense,
> Dowered his homely vision with more expansive an embrace,
> And the rotten foundation of old superstition exposed.
> That trouble of Pascal, those vain paradoxes of Austin,
>   Those Semitic parables of Paul, those tomes of Aquinas,
>   All are thrown to the limbo of antediluvian idols.[1]

But who now would claim that "that trouble of Pascal" has been rendered any less insistent by the discovery of the fossils of Neanderthal Man, or the Pithecanthropus of Java? We have returned to the old problems which arise not from lack of scientific knowledge, but from the very conditions of our nature.

It was in India that religion first reached this stage, owing mainly to local and climatic conditions which at once forced on and limited the development of a self-contained civilization. It is, however, a mistake to make these material factors responsible for Indian thought itself. The same process takes place eventually in every matured

[1] *Poems of Robert Bridges*, p. 421 (Oxford Edition).

civilization. Some peoples, like the Chinese and the Romans, have possessed a genius for social life, for organization, work and practical achievements, but even these have experienced at last the inevitable dissatisfaction with human life as it is, and the need for deliverance.

In India, these phenomena were exceptionally strongly marked and widespread, and the fundamental postulates of natural religion enter more deeply than elsewhere into the life and thought of the people. The sense of man's bondage to animal life and desire, and to the law of death; belief in the fruit of moral action, Karma, as inevitable retribution or recompense; and above all the need for deliverance from the animal life and the law of death (Nirvana) are at the root of all the great Indian systems whether Buddhist or Vedanist, Sankhya or Yoga, Sivaite or Vishnuite, though all this is woven on a background of animism, polytheism, and magic.

The Indians picture the whole life-process as an endless wheel of lives and deaths gripped in the claws of the monster Kama or desire; to be freed from that wheel is the end of all their efforts:

> Through birth and rebirth's endless round,
> Seeking in vain, I hastened on,
> To find who framed this edifice;
> What misery! birth incessantly.

But how can man escape from the domination of this power which seems the very power of life itself? Only, it was said, by turning his back on life, by seeing in the whole sensible world nothing but illusion, and by leaving the finite and the known for the unknown infinite. The sting of death is desire: destroy desire and you will destroy death, but you will destroy life also in so far as life is human and limited.

The classical expression of this attitude to life is found in Buddhism which excelled all other Indian religions in the simplicity of its reasoning and in the austerity of its morals. "Two things only do I teach, sorrow and the ending of sorrow," said the Buddha, rebuking those who would know whether Nirvana was existence or non-existence. Life is evil, the body is evil, sense is evil, consciousness is evil. Only in the destruction and cessation of all these can the true good be found. This is no less the message of the other great spiritualist religions of the East. Whether they teach a spiritualist monism, like the Vedanta; a spiritualist nihilism, like Buddhism; or a spiritualist dualism, like Manichæanism,—they agree in this, that what is wrong with man is not the disorder or disease of his actual existence but his very life itself. Evil is not in man's will, but is essentially bound up with the existence of the body and the material universe. Therefore this life must not be spiritualized; it must be left behind, and man must return to the one, absolute, undifferentiated Being, or Not-being, of which his spirit is a part.

This is the oriental solution of life, and with it all progress ends. Society loses its higher vitality which is transferred to the pursuit of the absolute, and man's spiritual energy is dissipated in theosophy and asceticism.

However progressive a civilization may be, eventually it realizes its natural potentialities, and then the tendency is for it to fall into an oriental or Byzantine state of fixity in which the life-impulse turns to religion.

There is no reason to believe that the modern scientific and industrialist civilization would ultimately escape that end any more than the great civilizations of the past. European civilization was tending this way under the early Roman Empire, in spite of the scientific genius of the Greeks and the essentially "Western" spirit of the Romans. The oriental spiritualist attitude to life was dominant alike in philosophy and religion, in Neo-Pythagoreanism and Neo-Platonism, in the oriental cults, above in Gnosticism and Manichæanism; and it was the great danger to the Christian Faith throughout the early centuries of the Church's life.

Yet these religions, with all their impressiveness and their fascination for minds that are satiated with material progress, do not solve the problem of human life. Man left to himself[1] is powerless to reconcile the antinomy of his spiritual and material natures. Either he may let himself sink back into the life of the body, disregarding the claims of the spirit, or he tries to satisfy these by the total rejection of the body and the life that it conditions. Yet man cannot be quit of his nature on such easy terms. In spite of his denial of it, the material world goes on, and the body must in time exact retribution from those who despise it.

Thus even Buddhism, the most uncompromising of all the spiritualist religions, was not proof against paganism and magic; and the way of renunciation and the law of moral discipline were succeeded by the superstition and obscenity of Tantric Buddhism

[1] i.e. man in his present condition of fallen nature.

which spread throughout Northern India and Thibet during the early Middle Ages.

In the case of monistic religions, the process of degeneration is even easier, for the vagueness and antinomianism of the pantheist attitude to life are apt to idealize man's lower nature, and to throw a cloak of symbolism over the indulgence of physical impulse.

III

Such reactions and degenerations can be avoided only by a spiritualization of the whole of man's nature, which will unite the life of the body and the life of the spirit in the service of a common end. Some force must be found which will spiritualize human life without destroying it, which will keep the life-impulse at work in the world without letting it dissipate itself in the aridities of materialism, or die down in the emptiness of world-negation.

This is the claim of the Catholic Faith, that a new power has in fact been brought into the world which is capable of regenerating humanity; not merely by reconciling human nature with itself—which is the unattained goal of human philosophy—but by uniting organically the whole of man, body and soul, sense and spirit, with a higher spiritual principle, thus making of him a new creature.

This restoration or recreation of humanity is the essential doctrine of Christianity. Jesus Christ is to the Catholic not a prophet and teacher like the founders of other great religions, nor even is He only the divine revealer of God to man: He is the restorer of the human race, the New Man, in whom humanity has a fresh beginning and man acquires a new nature. His work was genetic and creative in an absolutely unique sense, for it brought into the world a new kind of life which has the power to transmute and absorb into itself the lower forms of physical and psychical life which exist in man.[1]

It is the "new birth from above"[2] of which Christ speaks to Nicodemus, a mysterious force, the power and reality of which are manifest, while its cause and working are as invisible as the wind.

This higher life was of course not entirely absent from humanity before Christ, but it existed rather as a potentiality awaiting realization than as a force dominating the whole nature of man. For it is only through Christ, the second Adam, and in organic connection

[1] i.e. the Christian does not simply acquire extrinsic supernatural faculties, his whole life becomes supernatural, and finally even his body shares in the new life. Cf. St. Paul, Rom. viii. 19.

[2] St. John iii.

with Him, that the new humanity is to be built up. By the vital activity of the Spirit of Christ working through the Church and the Sacraments, mankind is remoulded and renewed; the disorder and weakness of human nature is overcome, and the domination of charity in spiritual love is substituted for the blindness of physical impulse and the narrowness and evil of selfish desire. The consummation of this work of restoration by the unification of humanity under the vital control of the Spirit of God may seem infinitely distant, since it involves the absolute conquest of matter by spirit, and the spiritualization and immortalization of the human body—in fact, a new world and a new humanity; but no lesser term is proposed by the Catholic Faith as the destiny of the human race.

Thus, the Catholic view of life involves a fundamental opposition between the new force that has entered human life through Christ, and the disordered material activity which it replaces. This opposition shows itself in Christian asceticism, in the monastic ideal of perfection, the cult of virginity, and the mortification of the body, all of which seem to betoken as drastic a world-renunciation as that of the Hindu ascetic.

Consequently, many moderns regard Christianity as the culmination of that wave of oriental spiritualism which overwhelmed the ancient world. But this is a fundamental misconception. Christianity comes neither from the East nor from the West. It is, even as it claims to be, the fulfilment of a unique religious tradition which denied oriental pantheism and nihilism as obstinately as it refused occidental humanism and materialism. It is founded, not on a metaphysical theory which denies the body and the material universe, but on a historical and social revelation—the Jewish faith in the Kingdom of God.

From the dawn of their history, the Jewish people were marked by an intense religious realism; they possessed a social genius no less strong in its way than that of the Greeks, but their political ideal was narrowly and literally theocratic: they were the one people of God—Israel.

Many other nations of the ancient world—Assyria, for example—likewise were governed by theocratic conceptions, but sooner or later these political religions gave way before the current of religious universalism, even as the states themselves were swallowed up in the Persian and Hellenistic world-empires. With the Jews alone, universalism did not destroy the national faith, but on the contrary strengthened and spiritualized their faith in their own God and in their peculiar destiny.

From the ninth century before Christ down to the final destruction of Jerusalem in A.D. 70, Israel passed through a long succession of misfortunes, crisis following crisis and disappointment crushing hope time after time: and yet in the midst of these troubles and disillusionments the Hope of Israel was gradually revealed.

It was the belief of the mass of the unspiritual Jews—the stiff-necked people and kings against whom the prophets wrote—that the covenant of Yahweh with Israel was such that the temporal welfare of the people was only limited by the strength of their god. If his service was neglected he would certainly send plagues in vengeance; but it was inconceivable that he should allow his people to be destroyed or enslaved by another, for that would be equivalent to acknowledging his inferiority to a "strange god."

It was against this conception of the relation of Yahweh to his people that the first prophets wrote. The earliest of them, Amos, declared that the kingdom of Israel was destined to destruction not because Yahweh was weak, but because the people had broken the covenant of justice and had ceased to be a holy people. Their avarice and the oppression of the poor had brought upon them the anger of God, which was not to be turned away by sacrifice or external service. Therefore the destruction of Israel was decreed by Yahweh, and the Assyrian world-power was but his instrument, "the rod of his anger" in the words of Isaias. Yahweh's power was not limited to his own people and his own land; the Gentiles also were subject to him, though they knew him not. Their cruelty and oppression would be punished in due time, as the sin of Israel had been; but first they had a work to do as unconscious instruments of the will of Yahweh.

And so the prophet Jeremias in the last days of the kingdom of Judah saw the divine purpose behind the victorious power of the King of Babylon, and set his face against the national and religious patriotism which would defend the Holy City to the last. He laid the curse of Yahweh alike on those who trusted in the arm of the flesh—the help of Egypt—and on those who prophesied falsely that Yahweh would never deliver his people into the hands of their enemies. For years he faced the intrigues and hatred of rulers and people, announcing in bitterness of heart the destruction of all that the traditions of his people held most dear. Throughout the siege of

Jerusalem and after the captivity, among the remnant that remained behind and went down into Egypt, he never ceased to warn the Jews that they must submit to the foreign yoke. Only after long suffering and humiliation might they hope for a time when Yahweh should restore his people under a king of the house of David, and give to them a new covenant, "written on the heart," whereby he would be for ever known with an interior and personal knowledge, in place of the external legal relation that existed under the old covenant of Moses.

This promise is perhaps the highest and most important utterance amongst all the sayings of the prophets, for it seems to anticipate, more than anything else, the Gospel teaching of the spiritual character of the Kingdom of God. It is, however, in the second part of the book of Isaias that the special vocation of Israel as the people of Yahweh is revealed in its widest and most exalted form. Here the prophet proclaims that Yahweh is not merely the God of Israel: he is the divine Governor of the universe who wills that all nations shall come to know him, and to obey the law of his Justice, as manifested in his people Israel. Therefore he has brought Cyrus, "His shepherd" from the north, to "humble the great ones of the earth, to break the gates of brass, to set free the captives," that all peoples from the rising of the sun to the islands of the west may know that the God of Israel is the one true God, the Creator and Ruler of the world.

And the prophet teaches that the sufferings of Israel had been inflicted not merely in anger, but for the fulfilment of this divine purpose. In the words of a later writer, "He scattered you among the nations that know Him not, that you may declare His wonderful works, and make them know that there is no other Almighty God besides Him."[1] In like manner, the restoration of Israel and the manifestation of God to the Gentile was also to be accomplished by suffering and obedience. Yahweh's chosen servant, on whom His spirit rests, is called to carry out the divine purpose in the spiritual order, as Cyrus is called to prepare the way for it in temporal things. The latter, unconscious of his call, has a mission of honour, the former, who shares in the Divine Spirit, has a mission of suffering and shame.

"By his knowledge shall this my just servant justify many, and he shall bear their iniquities." "Thus saith Yahweh, the Redeemer of Israel his Holy One, to the soul that is despised, to the nation that

[1] Tobias xiii. 4.

is hated, to the servant of rulers: kings shall see and princes shall rise up, and adore for the sake of Yahweh because he is faithful, and for the Holy One of Israel who has chosen thee."[1]

The passages of Isaias that describe the mission of Yahweh's servant have been more debated by the modern critics than any other part of the Old Testament, and every kind of interpretation has been suggested with regard to the character of the suffering servant. Most of their difficulties have, however, arisen from the inability of the critics to recognize the essentially mystical character of this prophecy. The Holy Servant is chosen from the womb to redeem the sinful Jewish people and to be a light to the Gentiles. Yet at the same time, in so far as the nation is holy and fulfils its vocation, it also is "the servant of Yahweh," and shares in the redemptive work; there is a mystical solidarity between the chosen individual and the chosen community, and the latter only attains to its destiny through the work of the former.[2]

It is not to be supposed that the Jewish people, even at its best, realized any of the depth of meaning contained in these utterances. They looked on the return from exile as the end of their trials, and the beginning of a glorious reign for the restored and purified theocracy. These hopes were destined, at least until the Maccabæan age, to complete disappointment. The external prospects of the Jewish state grew darker and darker, and the Gentile world-power grew ever more irresistible. Yet the more the rest of the Mediterranean world became united in a common civilization and a common syncretistic religious tradition, the more passionately did the Jews cling to their separation from the Nations, and to their special national, religious vocation. Since the disproportion between the material power of Israel and that of the Gentile empires caused any natural realization of this destiny to be inconceivable, pious Jews were driven to rely more and more on the supernatural character of the salvation which God had promised to Israel. As the prophets had foretold, the Kingdom of God would be established, not by the arm of the flesh, but by divine power alone; therefore it would be, not a mere episode in Syrian history, like the first kingdom of David, but a change in the whole world-order, the beginning of a new heaven and a new earth. So, too, the Messias would be, not a great prince like David, who would exalt Israel by successful wars, but One "like unto the Son of Man" whom the prophet saw in vision

[1] Isaias xl. 7.

[2] Cf. especially chaps. xlix. and lv.

coming in the clouds of heaven, and before whose everlasting kingdom would be the consummation of the whole world-age.[1]

It was to those who lived in the expectation of this supernatural deliverance, pious and spiritual Jews who, like Simeon, "waited for the consolation of Israel," that the preaching of Jesus was addressed and the revelation of His Messianic office was made. The kingdom that He announced was the kingdom that they had been looking for, but it was also something more, even as He, the true Messias, was greater than the Messias that had been hoped for. The Kingdom of the Gospel was not simply the restoration of Israel; it was internal and spiritual, as well as external and cosmic. Its newness lay not in the promise of a new world—that was the dominant hope of later Judaism—but in the conception of the new world living in germ in the bosom of the present order. It was like a piece of leaven hidden in a lump of dough, a seedling plant destined to grow into the greatest of trees, a hidden treasure; and the process of growth that these images foreshadowed was to take place in the human soul.

The Jewish expectation had conceived the Kingdom of God as a change in the external world coming from without, according to the decree of God's power, but the Gospel, whilst announcing an equally objective change, taught that the coming of the new world was consequent on an internal spiritual change in man. Judaism had hoped for a new world; Christ brought a new humanity.

Thus the primitive Christian idea of the Kingdom of God was essentially twofold. On the one hand there is the period of hidden life and growth, the kingdom in seed; on the other the state of perfection and glory, the kingdom in fruit. On the one hand there is the "little flock," persecuted, poor and without honour in face of the triumphant kingdom of this world; on the other the people of God reigning with Christ in a restored universe. In short, to use theological language, the Kingdom of God includes first the Kingdom of Grace, then the Kingdom of Glory.

Modern critics have as a rule failed to recognize this dual character of the Kingdom of God in the Gospels. Either they have realized the spirituality and universality of the teaching of Jesus and denied its supernatural character, or they have recognized the supernatural or preternatural nature of the kingdom, and conceiving this in an exclusively cosmic or eschatological sense, have denied its moral and spiritual character.

[1] Daniel vii. 13–14.

The organic connection between these two stages is set forth in detail in the writings of St. Paul, where for the first time the Christian doctrine of Man was fully elaborated. The Kingdom of God is shown to be nothing less than the restoration of the whole creation in and through Christ. The Church is the embryo of a new world, and the Spirit of Christ, which dwells in it, is the principle of its life and the source of its growth. With the Death of Christ, the old order came to an end, and His Resurrection,[1] together with the consequent gift of the Spirit to His disciples, inaugurated a new order which will only attain completion at His second coming "with power."

The life of the faithful during the present world-age is consequently of a double or intermediate character. They share in the life of two worlds, one dying, the other still in the womb. Their bodies are still "subject to the bondage of corruption," the powers of this world-age are against them, the force of spiritual evil is still unsubdued, but by their membership of the Church they already belong to the new world which is being built up invisibly under the veil of the old, and their possession of the Spirit and His gifts is a "pledge of the world to come," an assurance of the reality of the new life.

Thus the divine life that they possess now by grace is essentially the same as that which will be manifested in the next world in glory. Indeed, the true line of division runs not between Heaven and Earth, but between the natural and the supernatural orders in this present world. The gulf between the "psychic" or animal man who lives by the law of his body or by the law of self-interest, and the Christian who lives by the Spirit, is greater than the gulf between the Christian on earth and the glorified souls of the saints in Heaven.[2]

On this essentially divine and supernatural character of the Christian life all St. Paul's moral teaching rests. He established a far-reaching opposition between man left to himself, following his own will, and limited by his own nature, and man renewed by grace,

[1] St. Paul lays great emphasis on the position of the Resurrection in the economy of the Redemption. "The Resurrection is intimately connected with the fruit of the Redemptive Death, and with the gift of the Holy Spirit. It is at the moment of the Resurrection that Jesus becomes 'life-giving spirit.' Previously, indeed, He had the Spirit in its fullness; but the Spirit, which dwelt in Him, bound by the limitations inherent to the economy of the Redemption, could not then exercise all its vital power." Cf. John xiv. 18, and xvi. 7; Pere Prat, *Theologie de St. Paul*, II, 301; cf. also ibid., II, 453 and note.

[2] As Pere Prat remarks (*Theologie de St. Paul*, II, 25), the Apostle usually includes Grace and Glory in a single concept which he names sometimes "The image of the heavenly Man."

living by charity and spiritual love and admitted to a participation in the Divine Nature. This is not a Manichæan opposition between the essential evil of matter and the absolute good of spirit. St. Paul teaches that man is naturally good, and that the material creation, as represented by the human body, is an unwilling slave to evil. Humanity has been wrecked at the very beginning of its history by a disorder of the will which has sacrificed spirit to sense, and God to self; thus breaking the fundamental law of spiritual being and depriving man of the divine life which is his by grace.

This great refusal was Original Sin, the effects of which have been perpetuated through the whole course of man's development, and have influenced every side of his nature; and this refusal is renewed in each individual by actual sin, every instance of which is a fresh self-determination in disorder, and a new seed of death to humanity.

In a famous passage of the Epistle to the Romans, St. Paul gives expression to man's sense of this disorder in his nature,[1] and of the impotence of his spiritual will to dominate his lower nature effectually. The human will is free, otherwise there would be no room for these agonized feelings of struggle and of responsibility, since the physical instincts would meet with no resistance. But on the other hand, the disorder, which has been caused by sin, and by the consequent loss of the higher life of the spirit, affects both the mind and the will, so that man is powerless to restore the harmony of his nature, unless some new spiritual force comes into his life to liberate the powers of his soul from their morbid weakness, and to reunite his nature on a higher spiritual plane.

IV

The Christian life, therefore, consists in the gradual reformation of nature from within by the operation of the Divine Spirit, which is the actuating principle of the new life, just as the human soul is the actuating principle of the life of the body. This power manifests itself in the mind by faith, which is man's participation of God's Knowledge, and in the will by charity or spiritual love, which is

[1] Romans vii. 14–24: "I do not that Good which I will; but the evil that I hate, that I do. . . . For I am delighted with the law of God according to my inward man; but I see another law in my members, fighting against the law of my mind and holding me captive in the law of sin that is in my members. Unhappy man that I am, who shall deliver me from the body of this death?"

man's participation in God's Will.[1] This is the great dynamic force of the spiritual life, and upon it rests all Christian or supernatural morality, as opposed to natural ethics. It is not so much a virtue as the animating principle and motive of all virtues. Thus St. Augustine argues that all the virtues are nothing but love; Temperance is love reserving itself for God, fortitude love, bearing all things for God, justice love, serving God by well-ordering the things that are in man's power, and so forth. Hence his famous saying, "Love God and do what you will."

When man is introduced by Faith and the Sacraments into that new world, which is the Kingdom of God and the supernatural order, this new force begins to move his will. There is, as we have said, a natural love of God, for how can man not love the "Good of all good, the Good from which is all good, the Good which is alone good," but this natural love cannot dominate his life effectively.

The new power is different. It may be felt as strongly and as suddenly as the passion of personal love, or it may grow up slowly and imperceptibly, like the love of children for their parents, but in either case it is a genuine new psychical force which aspires to unmake and remake the personality. It checks physical impulse, and it denies self-interest. If it is strong—that is, if the whole mind is open to it—it may cause intense suffering, the birth-pain of the spiritual man. Yet though its power is so real and so evident, its source is not easy to discover. "The wind blows where it wills, and its voice thou hearest, but dost not know whence it comes nor where it goes; so is every one who has been born of the Spirit."

There is something mysterious about the whole supernatural life, whether of the mind or of the will. Man is moving in a strange world in which his own faculties no longer avail him. God's Mind, to which he attains by Faith, is so far above his own that he is unable to see, he can only believe. But already, if he gives himself up to the operation of grace, God's Will moves his own, and he is drawn strongly and painfully to the denial of his own will and the sacrifice of his natural activities.

It is a common error, especially among the non-Catholic Christian sects, to confuse charity, or supernatural desire, with devout feelings and religious sentiment. Charity, however, belongs essentially to

[1] *Caritas non potest naturaliter nobis inesse, neque per vires naturales esse acquisita, sed per infusionem Spiritus Sancti, qui est Amor Patris et Filii, cujus participatio in nobis est Ipsa Caritas creata.*—St. Thomas, S.T., 2*a* 2*ae*, Q. 24, A. 2.

the deepest and most spiritual part of the soul, a region beyond the reach of feeling or of self-analysis, and it is only indirectly and accidentally manifested in the consciousness or in the emotions. As St. Theresa says: "It is certain that the love of God does not consist in this sweetness and tenderness, which we for the most part desire, and with which we console ourselves; but rather in serving Him in justice, fortitude, and humility."

In the case of the ordinary Christian this force has not reached its full development. It has not absorbed into itself the rest of the psychic life, nor acquired immediate control over the emotions and the desires; but it exists alongside of the lower psychic activity which continues to operate although the higher will has turned itself deliberately towards the life of the spirit.

If this ultimate self-determination is adhered to, the final reformation of the personality on the supernatural plane is assured; but unless there is a continuous effort to bring the whole nature under the control of charity, this process may be so gradual as to be almost imperceptible. Moreover, there is always a probability that a resurgence of disordered natural activity may swamp the whole personality and detach the higher will from its adherence to spiritual love. With the saint—that is, the Christian in whom charity has fully matured—this is no longer so. The whole personality is unified. Every phase of the psychic life is animated by spiritual desire, which is no longer painful and unnatural in its operation, but has become instinctive—as instinctive on the higher plane as physical instinct was on the lower. Such is the charity of the saints, of St. Francis, St. Catherine or St. Philip, in whom the body becomes an almost transparent veil incapable of concealing the flaming energy of the spirit. The potentiality which the human soul possesses of becoming the vehicle of this supernatural spiritual force is the central point of the Catholic doctrine of Man. Thus, St. Paul speaks very little of man as he is in himself, but very much of the two forces by which human nature rises or falls. He is concerned less with its original constitution than with its dynamic possibilities, its aptitude for being transformed by the spirit of supernatural love or degraded by the spirit of self-love or of concupiscence.

This likewise was the standpoint of St. Irenæus when he had to meet the most profound of all the heresies that have ever attacked the Christian doctrine of man and his salvation. He describes the Christian as a threefold being consisting of Flesh, Soul, and Spirit:

that is to say, the Christian has three lives, the life of the body, the life of the rational soul, and the divine life which is given to him in baptism. "Of these, one, the spirit, saves and moulds; another, the flesh, is united and moulded; whilst that which lies between the two is the soul, which sometimes follows the spirit and is raised by it, but at other times sympathizes with the flesh and is drawn by it into earthly passions. The flesh without the Spirit of God is dead, not having life, and cannot inherit the Kingdom of Heaven, but where the Spirit of the Father is, there is a Living Man, living because of his share of the Spirit, man because of the substance of the flesh."[1]

Finally, in St. Augustine we have not only a system of psychology, but also a philosophy of history based on the conception of the two forces which may govern human nature. "Two loves," he says, "built two cities. The love of self builds up Babylon to the contempt of God, and the love of God builds up Jerusalem to the contempt of self." And so he sees everywhere these two loves at work, moving the depths of the psychic life, and manifesting themselves outwardly in two great hostile world orders.

"*Ex amore suo quisquis vivit, vel bene vel male.*"

"*Non faciunt bonos vel malos mores, nisi boni vel mali amores.*"

Such phrases are constantly recurring in his writings, and they show how deeply his thought was affected by this dynamic theory of the two loves. Yet he insists that both these loves spring from a single root, from the inextinguishable desire of man's nature for happiness—*vita beata*. All the difference between the two cities—between humanity as a "damned lump" and humanity as the deified Temple of God—depends on whether man follows the blind desire for life of his physical instincts and the dark wisdom of self-love, or whether he turns towards the true *vita beata* which is super-sensual and infinite, "the Beauty which is ever ancient and ever new," "nearer to man than his own soul, the life of his soul and the life of his life."

Nevertheless, this doctrine of the two men and the two loves, which is so ancient and fundamental a part of the Catholic tradition, is liable to misinterpretation. These pairs of opposites do of course correspond to the opposition between fallen nature and supernatural grace, but if they be applied *sans phrase* to the natural and supernatural *orders*, whether in their actual relations, or in their

[1] St. Irenæus., V, 9, 1, 2.

essential nature, the way is at once open to the Calvinist and Jansenist ideas of the radical corruption of human nature. According to Calvin, the good of nature has been literally killed by Original Sin, and nothing can restore it. God may shut His eyes to its corruption in consideration of the merits of His Son, but in itself it will always remain evil. Jansenism did not go so far. It admitted the objective restoration of nature, but it conceived this as an irresistible exercise of divine power, which found and left man passive, and which was, moreover, limited to the small body of the predestinate.

Both Calvinism and Jansenism shared the same practical error—a fatalism which excluded human nature from any co-operation in the work of its renewal, and which made of nature and grace two closed orders mutually exclusive and hostile to one another. At bottom it is the old Manichæan enemy in a new form. From the Catholic point of view, it is just as false to treat nature and grace as mutually exclusive things, as it is to oppose body and soul, or matter and spirit, to one another; for the union of nature and grace makes up the Christian, just as the union of body and soul makes up the natural man. The supernatural is not the contradiction of nature, but its restoration and crown, and every faculty of man, whether high or low, is destined to have its share in his new supernatural life.

Who has not felt that the life which is most truly *natural*—that is to say, most in harmony with man's true being—is not the life of the man who lives by sense-instinct, but that of the saint—of St. Francis, for instance—in whom the original innocence and harmony of man with himself and with outward things seem restored?

It is remarkable that this conception of the "naturalness" of the supernatural life was explicitly held by the very founders of Christian asceticism, those desert monks whose austerities have astonished and sometimes scandalized the mind of future generations. To St. Anthony and to his biographer, St. Athanasius, the ascetic life is the true "life according to nature." It is a process of simplification by which the monk may, as it were, recover the actual rectitude and harmony of nature in which man left the hands of his Creator.[1]

V

Nevertheless, this quality of simplicity and naturalness in the highest spiritual life has only been attained by intense effort: it is

[1] Cf. Newman, *The Mission of St. Benedict*, 3.

the result of a remorseless process of destruction and reconstruction. The disorder of nature is very real and very strong. It has rooted itself so deeply in humanity that it has become, as it were, an organized whole from which the individual or the society can only detach themselves with difficulty. Against the Christian ideal of social order as a co-operative effort based on justice and animated by charity, we see the reality of a naked reign of force, based on slavery, war, or economic exploitation, in which the strong prosper at the expense of the weak, and primitive peoples become the natural prey of more civilized powers. The reign of social and international justice is an ideal which can only be reached by a spiritualized humanity—a humanity set free from the domination of lust and avarice and cowardice, which drives men and nations blindly into disorder and cruelty. Hence the struggle between the spirit of Christ and that "spirit of the world" which is so real a force.

It is a common modern objection and one which is widely accepted as a damaging criticism of Catholicism, that our religion neglects the real things by which the progress of the human race is advanced—science, industry, and political organization—in the pursuit of imaginary goods of a visionary kind. In reality Christianity creates the motive power—spiritual will—on which all true progress must ultimately rest. Without this spiritual foundation, all progress in knowledge or wealth only extends the range of human suffering, and the possibilities of social disorder. All the great movements, which have built up modern secular civilization, have been more or less vitiated by this defect. Whether we look at the Italy of the Renaissance, the England of the Industrial Revolution, or the Germany of the last forty years, we see in each case that the progress and wealth which are founded on individual or national selfishness, lead only to destruction and suffering. A civilization which recognizes its own limitations, and bows before the kingdom of the spirit, even though it be weak and immature like European civilization during the Dark Ages, has more true life in it than the victorious material civilization of our own age. There is no hope for humanity in science and economic organization: these are but instruments, which may be used for death, instead of for life, if the will that uses them is disordered. Civilization after civilization in the past have stagnated and fallen into ruin, because they are tainted at the source, in the spiritual will which lies behind the outward show of things. The only final escape for humanity from this heartbreaking circle of false starts and frustrated hopes is through the conquest of the world by charity—the coming of the Kingdom of God.

The Catholic sees in the life of the Church, the progressive development and application to humanity of this supreme remedy. It is not, of course, a process which is susceptible of scientific demonstration; the forces at work lie too deep for reason to measure them, neither can we follow the action and interaction of human and divine activities. From the beginning the Church has taught that it is impossible to judge the inward growth of the Kingdom by outward signs; it is the field of wheat growing with the cockle till the time of harvest: but no less has she recognized the complementary principle, that where there is inward life, there must be outward manifestation.

Critics of Christianity are apt to judge of it as though it were an external system of law. This system is applied to a nation or a civilization, and if these prosper, well and good; if not, Christianity is a failure. They do not realize the infinitely tenuous and delicate nature of the supernatural life, which works as continuously and infallibly as a natural force through the sacraments and operations of grace, but which can only realize itself in man and transform human nature by the consent and co-operation of the individual will. Where it is accepted in a merely natural way as a law, as part of a human system, it is powerless to act.

Only in the saints, with whom the process is exceptionally advanced, is the whole external life conformed to the new inward principle. In the ordinary Christian, the natural life goes on almost unchanged, based on its own principle and following its own laws. It is to this region that much of what we are accustomed to look on historically as Christian civilization belongs. But behind all this the supernatural principle carries on its seminal activity and forms the embryonic life, which is destined eventually to absorb into itself and remake the whole nature, mental and physical, with all its vital activities.

Thus, although we cannot trace in society, as it is, even in Christian society, the clear evidence of the progressive development of the divine life in mankind, we can still see in every age new manifestations of the charismatic activity of the Spirit in the Catholic Church. Every age sees the Kingdom of God conquering fresh territory—the supernatural order more closely interpenetrating the natural world. Sometimes the conquests of one age seem to be lost by the next, but this loss is superficial. The achievement remains to be drawn in and represented at some future period.

The secularist naturally regards this kind of progress as unsubstantial and unsatisfactory. The end is never completed. Humanity keeps its old nature, whilst it loses the perfection that is really within its reach, in the pursuit of abstractions. But the goal of the Christian progress is far, because it is final. The Christian faith alone offers man a perfection which is not relative and transitory, but absolute and eternal. The Christian faith alone has measured how deep is the need of humanity and how great is the possibility of restoration. If it seems to neglect the material world, that is not because it treats the material world as unimportant, but because the restoration of the spirit must precede and condition the restoration of the body. The divine life that is in the Church is not limited in its effects to the human soul, it overflows on to the body, and hence on to the whole material universe:

Terra, pontus astra, mundus
Hoc lavantur flumine.

In the present order of the world, the relation of spirit and matter, as well as the relation of the natural and the supernatural, have become dislocated. The unification or harmonizing of the two former will follow eventually on that of the two latter. Then the body, and with it the whole material world, will be brought into a true relation with the soul, so that everywhere matter is the extension of spirit, and not its limit; the instrument of spirit, and not its enemy. St. Paul speaks of the material creation groaning and travailing in pain until the time in which it also will be delivered from the service of corruption and will have its share in the liberty of the perfected and glorified supernatural order.

This transfiguration of the material world is of course most vital in the case of the human body. That is why the Church has, from the beginning, attached such importance to the doctrine of the corporal resurrection, even though that doctrine was a source of difficulty and misunderstanding to the mentality of Hellenistic civilization, as now it is to the mind of modern Europe. Nevertheless without this final restoration of the body, the Christian doctrine of Man would remain incomplete. Man was created to be the soul of the material world, the link between the two creations; that through him, as St. Gregory of Nyssa says, the divine might shine as through a glass into the earthly world, and the earthly, elevated with the divine, might be freed from corruptibility, and transfigured.[1]

The very essence of man's nature and his true *raison d'etre* consists in this union of body with spirit. That is why death, the temporary dissolution of the compound, is a thing of such real horror for every man, even for the Christian. For though in one respect the death brings the soul nearer to God, delivering it from the veil of sense and from the dominance of animal needs; yet on the other hand it is a kind of annihilation, a loss of an essential half, even though it be the lower half, of his nature.

If that separation were final, a central purpose of the Incarnation would remain unfulfilled. In place of the Christian theory of redemption, we should have the Gnostic or Manichæan idea of the salvation of man by the separation of his true nature from its material envelope or prison—the return of the Alone to the Alone, as we find it in the typical Indian philosophies. "But," says St. Irenæus, "since men are real, theirs must be a real restoration. They do not vanish into non-existence, but progress among existent things. Neither the matter nor substance of Creation is annihilated, the form alone passes away. When this form has passed away and man has been renewed, there shall be the new heaven and the new earth in which man shall remain, ever new among the new, and always in communion with God."

In nothing less than this does the destiny of humanity consist, according to the teaching of the Catholic faith. Without losing his own nature, man is brought into an inconceivably close relation with God, so that he lives by the Divine Life, sees God with God's Knowledge, loves God with God's Love, and knows and loves everything else in and through God. The life of the Divine Trinity externalizes itself in the completed life of the Church, in humanity eternally and immutably deified. To that end, the Church on earth moves infallibly, irresistibly. In the Sacraments, in the life of faith, in every act of spiritual will and aspiration of spiritual desire, the work of divine restoration goes ceaselessly forward. In that work is the whole hope of humanity.

Ναί ἔρχομαι ταχύ. ἀμήν ἔρχου, Κύριε Ἰησοῦ.

[1] It may be objected that this view of man's function implies an anthropocentric view of the universe essentially bound up with the conception of the earth as the unmoving centre of the stellar heavens. But in reality this function of man depends not on his being the ruling creature in the central sphere of the universe but on the essential duality of his nature. The truth and importance of that duality is in no way affected by the progress of astronomy.

IV
THE PROBLEM OF EVIL

BY

E. I. WATKIN

I

THE problem of evil, always the weightiest, as it is the most obvious, objection against belief in an almighty and all-loving God, lies with a peculiar urgency upon the spirit of modern men. The existence of evil has always cast its dark shadow across the sunlit spaces of God's creation. Never before has that shadow appeared so utterly, so impenetrably black. This is not to say that there is more evil in the world now than in former ages. It is true that the late war with its concomitants and its consequences has constituted one of the most appalling revelations of evil alike physical and moral in the history of mankind. But a clearer manifestation is not necessarily an actual increase. A disease is not necessarily intensified by the extension of its outward symptoms. Indeed, to attempt any estimate of the comparative balance of good and evil as between different periods, is to undertake a task essentially impossible; for such an estimate would require objective standards of measurement, and these in the nature of things are unattainable. Who can strike a balance between the diverse kinds of evil which differ in quality, not merely in degree? How is it possible to eliminate the subjective element in a judgment of values? The pessimist and the optimist, the devotee of progress and the *laudator temporis acti*, the happy man and the unhappy, the successful and the unsuccessful, the idealist and the realist, the religious and the irreligious, men of such diverse temperaments, and men who approach life from standpoints so remote each from the other, can never hope to reach even a proximate agreement in the comparative valuation of historical epochs. Hence the modern urgency of evil, the modern preoccupation with evil, the modern pessimism, are not due to any increase of evil in our days, even if such increase exists. It was strongly established in modern culture long before the fatal summer of 1914 dawned upon it. Its causes will, I hope, be at least partially unveiled in the course of this paper. For the present I desire merely to emphasize the fact. We have but to take a glance at modern literature, to recall, for instance, the dramas of Ibsen and in general the realist problem-drama of which he was the father, the novels of Thomas Hardy, the modern Russian novel, the poems of Masefield, to perceive an intense realization of evil, if not a fundamental pessimism. Of art I am scarcely qualified to speak. But I doubt if anyone would derive from such modern work as the portraits of Augustus John or the sculpture of Epstein, that sense of the moral nobility of man to be obtained even from such naturalist art as that of the ancient Greek sculptors or the most purely humanistic painting of the Renaissance.

Nor is this pessimism simply regrettable. It is well that those who believe in the loving Father of Christian theism should be compelled by the challenge of modern thought and feeling to face the reality of evil in its most uncompromising manifestation. Not of course that it is good to contemplate, as certain modern writers and artists would have us contemplate, the polluting details of unbridled impurity. But it is a good thing that we should be obliged to realize both the terrific fact of evil in all its extent and intensity and the difficulty of the problem which it raises. A faith in the love of God which lives only because the blinds are drawn close over the windows through which the soul looks out on the universe and on human life, is a sickly faith, and an endangered faith. Certainly it is a faith impotent to assist others to belief. At any moment experience may pull up these blinds and make us look out at the hideous countenance of evil. In the shock of that discovery we might see nothing but the evil and lose our faith. Still worse is an attempt to keep our faith by shutting our eyes to the evil we know to be there all the time, in imitation of the ostrich who buries her head in the sand at the hunter's approach. Such faith is unworthy of the name. It is rather a credulity fundamentally incredulous, a lack of faith without the courage to avow itself. If possible even worse is it to accept inadequate solutions of the problem of evil and to pretend to ourselves that they are adequate. This is that lie in the soul, which, as Plato perceived, is the worst of all lies. Indeed it was precisely this acceptance of inadequate solutions as fully adequate in the face of an honest refusal to be content with such inadequacies, that drew the divine condemnation upon the friend of Job. If, therefore, the modern insistence upon the world's evil has rendered some of our ancestors' solutions of the problem less convincing than they once seemed, or has in any way enlarged the scope or increased the weight of the objections to a divine Providence arising from that evil, or again has brought to light a superficial and in so far unwarranted optimism in the old outlook on life, it has in this rendered us a valuable service.

Now I take it that when every deduction has been made for exaggeration and distortion of perspective by individual temperament, it must be admitted that the modern man does see with a novel clearness of vision, and feels with a peculiar acuteness, the amount and quality of evil—even moral evil—due not to the immediate and avoidable free choices of men but to the inevitable operations of nature. By nature is here understood not only inanimate nature, but individual human nature as determined by heredity and environment, and social human nature as determined by physical and economic forces or by irrational subconscious instincts and impulses. The ancients, for example, found it easier than we find it, to see non-human nature as subservient to man and existing for his good; or they saw it as the immediate and obvious reflection of a spiritual world and a moral order. Thus did mediæval art as exemplified in the sculpture of a Gothic Cathedral, read nature as a religious and moral picture book in which any natural object was by its very nature a type of some religious or moral fact, a second Bible in obvious harmony with the written Scripture whose lessons it illustrated and enforced.

The seventeenth century nature-mystic Traherne insists again and again—not as the final conclusion of religious faith or philosophic argument, but as an all but self-evident truth—that the world is the mirror of the divine attributes, particularly of the divine goodness, and that it is created for the service, both material and spiritual, of man. "The beauty of God," he says, "is invisible, it is all wisdom, goodness, life and love, power, glory, blessedness, etc. How, therefore, shall these be expressed in a material world? His wisdom is expressed in manifesting His infinity in such a commodious manner. . . . His goodness is manifest in making that beauty so delightful and its varieties so profitable: the air to breathe in, the sea for moisture, the earth for fertility, the heavens for influences, the sun for productions, the stars and trees for innumerable uses. Again His goodness is seen in the end to which He guideth all this profitableness, in making it serviceable to supply our wants, and delight our senses: to inflame us with His love, and make us amiable before Him and delighters in His blessedness."[1] "The World is our storehouse

[1] *Centuries of Meditations*, 2, 21.

and treasury. That our treasures should be endless is a happy inconvenience: that all regions should be full of joys."[1] "The world . . . is a region of light and Peace, did not men disquiet it. It is the Paradise of God" (1, 31). "The laws of God discover all that is therein to be created for your sake" (1, 20). "Everything is ours that serves us in its place. The Sun serves us as much as is possible. The Clouds and Stars minister unto us. God gave . . . all the world to me alone" (1-14, 15). This is typical not so much of the author who is peculiar only in his extraordinary emotional appreciation and in the felicity of his expression, as of our ancestors' normal view of nature and its order. With this we may contrast the outlook on nature of a modern man, like Traherne an ardent lover of natural beauty, like him also a nature-mystic, Richard Jefferies. "There is nothing human in nature. The earth, though loved so dearly, would let me perish on the ground, and neither bring forth food nor water. . . . Those who have been in an open boat at sea without water have known the mercies of the sun . . . dying in misery under the same rays that smile so beautifully on the flowers. . . . Water man can drink, but it is not produced for him; how many thousands have perished for want of it? Some fruits . . . he can eat, but they do not produce themselves for him; merely for the purpose of continuing their species. In wild tropical countries, at the first glance there appears to be some consideration for him, but it is on the surface only. The lion pounces on him, the rhinoceros crushes him, the serpent bites, insects torture, diseases rack him. . . . We utilize the wheat, but its original and native purpose was for itself. By night it is the same as by day; the stars care not, they pursue their courses revolving and we are nothing to them. . . . All nature, all the universe is absolutely indifferent to us. If the entire human race perished at this hour, what difference would it make to the earth? What would the earth care? As much as for the extinct dodo. . . . On the contrary, a great part, perhaps the whole of nature and of the universe is distinctly anti-human."[2] These two contrasted pictures epitomize a revolutionary change in the valuation of nature.

Wherever the truth lies as between these contrasted valuations we cannot deny at least a considerable element of truth to the modern and pessimistic estimate. For it is a commonplace that palæontology has revealed a pre-human world-history deeply stained with suffering and brutal violence, marred by enormous waste and fearsome ugli-

[1] Ibid. 1, 37. [2] *The Story of my Heart*, chap. iv.

ness. However exaggerated be the picture of "nature red in teeth and claw," however much can be said for the operation in this pre-human world of forces of progress and co-operation, we cannot see in that history a clear reflection of ethical law, nor find an obvious and immediately demonstrable manifestation of divine wisdom and love. Indeed the law of evolution and life seems to be revealed as a law of reckless waste alike of individual and of species. And at this present time the earth is filled with non-human suffering. There is the pain and the fear of animals, if not also, as certain recent discoveries indicate, a certain suffering even of plants. In every sphere there is wasteful destruction, and premature blighting of life. Of animals and plants alike but a minute minority attains the perfection of its species. If attained, that perfected life hastens on the downward path to decay and death, often—as the blossoming of plants, and the day life of many insects—perishes almost in the act of unfolding. And all this lacks any apparent connection with the sinful volition of men. And when we turn to mankind we are compelled to realize—unless we wilfully blind ourselves to facts—a vast mass of evil, even moral, which no act of the sufferer's free-will has caused or even controlled. There is the far-reaching extent of undeserved suffering—diseases, loathsome and agonizing, lack of opportunity, tortures of body or mind inflicted by the neglect or evil-doing of others or of society as a whole. Hereditary disease and, worse than disease, hereditary tendency to vice apparently so strong as to overpower the resistance of the will, even to render any resistance impossible; an environment which debars its victims from any opportunity of educating or developing those distinctively human faculties whose education and free exercise are essential to a fully rational or moral life; madness and neurotic complaints which at the least seriously attenuate moral responsibility and rational control; subconscious tendencies which rule men's actions and nevertheless, escaping their detection, escape also their control—such facts as these though never wholly ignored have impressed themselves upon the modern psychologist and student of human nature, with a force and an urgency hitherto unknown. Moreover, we perceive with a new clarity the immense and often to all appearance irresistible force in the determination of conduct exercised by herd-instincts frequently of the most irrational character. It is not by the exercise of man's reasonable, and therefore free, will but rather, as Jung points out,[1] by the

[1] *Collected papers on Analytical Psychology.*

play of infra-rational subconscious group-instincts that the groups which compose in their mutual membership a common civilization, divide themselves one from the other in an internecine conflict and bring to ruin that civilization itself, thereby risking the destruction of a structure that has been built up by the slow and costly progress of millenniums of painful toil. These are but a few features of the "black image" of evil which to the soul of modern man seems unconnected with avoidable human sin. Who dare say that the picture is false to the facts? Who can disprove its hideous reality?

If in face of all this evil we still affirm with the sure faith of our fathers as the Cause and Ruler of a universe so constituted, a God Who is at once almighty power and tenderest love, how shall we defeat the mocking challenge of the convinced unbeliever, or still the bitter cry of many a soul under the torment of anguished doubt? The dilemma seems so cogent, so utterly inevitable. If God is almighty, He could have prevented this evil; if He is good, He would have prevented this evil. Therefore, either He is not almighty or He is not good. Whatever be the nature of the ultimate reality, it is not, it cannot be, the God of Christian belief, the Father-God of prayer and loving faith. When the vision of evil dawns in cold clearness, especially when it is a sudden vision, and when the dilemma just stated is brought home thus to the entire being, it seems scarcely wonderful that many souls share the bitter experience of Pearce's Singer, when he had experienced the reality and power of life's evil and life's pain. "Once, as I knelt by the cross of Kilgobbin, it became clear to me, with an awful clearness, that there was no God. Why pray after that? I burst into a fit of laughter at the folly of men in thinking that there is a God."[1]

"What shall we say to these things," we who nevertheless believe in a God both omnipotent and all-loving? First of all we must make it quite clear that there is no adequate solution possible of the problem of evil. People are often irritated because apologists and preachers of theism or Christianity, offer or appear to offer such a solution. They are often so irritated that they will not give unprejudiced audience to any considerations or arguments on the subject which the apologist or preacher may produce. It is indeed scarcely credible that any apologist has ever explicitly propounded any solution as adequate. He may, however, so treat inadequate and

[1] Pearce was indeed himself a convinced and fervent Catholic; and his "Singer" in this drama soon recovers his lost faith.

partial considerations, as apparently to regard them as possessing the cogency and completeness of an entire solution. But evidently evil has a providential purpose or it has not. If it has not, there is of course no solution of the problem, indeed (and be this noted) there is no longer any problem of evil: if it has, then it is clear that an adequate and complete solution would defeat the realization of that purpose. For if evil could be demonstrably shown to be in every case an operation of good to its victim, indeed the best thing that could befall him, and if evil as a whole could similarly be proved the best provision of good to the universe and to all its parts, evil would lose all value as a test of faith, or as an exercise and development of moral character. But if there be a providence in the permission of evil, and therefore a solution of its problem however to us insoluble, undoubtedly one at least of the good results intended from evil is precisely this religious and moral trial and education.[1] Hence an adequate solution of the problem is *a priori* impossible. If, however, the problem were utterly and completely insoluble, it would constitute a difficulty against divine Providence too great for a rational faith to be maintained in its face. It would also be a burden too heavy for man to endure and overcome. Therefore, though we cannot expect a complete solution of the problem of evil, if there be a Providence in it, we may expect to discover a number of partial solutions, to catch sight of various lines of thought which, starting from diverse aspects of experience, lead in the direction of a solution, and more or less converge towards a common goal, and to apprehend, however dimly and incoherently, fragments of an answer which give us good ground to believe that there is a complete answer beyond the limited ken of our vision.

Now it is just those fragmentary and inadequate, but on the whole harmonious and converging answers, or rather indications of an answer, to the problem of evil that we do in fact find. Some of these I hope to point out. I will first clear from the path certain suggested answers which are philosophically or theologically inadmissible. I will next bring forward a few general considerations bearing on the problem of evil as a whole. After this I will discuss certain considerations whose application is more or less peculiar to each of the three categories into which evil may be divided: physical

[1] This much of truth is there in Bishop Blougram's exaggeration:—
"Some think Creation's meant to show Him forth;
I say, it's meant to hide Him all it can,
And that's what all the blessed Evil's for."

evil or pain; defect and waste; moral evil and especially its worst, because voluntary, form—sin. Finally, I will bring forward considerations tending to subsume the results of our enquiry in a final view of the problem as a whole, as it appears in the light of those results.

II

In the nature of the case my treatment cannot be rigidly determined by these divisions. The farther a sphere of being is removed from the purely physical and therefore externally demarcated world of matter, the greater is its internal unity in multiplicity, the more is it an organic whole of mutually implicit parts as opposed to a mere aggregation of mutually exclusive units. Therefore the subject-matter of a largely metaphysical discussion, such as is this present problem of evil, will possess an internal unity or totality which will involve in its treatment an inevitable overlapping and mutual presupposition of its various aspects however distinct. Hence it is impossible to follow consistently and with accurate demarcation the divisions of treatment above indicated.

It should also be made clear that the problem will not be handled from a purely philosophic standpoint. The writers of this book are not expounding a metaphysical theism, but the fundamental doctrines of a revealed theology. For this reason alone my essay would necessarily discuss the problem of evil in the light of this revelation, and with the aid of any data towards a solution which that theology may afford. But indeed I should despair of the problem of evil were I left to face it with the sole assistance of philosophy. Though there are indeed philosophic arguments for immortality they are not to me so secure that I should care to rest in them my hope of a life beyond the grave. But if there be no other life than this, I do not see any possibility of indicating any rational purpose in human suffering and permitted sin, any reconciliation of evil as we know it with a divine Providence of individual love. And when I contemplate—I must speak here from a personal standpoint, since in matters of moral valuation the subjective factor can scarcely be excluded—when I contemplate the terrible fact of evil, as I have attempted to sketch it above and as it has burnt itself into the heart and mind of so many men to-day, I could hardly hold to any faith in a personal God, almighty and good, Who permitted its existence with the seeming lack of purpose in its cruelty and in its incidence, did I not also believe that this God took on Him our suffering humanity and in that humanity bore to the utmost the evil of the world, all—far more than all with the exception of personal sin—that any child of Adam is called upon to bear. In any case evil is a stern trial of faith, a heavy burden on the spirit, even when considered theoretically from without, still more as it must often be experienced in practice. But it would seem *impossible* to reconcile with theistic faith, if we did not believe that the God who created a world in which there is so much evil, also redeemed it by sharing in person the burden of that evil; if in face of the challenge which evil raises for the believer: "Where is now thy God?" we could not for reply point to Jesus Christ agonizing and dying on the cross, and say: "Here—not on some remote throne of glory, but here in the very heart of the world's evil and pain—here is our God." Therefore, I will treat of evil on the assumption that the full Christian and Catholic faith is true. Without weight, too, for the Catholic, are the many objections to the divine goodness based on the denial of any portion of Catholic faith; for instance, a denial of free will, or a denial of a future world of just recompense, of the purgatorial value of some pains, or again of the spiritual solidarity of mankind with its consequence, the possibility and worth of vicarious suffering.

It is easier, far easier in face of the problem of evil, to believe in the Christian revelation than in the bare philosophic theism of a natural religion however pure. Where Christian faith can behold evil undismayed, a simple Deism without dogmas will often fall to pieces. On the other hand, we may and must make large use of philosophic arguments and, in general, of the data of natural human experience.

(*a*) A solution radically false is that of those optimistic philosophies or mystical systems of metaphysics that regard evil as illusion—an illusion due to our incomplete understanding of the universe. If we could but attain, we are told, to a complete knowledge of the whole, a knowledge sometimes indeed promised us as the result either of philosophic study or of mystical experience, we should see evil in its true character as good: since evil is good either partially viewed or unduly isolated.

Such a solution does violence alike to experience and to the deliverance of the human conscience. That his pain is mere illusion, is to the sufferer self-evidently absurd; that wickedness is from any conceivable point of view morally good, is to the unsophisticated conscience self-evidently immoral. Certainly, as we shall see, there is a very true and most important sense in which evil is unreal, and in which evil is merely relative. But the metaphysical unreality of evil does not prevent its being in the ordinary sense very real indeed, nor does its relativity prevent some of its forms being absolutely bad. Although all created being, even the most positive, is relative—for otherwise it would be the Absolute Divine Being—yet since this relative being possesses true existence and definite character, it is to that degree and in a secondary sense, absolute. Purely metaphysical considerations as to entity and relativity cannot in themselves solve the problem presented by a far-extending series of ineluctable facts. Moreover, the view of evil as illusion tends to pass into a cosmic pantheism; the view of evil as relative or partial good, into cosmic pantheism.

(*b*) Nor can we maintain that this evil-stained universe is the best of all universes absolutely possible. Such a proposition limits the power of omnipotence to the one particular manifestation of which we are witness; a limitation which is, to say the least, unwarrantable dogmatism on the part of creatures possessed of such imperfect knowledge as ours.

(*c*) Neither can we affirm that all the evil of the world is the direct and proportionate result of human sin. For suffering, as we have already considered, existed for millenniums before man appeared on earth; and there is an enormous mass of evil not immediately referable to the deliberate fault of any individual. There is, however, a larger element of truth in this solution than is often supposed. Indeed there is a sense in which it may be altogether true.

(*d*) Nor yet is all human suffering such in quality, quantity, and incidence, that it is of moral value to the actual sufferer. The suffering of children before the age of reason, of maniacs, and indeed of persons obviously too weak in moral or intellectual calibre to utilize the pain inflicted upon them, disproves immediately a theory so false to patent facts. Still, as we shall see, such suffering does subserve the good of the world as a whole.

(*e*) Nor can we even lighten the burden of evil by maintaining that the Godhead shares it by participation in the pain of His creation. Such a god would not be all transcendent, therefore not the God of Christianity, not the God Who can and will reward with the eternal happiness of His own self-fruition, souls who by His grace endure all the passing sufferings of our short life. Such a god would be finite, a god who is himself conditioned and therefore to some degree constrained by an evil which he cannot altogether overcome; in a word, a god whose power for good is at once imperfect and imperilled. This, however, is the finite god of Mr. Wells—and of Fr. Tyrell in his final position,[1]—a god who needs our human aid, not simply to overcome evil *in free-willing man*, which is true; but to secure the defeat of evil in the world order. For such a deity one might well feel admiration and love; but he would be no object of religious faith or divine worship. And if, as the hypothesis demands, he is so finite that he cannot even diminish the enormous evils, the pain, the waste, the wanton injustice and cruelty, inherent in the present condition of the world without the help of man, his power must be so slight that he can scarcely be greater than man himself. Certainly his ultimate victory over evil is doubtful in the extreme. If, however, Mr. Wells, or any other adherent of this creed, reply either that he could help man more than he does against evil but will not because of the spiritual value of human struggle, or that he cannot do so without violating human free will or in some other way disturbing a cosmic order whose maintenance makes all the evil worth while, he indeed answers well the difficulty of evil; but he takes away all need for the hypothesis of his finite, struggling, deity. For this answer consists as well, if not better, with the Christian doctrine of a God all-mighty and all-wise.

III

We turn now to certain general considerations bearing on evil in all its forms.

(*a*) And first I would insist as a truth certain to any unprejudiced mind that good exceeds evil. In every department of experience, I maintain it with the utmost confidence, the amount and force of good far exceeds the amount and force of evil. We must not, with so many modern observers, exaggerate the world's evil. If evil were equal to good in degree and in quality, in power and reality, why do we regard it, rather than good, as a problem requiring solution? Why should we expect to find goodness in the universe, in our fellow-men, unless man's fundamental nature is good, and the fundamental nature of the universe is good? If anyone tells you he has found more evil in his fellows than good, we may well enquire of him whether he believes himself to be more evil than good. I do

[1] See Essays on "Faith and Immortality," a posthumous publication.

not think he will readily admit this preponderance of evil in his own character. It is true that the saints speak as though the evil in them enormously exceeded the good, if, in deed, they are not wholly evil: but this language is explained by their realization that the good in them is the gift of God (the sole source of all goodness natural and supernatural), the evil alone from themselves. This, however, is not the position of our pessimist. His complaint is that there is actually more evil than good in men. If, however, he is unwilling to apply this to himself, what ground has he to place himself among a favoured minority?

Mr. Bradley in his *Studies in Shakespearian Tragedy*, whose treatment penetrates beyond any merely literary criticism to a very deep and acute philosophy of life, insists on the witness born to the predominance of good even by the darkest, most seemingly despairing, tragedies. We see in these, he points out, a universe essentially hostile to evil, since it is auniverse in which evil, though it may destroy much good, destroys also itself, and destroys good only in virtue of some defect of goodness in its victims. "In Shakespearian tragedy," he observes "the main source of the catastrophe which produced suffering and death is never good: good contributes to this conclusion only from its tragic implication with its opposite in one and the same character. . . . If it is thus chiefly evil that violently disturbs the order of the world, this order cannot be friendly to evil or indifferent between evil and good."[1] The ultimate power which shows itself disturbed by this evil reacts against it, must therefore have a nature alien to it. Indeed, its reaction is so vehement and relentless that it would seem to be bent on nothing short of good in perfection and to be ruthless in its demand for it. Mr. Bradley also remarks that whereas Shakespeare, and his readers with him, ask of Regan and Goneril what cause in nature breeds such hard hearts, they do not ask of Kent and Cordelia what cause makes these kind hearts.[2] For he and we alike regard the good heart as natural, the evil heart as unnatural, a monstrosity requiring an explanation of its existence; thereby implying that nature is ultimately and essentially good, not evil. A further proof of this fundamental optimism is afforded by the Utopian dreams of a Shelley, who without any theistic belief to warrant him, believed that the mere progress of humanity would effect for man and his environment such a reign of good as the Church believes will be supernaturally established for redeemed

[1] Op. cit., p. 34. [2] Ibid., p. 305.

mankind at the parousia.[1] This optimism is equally evident in Nietzsche's triumphant affirmation of life in the teeth of his theory of an endless and unprogressive revolution or return of all things, a doctrine which logically should have bred utter despair.

The course of evolution, as has been pointed out by Mr. Massingham among others, shows a progress through increasing co-operation and individual self-sacrifice. It is a mistake to see in the pre-human world only "monsters that tore each other in the slime." Certainly neither in past evolution nor in the present order, is nature immediately ethical. Nowhere do the laws of nature immediately and patently reward good conduct and punish evil. It is also true, as Jefferies so eloquently pointed out, that nature does not directly subserve human purposes. If, however, nature did thus immediately reflect an ethical order, there would be no moral test: man would be compelled to be good by obvious self-interest. If the course of evolution had been perfectly and immediately ethical, or if natural laws immediately served man's moral and rational needs, moral and intellectual conflict, his toilsome and painful advance and struggle towards good, would be at the least gravely attenuated. But what if this struggle, this toilsome and painful advance, were itself among the highest goods, among the most ethical and spiritual ends of creation? No one of a truly spiritual insight would, I think, deny this. Nevertheless spiritual progress and struggle need not have been *so* slow, *so* toilsome, *so* painful, *so* costly of waste and failure as they have in fact been; and we are compelled to seek a further cause for these apparently unnecessary evils. Catholic doctrine declares this further cause to be sin—original and actual. But of this, more hereafter.

While a predominance of moral good over evil is thus a demonstrable fact of experience, there is perhaps more to be said for a predominance of the lesser evils, pain and sorrow, over pleasure and joy. But if the greater good—that is, moral good—predominates over the greater evil—that is, moral evil—then it must be admitted that good still predominates over evil, even if we must grant that the lesser—the physical—evil of suffering outweighs the lesser—the physical—good of happiness. Whether this be actually the case is highly debatable. Much can be said on both sides of the question.

[1] See especially the concluding acts of "Prometheus Unbound." We may however observe that Shelley's optimism drove him to the implicit theism involved in the supremacy assigned to Demogorgon which is actually God.

Most probably it is impossible to reach a certain answer of universal application. In any case the goodness of God is not refuted even if suffering weighs down the scale. For if the Christian doctrine be true, and we are discussing the problem from that supposition, there is no reason to expect an excess of happiness in this life. On the contrary Christ has promised His followers suffering in this world, joy in eternity; the cross here, the crown hereafter. Indeed, the Church teaches, and with the Church is the unanimous consent of all mystics and deeply religious souls, sinful man cannot in the very nature of things[1] attain to the spiritual happiness for which he was created, without suffering. Purgatorial suffering, whether in this world or in the next, is the inevitable passage and entrance into the divine Joy. There is, moreover, so the experience of the noblest and holiest souls bears its consentient witness, a peculiar and a sovereign joy in the suffering itself when rightly borne; a joy which surpasses all other joys attainable on earth, and renders the suffering as desirable to them as it is hateful to us who do not share their secret.

(*b*) That modern man tends to adopt a world outlook in which evil predominates, is largely due to a psychological change. This psychological change, in virtue of which his valuations are differentiated from those of his ancestors, may be described as an increased sensibility to suffering, a decreased sensibility to sin. The latter is not a decreased sensibility to all forms of moral evil, for the modern man often possesses a heightened sensibility towards many forms of such evil. But it is a decreased sensibility to the evil of a will freely averted from the divine law. The increased sensibility to suffering is clear gain. For the increased sensitiveness of any organ means an increased utility and delicacy, an increased perception. To charge the modern soul with a weak sentimentality because of its keener and more delicate apprehension of pain, is as if the short-sighted man charged the keen-sighted with a perverted imagination, or the pagan polygamist taxed the Christian monogamist with a hypersensitive conscience in the matter of purity. But the decreased sensibility to sin has produced an exaggerated notion that evil in all its forms is independent of free will; and a failure to see also the purgative and expiatory values of suffering. It also leads men to regard suffering as an evil equal to, if not worse than, moral evil. This radical perversion of values cannot fail to give birth to a distorted vision of experience, an unfounded pessimism which is unable to

[1] That is as things are in the actual order of our existence.

deal with the problem of evil because it sees that problem in a false perspective. If, on the other hand, we realize that good is more natural, more powerful, more real, more widely extended, more deeply rooted than evil, we shall be able so to perceive the divine origin of the world, and God working in the world of human experience, that we can in peaceful faith commit its unsolved and insoluble problems into the hands of our heavenly Father.

(*c*) Not only is evil less extensive, less potent and less real than good, it has no existence apart from the good: in this sense, and in this sense only, it may be said to be unreal. For evil is not a mere absence of good, it is an absence of *due* good, of good that ought to have been present; hence, a privation. A privation, however, may be extremely real. What more real than famine? To people slowly dying of starvation, their lack of nourishment is the most actual and dominant reality of their experience. Yet privation of food is obviously a nonentity. If it is asked how evil, being merely a privation, can possess its hideous force, its power of destruction, of infection, I reply that this force, this power to infect and destroy, is grounded not in the evil as evil, but in the positive and therefore good thing or person in which that evil inheres. Evil as such is powerless. Only *sub specie boni*, that is, in virtue of something good to which it belongs is it a force whether of attraction or destruction.[1] The destructive power of gunpowder is *per se* a good thing, capable indeed of good use when, for instance, it destroys not a Gothic cathedral but a piece of rock which obstructs a line of railway. Men never sin for the sake of evil but for the sake of some good. Consider even wanton cruelty, sheer delight in the infliction of pain for its own sake. Psychology shows that even this apparently unmixed love of evil is a perversion of the desire to exercise power—in itself a good desire—combined in extreme cases with a nervous perversion whereby the infliction of pain causes pleasure. Consider again the infectious power of manufactured war or class-hatred. This power depends on an appeal to positive instincts in themselves good; social instincts of love and loyalty to a nation or class of our fellow-men. The evil lies in limitations such as blindness to the good in other groups, ignorant credulity, mental laziness, lack of self-criticism, and the like.

[1] There is indeed a difference between the two; goodness, as such, attracts, and it destroys only accidentally. In wanton destruction only the power to destroy is good together with the positive self-affirmation of the destructive force.

Evil, then, is a negative thing, even whilst it is something very real. If we admit a positive entity in evil, we cannot escape one of two alternatives. Either there is a radical dualism in the constitution of reality, a bad principle in opposition to the good God, or evil is a reflection and participation of the one ultimate Reality, that is to say, a reflection and participation of Divine Nature in one of its aspects. Not only is the former alternative contrary to the Catholic faith, condemned long since in the Manichæans, it also involves the consequence that some creatures are of their very nature evil. What are these natures? Human experience at least has never been able to find an example. A wholly evil devil is a mere figment. We can only be *certain* of the existence of evil spirits from the teaching of the Church, and the Church has never taught that the demons are wholly devoid of good, or are bad in their positive nature as creatures of God: Satan is not Ahriman. The second alternative, equally contrary to faith, is a denial of the divine goodness, and therefore of any theism of the least religious value. It is, of course, true that this metaphysical negativeness of evil leaves the practical problem unsolved; for undue privation of good remains a bitter reality, marring on every side the positively good universe. The loss of half a picture is also metaphysically negative; but it leaves the picture ruined and all but worthless. But this negativeness of evil does cut at the root of any pessimism which would see evil as more than, or as equal to, the good in the world; or which would ascribe evii to the fundamental nature or the source of reality.

These general considerations directed against an exaggerated pessimism should make us see evil not as the dominant fact of experience, but at most as an imperfection however extensive in a universe essentially good. But if the universe and its order are essentially good, the goodness of its Author is not rightly called in question by an imperfection whose cause is at worse unknown. It would be equally unjustifiable to deny the genius of an artist because a portion of his picture was seriously damaged, or because even a considerable portion of that picture were in such darkness that no coherent design could be made out.

IV

Before, however, we enquire whether we can obtain at least glimpses of the cause or causes of the evil which disfigures the present condition of our world, we must discuss briefly a few considerations having special reference to particular categories of that evil.

Suffering.—Pain, whether sensible or mental, is undoubtedly the most difficult fact to reconcile with the negative character of evil. Painful consciousness is evidently as positive as pleasurable consciousness. Pain and sorrow are obviously quite other than mere absence or privation of pleasure and joy. I do not claim to solve this difficulty. I would, however, ask a question whose answer will take us into the very heart of the problem of suffering. Is suffering evil? Unpleasant it undeniably is of its very definition. But the unpleasant is at least not simply identical with the evil.

The majority of mankind will, no doubt, if we are honest with ourselves, answer unhesitatingly that suffering is evil. But there is another class of men who answer otherwise: they are the saints. These, as is well known, have embraced suffering with joy, have desired suffering. *Aut pati aut mori—To suffer or to die*: so spoke St. Teresa, and she spoke not for herself alone but for all the holiest and most religious souls, inclusive even of those outside the pale of Christianity. Nor have these souls merely desired suffering as the unavoidable price of an other-worldly reward. As has been pointed out already, they have found in suffering itself a present and unique joy absent from pleasure or happiness however innocent or elevated. We cannot reject this attitude as a mere neurotic perversion. We might just as reasonably reject the æsthetic perceptions of the artistic genius, or the intellectual perceptions of the scientist or philosopher, because we cannot ourselves share them. Majorities are no test of truth. Wisdom is not democratic. The more delicate instruments reach farther and register more accurately than the blunter and the more imperfect. And in our own deepest moments, despite our natural aversion to pain, we bear witness in ourselves to the message of the saints. We recognize that there is in suffering a value which happiness does not possess. Not only my faith but my reason, compels me to affirm this, notwithstanding all my loathing of pain and my thirst for pleasure. Someone I once knew said there could be no good God who allowed the suffering of the innocent. That same person on another occasion told me that no one was really understanding and sympathetic, who had not suffered.

This does not prove that all suffering possesses this goodness. If it could, there would be no problem of suffering. Nor is it to say that suffering is ultimately better than happiness. Even the saints look forward to an eternity of happiness beyond the suffering of this life, although, as Baron von Hügel points out,[1] even in heaven we may look for the abidingness in another form of the positive value of noble pain. But the experience of the saints, and the deepest if occasional experience of the average man, does reveal in suffering a value for which we can conceive no other equivalent. Hence the existence in the world of suffering, pre-eminently of that personally undeserved or vicarious suffering which alone possesses in its fullness this peculiar worth, is a good not an evil. We have seen the Singer lose his faith in God through his undeserved suffering. It is by a wider and a deeper knowledge of the world's undeserved suffering that his faith is restored. "He has revealed His face to me. His face is terrible and sweet. . . . I know it now. His Name is suffering. . . . The people, the dumb suffering people: reviled and outcast, yet pure and splendid and faithful. In them I saw, or seemed to see again the Face of God. . . . It is a tear-stained face, blood-stained . . . but it is the Holy Face."

Even though we must grant that much suffering is, as far as we can see, evil, yet such suffering is not thereby proved an absolute evil. An evil it may be viewed from the standpoint of the individual, and yet a good when viewed from the standpoint of mankind as a whole, or of the entire world-order. Nor is it unjust that the individual should thus suffer for the whole body, if, as our faith teaches us, the innocent sufferer will undoubtedly reap the full fruit of his pain in eternity, in his joy in redeemed humanity, even if he does not reap it here in this brief passage of time.

There remains, however, perhaps the greatest because the most insoluble difficulty against a divine Providence, the suffering of animals. We must not unduly minimize this difficulty by minimizing the fact of this suffering. Certainly there is no ground to equate the suffering of even the highest animals, with the suffering of man with his enormously more developed nervous system. But the fact remains that animals do suffer, often most acutely, both from man and from their fellow-animals. In modern man, or rather in a few modern men, there is a heightened sensibility to animal suffering. An appalling callousness and cruelty towards animals is still existent in modern civilization as a whole, for birds are tortured and slain almost to extinction, not for the supply of human need but for the

[1] *The Mystical Element of Religion*, Vol. II, p. 155 *sqq.*, Article in *Church Quarterly*, April, 1917.

mere service of a useless vanity. Therefore let no words of mine, or of any Christian man, appear to condemn sensibility to animal pain because of the excesses of a handful of fanatics, or of foolish statements like that of Mr. Bertrand Russell that from the point of view of an amœba an amœba is as valuable as a man.[1] There is, however, no ground either in revelation or in philosophy to suppose the individual soul of any animal to be of such real spiritual worth as to require, or even to render possible, its individual survival. On the other hand, when we consider that animal pain is at most far less in quality and intensity than human, and that if we take animal consciousness as a whole there is reason to believe in an excess of pleasure, so that animals would, had they the choice, prefer to be born into this world rather than not to exist at all, then our difficulty is at least diminished. Can we go further and, with Canon Peter Green, consider that there is such solidarity between mankind and animals, that the sufferings of animals possess value for the restoration of a fallen humanity? "If," he says, "the universe bears to the totality of human spirit something of the relation of the human body to the individual soul, may we not hope that no pang of agony is altogether hopeless, but that every mite of pain, from the pain of the bird in the claws of a cat to the willingly borne pains of the martyr, pays off something of the debt, effects something for our restoration?"[2] Assuredly we cannot ascribe immediate supernatural redemptive value to any pain save that of Christ's members, human souls in supernatural union with the Redeemer. But in view of the fact possibly indicated[3] in Romans viii. vv. 20-23, that creation as a whole is bound up in the solidarity of man's fall, and will share in the solidarity of his redemption, we may, surely, see even in animal suffering an indirect and mediate value in virtue not of any supernatural worth it has of itself, but of its subordination in the world-order to mankind, and therefore to the redeemed humanity whose Head is Jesus Christ. If this be so, the difficulty of animal suffering is still further diminished. In any case and at the most we must balance against the insoluble problem of animal pain the entire weight of the arguments for a divine Providence of wisdom and love, especially the indications of that Providence operative in the pain of humanity.

[1] *Mysticism and Logic.* [2] *The Problem of Evil*, p. 162.
[3] I say "possibly" since Fr. Joseph Rickaby (*Notes on St. Paul*) maintains that every creature here means simply every human creature.

Waste and Defect.—Modern discoveries in palæontology have brought home to us the immense waste, specific and individual alike, in the enormously slow and costly progress of organic life. The same waste obtains throughout the organic kingdom to-day.

One question I would put to the objector in regard to non-human waste. Suppose after a lifetime of failures and misdirected effort, an artist produces but one masterpiece; is not that masterpiece worth all the previous failure and waste? Not only is it worth the price, but most probably it owes a peculiar value to that costly price which has been paid. Let the critic but take a walk through the countryside in springtime, when the woods are fragrant with the honey-sweet flowers of the mountain-ash, when the heaths are aflame with gorse, when the hyacinths are in blossom and the primroses and the sweet violets, when the beech-trees are unfolding their first leaves, and when in hedgerow and orchard the apple-blossom reminds us of One "white and ruddy" of Whom it is written, "As the apple-tree among the trees of the wood, so is my Beloved among the sons." Here is a masterpiece incomparably fairer than the masterpiece of our imagined artist. If such be the end and achievement of æons of evolutionary waste and misdirected efforts, who shall count that waste profitless, those efforts vain? For the further difficulty as to the need for such waste at all, I must refer to our final considerations.

As to the human waste and defect, whether in the lives of individuals or in the course of human history, this question cannot profitably be considered apart from the specifically human evil of sin. We may, however, remark that mental and moral deficiency—the most extreme form of human defect—remove the danger of grave sin while preserving intact the soul's capacity for its supernatural and eternal destiny. The investigations of Jung, for many years head of a mental hospital,[1] go to show that the lunatic, far from living in a continuous agony, more usually lives in a self-created paradise of his own construction, so that the madman is in reality an artist who mistakes his own creations for reality. If these creations are better than his real environment he has at least some compensation for his loss. If they are worse, the cause may be in most cases traced to personal fault in the sufferer's past life. In many cases human madness is a merciful invasion by the subconscious in relief of a conscious life overstrained beyond bearing. The congenital lunatic or imbecile is on the other hand more like a child,

[1] See his *Collected Papers on Analytical Psychology*.

a child saved by this abnormal prolongation of childhood from the pain and sin incident to the knowledge of maturity. If, notwithstanding, we are certain that this security is not worth the price paid by the lunatic and imbecile, we prove thereby our conviction that a full human character is worth the suffering and the possibility of sin involved in its formation.

Moral Evil: Sin.—The possibility of sin for all, and consequently the practical necessity of sin for some at least, is involved in the existence of human free will.[1] Certainly that free will is most perfect that is so fixed in good that it is beyond the possibility of sinning. Such is the divine Free Will to which our own is but analogous. In creatures, however, free will rightly used comprises two distinct and mutually incommutable species of moral good. One is the good of temptation conquered, the other and the higher is the good of temptation unfelt. It would appear scarcely possible without a loss of moral values simply to substitute the latter good for the former. Moreover, temptation unfelt, if it is to have supreme worth, must somehow include temptation conquered. If confirmation in good be the crown of a successful struggle against moral evil, the supreme value of that confirmed good will is enhanced by the precedent value of the moral struggle and victory. Though Origen was wrong in playing with the notion that perpetual liability to fall is involved in free will, yet the most complete form of human, indeed of angelic, free will does appear to involve temporary liability to fall, a period of probation in an order open at least to evil.[2]

But it will be said, many men and women have no fair moral chance. They enter the world with such a psycho-physical constitution, or in such an environment, as will make a life of immorality or criminality inevitable. But the specific evil of sin is constituted by its deliberate and free malice. This and this alone is a spiritual and, if unrepented, an everlasting evil to the soul. No amount of inevitable, and therefore irresponsible, immorality or crime is comparable in its evil to the most petty act, the most trifling thought that is a deliberate, freely willed, defiance of a divine or moral law known as binding and possible of fulfilment. Canon Green quotes a most helpful passage from the Anglican, Fr. Dolling, in which from years of intimate experience of the Portsmouth underworld,

[1] Fr. Joseph Rickaby, S.J., *In an Indian Abbey*, pp. 143–5.

[2] The case of children dying in infancy does not invalidate this providential law. We cannot believe that these infants possess the same degree of divine union as adults who have worked out their salvation in conflict with sin.

an environment of almost inevitable vice and crime, he maintains the comparative spiritual innocence of these inevitably vicious and criminal slum folk. "Our falls in Portsmouth entailed no complete destruction of character, hardly any disfigurement at all. Boys stole, because stealing seemed to them the only method of living . . . girls sinned . . . unconscious of any shame in it, regarding it as a necessary circumstance of life if they were to live at all. The soul unquickened, the body alone is depraved, and, therefore, the highest part is still capable of the most beautiful development."[1] Nor should we imagine that such people possess no moral code, by obedience or disobedience to which they can save or lose their souls. Mr. Masterman has pointed out that the slum poor have a peculiar moral code of their own, a code in which loyalty, generosity and mutual self-sacrificing help are the dominant virtues. No doubt it is lamentably imperfect; but, in view of the Gospels, we dare not pronounce it more imperfect, less Christian, than the equally imperfect, though highly legal and respectable, codes of the middle or upper classes.

V

We have now to consider a sin whose very existence is ignored or contemptuously rejected by most modern men, a sin indeed whose existence and nature can be proved only from revelation, though its effects are but too obvious in history and experience, a sin commonly dismissed as an ecclesiastical figment, a sin whose very introduction seems at first sight a needless complication of the problem of evil already difficult enough, yet a sin which in reality introduces us into the very heart of that problem and of such imperfect solution as is possible in this life. This sin is original sin. On no other subject does the modern ignorance of Christian theology—an ignorance which imagines itself competent, without the shortest course of previous study, to pronounce on what is at least one of the most carefully elaborated structures of human thought—flaunt itself with more blatant self-assurance. I have listened to a table full of otherwise intelligent people making merry over the notion of infants born into the world vile and hateful to their Maker, merely because in the dim dawn of human pre-history one man ate a forbidden apple.

[1] Dolling, *Ten Years in a Portsmouth Slum*, quoted by Canon Green, *The Problem of Evil*, p. 199.

Yet the least study of the Catholic doctrine of original sin would have sufficed to explode this calumnious parody. On the other hand, we must in fairness admit that since the dogma of original sin, like many others, has been elaborated as the result of a long historical development, in the course of this development inaccurate explanations have been propounded which lend colour to these popular notions; and that traces of these explanations still remain in language unexceptionable when understood as theologians understand it, but misleading or false if taken in a popular and untechnical sense. Yet our critics should remember that the language of any science is of necessity more or less technical, in theology largely analogous, and therefore does not claim to be immediately intelligible. But in truth for the Englishman a cloud of Protestant distortion still veils the Catholic doctrine of original sin.

I cannot even briefly sketch the doctrinal history of original sin, as it was developed first in one direction by Augustine and his successors against Pelagian naturalism; later in another and complementary direction—a direction taken by the mediæval schoolmen with their lucid distinction between the two orders of nature and supernature hitherto somewhat confused, and later in opposition to the perverse and exaggerated supernaturalism of Baius and Jansenius. I can but summarize the doctrine as it is taught to-day in its maturity of exposition.

Original sin presupposes two distinct orders, nature and supernature. The latter is an elevation towards the unlimited life of God, whereby man is released from the limits inherent in his created nature, and made in very truth a superman, a partaker of the Divine Nature, an adopted son of God. It is, therefore, in no constituent a perfection of human nature, but an added free gift of God. It was, however, bestowed by God on our humanity when He created the first man. It was given to him not as a merely personal possession, but as an endowment attached to his nature. It carried with it as by a connatural consequence certain special graces by which human nature as such was so delivered from defects naturally inherent in it, as to be thereby enabled perfectly to receive and obey the power and operation of the supernatural life. Among these gifts were bodily immortality, freedom from suffering, and the perfect subordination of man's animal life to his reason, and of both to the will of God. This supernature and its effects were given to human nature, not to Adam as an individual; they were given to humanity as a solid whole with

Adam, a body of which Adam was the divinely appointed head. It would therefore have been ours by natural descent from Adam, in virtue of our solidarity with him as incorporate into his body by generation. When, however, Adam fell, he lost this supernature for human nature as such, for humanity as a whole. As we should have partaken of supernature in virtue of our natural solidarity with Adam, we now partake of his lack of supernature in virtue of the same natural solidarity. Henceforth we are all (our Lady alone by peculiar redeeming grace excepted) generated with a nature deprived of that supernature which in God's original plan for humanity was to have been its complement and end. This state of mere nature thus *unduly* deprived of supernature—this "lack of the superadded gift" of supernatural union with God—constitutes the state of original sin. The further evils from which we suffer in the natural order as a result of Adam's fall, are not natural defects nor punishments extrinsically inflicted.[1] They are the natural consequences of our human nature, no longer supplemented and corrected by supernatural grace. We die because we are human beings, we suffer because we are human beings. Moreover, because we are human beings our animal desires and in particular the strongest of all these, the impulse of sex, rebel against the control of reason; and from the same cause our rational will labouring under ignorance and selfishness, is prone to prefer an immediate but limited good to the supreme and unlimited, but more remote, good of obedience to the divine law. This twofold deordination is called concupiscence, though that name is more particularly given to the lower deordination of sense as against reason.

We may see in original sin the limited self-assertion of the natural man going forth to the goods of mere nature and, imprisoned in the limits of nature, unable to rise to the supernatural and unlimited union with Infinite Godhead. Such a confinement within the limits of nature in opposition to man's original call to supernatural union with God, is an exclusion of that supernatural union with God, and therefore of God Himself as man's supernatural end. But this unrighteous exclusion of God by imprisonment of the soul in created limits, is essentially a sin (peccatum) or fault (culpa); not, however, the personal sin or fault of the individual, but, as Odo of Cambrai clearly explains, the sin of humanity itself in which the

[1] They are punishments in the sense that they are the result of a sin freely committed.

individual shares in virtue of his humanity.[1] If dirt has been aptly defined as matter in the wrong place, original sin, being essentially nature in the wrong place (that is, exclusive of supernature) is truly termed an uncleanness, and baptism a cleansing from stain. No physical defilement, nor uncleanness of nature as such, does the Church intend by such language, but simply and solely birth into a nature-self deprived of the supernature which should have completed it. Thus the personal innocence of the new-born babe, its innocence in the natural order, is compatible with a guilt of its nature in relation to the supernatural order. Thus also is it dear to God because substantially united to Him as its natural ground and end, yet a "child of wrath"[2] in its separation from Him and aversion from Him as its supernatural end.

This law of solidarity implied in the doctrine of original sin, is neither unjust nor arbitrary. It is a fundamental law of the providential order. We are not intended to be raised to supernature, to attain our supernatural destiny and live our supernatural life as unrelated units, but as members of a social organism. This organism would have been humanity as one whole with the first man its head. Now it is redeemed humanity—the church-body of the God-Man who has taken our humanity to raise it once more in Himself to supernatural communion with God. If our fall and redemption were not thus effected in and through human solidarity, that would have been a difficulty indeed, for it would have been in disharmony with the fundamental nature of humanity.

But it is objected that many, perhaps most, individuals do not share in the new supernatural solidarity of the redeemed and die in the grace-excluding nature of Adam. Even so, they suffer on that account no loss of any good, not even of a rational union with God, which constitutes the integrity of purely natural happiness, the fulfilment of man's nature in its strict exigency. If God were unjust, because He does not raise all men to supernature, He would be equally unjust in not raising animals to human nature. The super-

[1] "I did not sin in Adam, but my nature sinned. I sinned not as Odo, but as a human being, my substance (i.e. nature as a solid reality) sinned, not my person (individuality). Because a substance (nature) only exists in a person (an individual) it is the sin of this substance, it is indeed a personal sin, but not the sin of a person." Bl. Odo of Cambrai, quoted by Pohle, *Treatise On God the Creator*, Ch. 2, 3, arb. 3.

[2] Yet surely such language as "child of wrath" or "hateful to God" should not be used of naturally and personally innocent children without careful explanation of its highly technical and non-natural sense.

natural life is no more necessary to the happiness of man in pure nature, than is rational life for the happiness of a horse or dog.

The progress of psychology is revealing to us ever more clearly this basic fact of solidarity to the utter confusion of the Victorian objection to original sin grounded on a radically false individualism. Psycho-analysis is as yet very imperfectly developed. No one therefore can at present safely rest a conclusion on the theories of any psycho-analyst. The onesidedness and crudity of Freud has been corrected by Adler and Jung. But we can, I think, see already in the general trend of psycho-analysis, ample confirmation of the "solidary" operation of original sin, though not of the fact of that sin as such, for no psycho-analysis can discover the presence or absence of supernature, or discriminate between unaided nature and grace. But psycho-analysis displays the power and extent of concupiscence. No doubt Freud has grossly (in both senses of the word) exaggerated the supremacy of sexual concupiscence even in the most personally innocent people. But when all deductions are made, his analysis of dreams discloses the scope and power of this concupiscence as enormously greater than the individualist Victorian, confined to knowledge of the conscious alone, allowed or suspected. Liberal theology in the nineteenth century, as exemplified in Harnack's "*Dogmengeschiste*," accused Catholic and particularly Augustinian theology of an unhealthy pruriency because it has insisted on the fact of sexual concupiscence, and has therefore stressed as no other teaching has stressed the importance and worth of chastity; but the exaggeration of Freud revenges the despised common sense of Augustine.[1] For this concupiscence is precisely the supreme and most powerful operation of the natural life-force in fallen man, and consequently of his self-determination towards the limited life of nature as opposed to supernature, and of animal instinct as opposed to rational will. It is precisely as such that Freud reveals it at work in the subconscious field when education or reason has suppressed it in the conscious. To the revolt of the higher or spiritual concupiscence corresponds the power-impulse with which Adler replaces the sex or pleasure-impulse of his master Freud as the dominant subconscious motive revealed by analysis. As Jung rightly points

[1] The Augustinian and scholastic doctrine of the peculiar transmission of original sin by paternal as opposed to maternal generation, long despised as an unscientific figment, is confirmed by Jung who maintains the dominance of the paternal element in generation and in psycho-physical inheritance (*Collected Papers on Analytical Psychology*).

out, both are powerful motives, dominant according to individual temperament. Both alike on diverse planes manifest the disordered operation of concupiscence towards the limited good of nature away from the unlimited God. Both alike are radically self-centred and immediately or mediately self-regarding. Both alike are the natural love that builds up a world-order opposed to the city of God built up by charity in which the natural will is emancipated by grace from the limits of nature and self. Even the term concupiscence is practically restored to use by Jung who calls this natural impulse *libido*. Jung demands for our well-being its "sublimation" into a higher moral and altruistic volition. But on the natural plane he does not show the possibility of any general and constant sublimation; only supernature can effect this by sublimating and sanctifying this *libido* or concupiscence by charity. Thus is supposedly outworn theology shown to be in vital relation here as elsewhere with the data revealed, and the problems raised, by the most modern scientific research.

One outstanding difficulty, however, remains. Modern anthropology knows nothing of any fall. It knows only progress from primæval savagery. I frankly admit the difficulty. We cannot pretend that natural knowledge on all points confirms the data of revelation. Indeed, if it did, what need would there be for revelation, what value in faith? But scientific anthropology cannot, in fact, disprove the Fall. For as a natural science it can at most reveal only man's progress on the natural plane—his advance in natural civilization. But, as we have seen, the Fall concerns man's supernatural condition. Even suppose it possible to discover the fossilized remains of our first parents, we could learn from them nothing of their supernatural endowment or its lack. Genesis admits a natural progress among primitive men, a gradual discovery of the arts of a rudimentary culture. On the other hand, there is a common tradition through the world of a Golden Age at the beginning of human history: witness Hesiold's Golden Age, the Alcheringa time of the Australian bushmen. In these Golden Ages, so the traditions affirm, man was in closer communion with the gods than he now is. This is certainly no proof of original justice. It may be but the reflection into the past of man's ideals, so hopelessly unrealized in the present. But it is surely at the least not unreasonable to see in this belief an instinctive knowledge that man has fallen from a higher state in which he enjoyed a special union with God.

Nor need we be troubled by the folk-lore details of the inspired story of the Fall. Canon van Hoonacher of Louvain, one of our leading Catholic Old Testament scholars, has suggested in an illuminating article in the *Expositor*[1] that the inspired writer has taught the doctrine of the Fall by the employment of a story taken from Semitic folk-lore. This folk-lore, it seems, told of a garden prepared for the inhabitation of the Cherubim. There these angels sustained their immortality by the fruit of the Tree of Life. Into this Paradise man was admitted as a guest on probation. He disobeyed the divine command and was driven forth into his natural environment the world outside. Evidently this garden of the Cherubim represents the supernatural order to which at man's creation the good angels finally and irrevocably belonged, receiving from the divine self-communication the eternal life of God Himself. But man enjoyed this supernature in a lower degree and on trial, lost it and fell into the state of mere nature, till in Christ he is restored to supernature.[2] On such a matter anthropology neither has said nor ever can say a word. On the other hand the present condition of humanity and of our earthly environment is obviously out of harmony with our highest possibilities and aspirations and therefore with the divine ideal for man. It is plainly not a condition of progress as far advanced as it could possibly be, but a condition that is and is felt to be evil, a condition that ought not to be, in other words a fallen condition.

Certainly the pre-human environment was not without much evil. That, palæontology has amply proved. But eternity, though manifest in time, is not itself temporal. The redemption began before the Incarnation of the Redeemer. Before God was incarnate in the historic Jesus, He began to restore us to grace in solidarity

[1] *The Literary Source of the Fall Story* (Dec., 1914).

[2] If the tree of life represents sanctifying grace as conferring on nature immortality by "enspiriting" it, the tree of the knowledge of good and evil will represent the knowledge of the natural order as, when exclusive of supernature, inevitably good and evil; good in its participation of God, evil in virtue of its created limitation now unduly excluding the supernatural. (The employment of a folk-lore story, if van Hoonacher's theory be admitted, in no way militates against the authenticity of the Scriptural narrative as setting forth the "facts" of the Fall which are embodied in the Christian Faith, viz. that our first parents lost their original state of supernatural grace through disobedience to a divine law at the instigation of the devil, and in consequence were cast out of the Paradise of their primæval innocence. The Church in her dogmatic teaching, is concerned with these facts; not with the literary form in which they are set forth by the inspired writer. (See the Response of the Biblical Commission concerning the historical character of the first three chapters of Genesis, 30 June, 1909, in *Acta Apost. Sedis*, 15 July, 1909.)—Ed.)

with the Christ to come. So also we may well believe, did the pre-human world suffer from its solidarity with fallen man—by being left from the outset to the evils arising from its natural limitations which had otherwise been remedied by a supernatural operation of God.

But "where sin abounded, grace did yet more abound." Not to leave humanity in the mire of grace-excluding nature did God permit this solidarity of fallen mankind. He has permitted it in order to restore man by another and a far higher solidarity even than the lost solidarity of original justice in Adam. In contrast to that tree of death tasted by Adam God has planted in the midst of the new garden of Eden the Church of the redeemed mankind, another tree of supernatural life through nature's death, the cross of the Redeemer. Into the very midst and utmost of suffering and sin was born the sinless God-man to share our suffering and bear our sin.

In an old Missal there is a picture of angels offering earth's gifts to the new-born Babe of Bethlehem. Those gifts are the instruments of the Passion. Those instruments are themselves the suffering of mankind, and in virtue of solidarity the sin of mankind. If original sin in its solidarity illuminates for us the source and presence of evils disproportioned to personal sin, redemption in its counter solidarity illuminates the value and operation of this evil. In view of the cross any murmur that might rise to our lips against divine Providence for the world's evil, should be changed into the joyous and grateful cry of the Paschal deacon: "*O certe necessarium Adæ peccatum—O felix culpa quæ talem ac tantum meruit habere Redemptorem*"—"O sin of Adam truly necessary. O happy fault that hath merited such and so mighty a Redeemer."

But, it will be urged, all are not saved in Christ. Of those, how many God only knows, who are never effectually called to supernature I have spoken above. I need but add a conjecture and a consideration. The conjecture—a mere possibility for reflection—is that had Adam never fallen those souls would never have been born at all, that only the number, now actually called to the supernatural would then have been created. Thus my conjecture. The consideration is borrowed from Baron von Hügel.[1] He has pointed out that the lack of the supernatural call, though it involves the loss of supernatural happiness, precludes also the possibility, the awful possibility, of wilful and final rejection of supernatural life. We of the higher

[1] Article in the *Church Quarterly Review*, April, 1917.

call, of the supernatural possibility, have also in its completeness this awful choice. Nor, till the hour of death, can any man be secure of his salvation. But we are here brought face to face with the worst, because the only irredeemable, form of evil—the black shadow it casts on the universe, the possibility of eternal damnation.[1] We cannot escape the fact that eternal punishment is an essential constituent of the teaching alike of the Church and of her Divine Lord as recorded not once only but in many places throughout the Gospels. Even if for argument's sake we allowed the utmost claim of modern non-Catholic biblical criticism, short, that is, of the obvious irrationality of the school which denies an historical Jesus, it would remain true that our Lord taught an eternal punishment. Indeed, as Baron von Hügel insists, the entire character of the Christian religion as opposed to all religions of reincarnation, demands abiding, that is, irrevocable and everlasting, consequences of our free choice in this life of probation. Nor is it Catholic belief that God casts into hell souls who would turn in repentance to Him. Those only are in hell whose wills are fixed in obstinate rejection of God. Moreover, strictly speaking, He does not send any soul to hell. Rather does the soul in virtue of its own wilful rejection of God cast itself into hell and keep itself in hell. Or, perhaps, it would be more true to say that God places the soul in hell by the very act of being Himself, of being the one absolute Good—in face of the evil will of the soul which rejects His goodness. The free and deliberate rejection of God's love by the soul's self-identification with evil—this is and ever will and must be, hell. Hell with all its implications—about which we really know very little—is thus simply the eternal and necessary relationship between a soul that rejects and excludes the love of God, which is God Himself, together with the consequences that flow from this freely willed relationship. Since God is the Ultimate Reality in whom all creation is grounded, it is obviously impossible that a being in revolt against Him and in wilful disharmony with Him should find happiness in His universe. Even in this life the happiness of the wicked is superficial, and leaves the depth of the soul hungry for lack of its sole possible satisfaction. Hereafter, when the superficial and the temporary have passed away, the bare essence of the soul is left confronting the One Reality, God.

[1] Baron von Hügel has treated this intensely difficult subject with masterly suggestiveness and delicacy in *The Mystical Element of Religion*, and again in the article already mentioned (pp. 218–30). To these sources I must refer readers who desire fuller discussion than the scope of this essay permits.

If that essence be found excluding and denying this One Reality, what is this but eternal imprisonment within a self that cannot satisfy, and in a universe which now stands revealed as in its very constitution hostile to all who choose to be excluded from God? To be in opposition to God is *ipso facto* to be in opposition to His entire creation. Only a creation marred by evil can offer any support to the evil will. The restored creation wholly subservient to good, wholly penetrated by God, wholly reflective of God, must essentially reject and resist every soul that rejects Him. No longer for merciful teaching, but as the terrible revelation of the innate justice of a universe created by justice, the lost soul shall learn too late the law of the universe; "Lo, naught contents thee, who content'st not Me, All things betray thee, who betrayest Me, Naught shelters thee, who will not shelter Me." Nor indeed could God provide any happier condition for such a soul. So long as He is Himself, and the soul abides a free willing spirit in opposition to His love, that soul can only be in hell. To maintain that it could be in heaven or even in purgatory would be to maintain a self-contradictory proposition. How far the love of God may and does attenuate certain of the accidental consequences of a state so intolerable, is His secret. We surely may trust that to His love.

But, it will be asked, why does God create souls that will thus damn themselves? The answer is that the possibility of damnation is the other aspect of the possibility of attaining to everlasting life. "Lo, I have set before thee this day death and life." To set forth the possibility of an eternal freely chosen life, is by that very fact to set forth the possibility of a free choice of eternal death. "But God could annihilate souls wilfully impenitent." Absolutely He could: but in the present order of values which He has chosen, there is no reason to affirm this possibility. If even the electron, or whatever be the ultimate constituent of matter, is indestructible, how should the soul of man be liable to annihilation? Further, as Baron von Hügel has pointed out, the deepest religious sense of mankind witnesses to the abiding consequences of free choice for the individual, and to the appalling possibility of eternal self-identification with evil, as involved in the possibility of eternal self-identification with absolute Goodness. To deny this is to show defective realization of the seriousness of moral issues, a blindness to the gravity of wilful sin, which tends to result in a falsely optimistic and immoral pantheism.

VI

These special considerations of particular forms of evil, in conjunction with the general considerations bearing on evil in all its forms, have led us to a view of evil which would sum up its fundamental purpose in two words, *struggle and solidarity*, or, perhaps more accurately, *struggle in and through solidarity*. It was especially the consideration of original sin and its redemption that revealed the law of solidarity. The insistence on free choice displayed the supreme value of struggle. If we consider the course of evolution as discovered by the researches of modern science we find its progress dependent on the operation of these two factors. In pre-human times the struggle was non-moral, confined to the physical or sub-rational psychic plane, a struggle of physical strength and agility, of instinctive device, a battle in which the prize went at first to the physically fittest, and later to the most cunning. The solidarity also was but the instinctive cohesion of limited groups—the family, the herd. With man since his sin the struggle is still largely waged on the physical, merely animal, plane to which mere nature, in so far as it is unsanctified by grace, is ever dragging him down. But it is no longer confined to that plane. We are called to a higher struggle, a moral and spiritual struggle with evil both within and without ourselves. "Our wrestling is not against flesh and blood: but against principalities and powers, against the rulers of the world of this darkness; against the spirits of wickedness in the high places."[1] Fr. Rickaby in his dialogue on this problem of evil[2] insists on this supreme value of spiritual struggle as the purpose of God's permission of evil. He refers us to the blessings pronounced in the Apocalypse on *victors*. Throughout Scripture, indeed, runs this refrain—fight, conquer, in order to win the crown of the conqueror. "Man's life is a warfare on earth." Faith itself must be kept and affirmed by struggle against a world that often seems to overthrow its very foundations. We are told that the very name Christian, Christianus, is formed on the analogy of words such as Cæsarianus, Pompeianus, which meant a soldier in the army of Cæsar or Pompey, and signifies therefore a soldier in the army of Christ. The Passion-tide hymns set forth the Crucifixion as a triumphant battle against the utmost power of evil, in which Christ did not explain away, or simply remove evil, but met it and overcame it.

[1] Eph. vi. 12. [2] *In an Indian Abbey*, p. 245.

And this our struggle against evil is to be fought by no solitary combat, but in the army of Christ, in the solidarity of His mystical body. In union with the victory of Christ on the cross, in virtue of the indwelling Spirit of God operative in Jesus' victory and in ours, is the struggle of every Christian to be fought out. Christ as the God-man could have overcome evil without us, but He will not complete alone the victory begun by solitary conflict. The whole of redeemed humanity, both Head and members, must conquer evil. When this is effected in its fullness, humanity will partake of its victory and then it will be set free from all kinds of evil. The restored and sinless race will dwell in a new and perfect heaven and earth.

True, God could have bestowed the prize of victory without the struggle; but the victory He could not bestow: and in the divine economy of man's life that victory is an indispensable constituent of the prize. It is a commonplace that character is formed only by personal effort and struggle with its inevitable possibility of falls. More and more we are learning the educational mistake of such interference with a child's environment that it is saved, so far as is humanly possible, from all danger of going wrong by the removal of all possibility of free choice of right. We learn by our mistakes the lesson which otherwise we could not have learnt. And that lesson is the lesson we are born to learn, the only lesson worth learning. Certainly we need not learn it by actual sin, but only by the possibility of sin can we learn it. Indeed, solidarity itself is only revealed in and by struggle. It was physical struggle that led to the evolution and appreciation of natural solidarities. It is the spiritual struggle that realizes and renders effective spiritual solidarity in Christ.[1]

And now we return to the objection that evil is a denial of God's providence in the world. Here I would ask: Which, even to our feeble vision, is better and worthier of God—to permit no suffering or to reveal Himself in a suffering humanity? To remove the possibility of defeat and failure or to give the possibility of conquest and attainment? To obtain external mechanical perfection by quick but mechanical methods productive only of machines, or in the patience of humanity's slow travail to bring about a living and therefore free organism? To make of man a slave who knows not his master's purpose, or a son who by the very means of suffering and sin has

[1] Even had Adam never fallen, each of his descendants would have been tested, and some, it is morally certain, would have failed under the test. So very truly says Fr. Joseph Rickaby in the above-mentioned dialogue.

come to a son's free service in communion and free self-identification with his Father's purpose and life? The alternatives surely give their own answer, and I might here end but for one final objection that may still be raised. Why, it may be asked, these alternatives? Could not an omnipotent God have achieved all the good attainable by the permission of sin and suffering, without that permission?

Let us reflect a little. An omnipotent God is as such an infinite God. But an infinite God, though infinite and therefore omnipotent in Himself, cannot be infinite and therefore omnipotent in His creatures. For they, because they are creatures, are limited, not infinite. But in this limit evil is grounded. Every limited being excludes, by its essential limitation, some being and therefore some good it might have possessed. Even the negation constituted in its specific nature, is of necessity a privation, though not felt as such. Too sharp a line cannot be drawn between simple limitation and the evil of privation, evil strictly so called. Though from the point of view of the universe it is no evil that cows by their nature cannot fly, it is in a true sense an evil, though unrealized as such, to the cow. Suppose a cow could in time of drought fly from bad pasture to good, and thus save its life, it would clearly be good for that cow, though not for the natural order. Its lack of that power is therefore *pro tanto* an evil. On the other hand, as we have seen, all evil except sin is an evil only in relation to its subject; from the point of view of the universe it is good. Even of sin this is true as regards its possibility, and *in so far* as that possibility to be a true possibility involves a certain actualization, it is in this sense true even of actual sin. Though the sun has no shadow in itself, it of necessity casts a shadow when objects on earth exclude its rays. In like manner the shadow of evil on a universe otherwise sunlit with the reflection of its Maker, is not indeed in the Divine Sun, but it is necessarily involved in the relation of creatures to God through the exclusion of His rays by the creatures' limitations. Creatures by their existence involve evil, as shadows are involved by the existence of objects that intercept the sunlight. Therefore even an omnipotent God could not exclude evil from creation. Otherwise creation would itself be the Creator. The evil actually existent in all its terrible hideous extent and quality, above all the supreme evil of sin, is not indeed thus involved in creation as such: it is, however, involved in the special creation which God has willed, a creation whose end is the free-willing man, victory through struggle, and "the consummation of that unity in multiplicity—the love-life of the world, and the world with God," which is achieved through struggle and victory. It may be that God could have created another world-order better in itself. But it certainly *could* not be a world-order containing these good things.

In conclusion let it be said, if we in our human ignorance can dimly perceive the supreme and unique value of free will and victory, and the love which involves struggle and victory, we can surely believe that it was in infinite wisdom and love that God willed their existence even at the cost of all the evil, alike of suffering and of sin, involved in their attainment. The problem of evil remains, and must remain unsolved. But in the divine revelation given to us in Christ and His Church of the divine purpose in the world, we have at least an indication of the nature of the solution. A ray of light emerging from rain clouds on the faint orange dawn in the eastern sky, reveals to us the presence of a hidden sun and the quarter whence to expect its appearance. Such is the light of Christ to the evil in the world.

V

THE DIVINE ATONEMENT

BY

FATHER CUTHBERT, O.F.M.Cap.

I

THE doctrine of the Atonement in Catholic theology is the doctrine of our Lord's actual coming amongst us: *Qui propter nos homines et propter nostram salutem descendit de cœlis et incarnatus est*—Who for our sake and for our salvation came down from heaven and was made man. Whether the Divine Word would have become incarnate had man not sinned, is, as we have elsewhere remarked, a matter for speculation: that His actual Incarnation took place for the purpose of our redemption, and that in His incarnate life on earth He did redeem the world and open the way for our restoration to the supernatural life with God, is an article of the Catholic Faith. Moreover, as the Church teaches, there can be no redemption from sin, and consequently no attainment to the supernatural life, except through Christ and by the grace of His redemptive work; no sin can be forgiven except it be forgiven in and through Him; no divine grace can come to us except as the fruit of Christ's atoning life and death. Christ is our salvation: not merely in the relative sense in which we speak of ordinary men being the salvation of their erring brothers, but in the absolute sense of one who is the very principle and source of our redemption, and apart from whom there can in truth be no salvation.

Further, the Church teaches that Christ wrought our redemption by taking the world's sin upon Himself and in His own Person suffering the consequences of sin, making Himself a sacrifice, and in His self-sacrifice reconciling our human nature with God. Our redemption is won at the cost of our Lord's own self-sacrifice for us. By His suffering and death we are saved.

Against this doctrine objection has been taken on moral grounds. No one, it is urged, can morally relieve another of the responsibility and guilt of his own sin: vicarious atonement, so it is said, strikes at the very root of moral activity: whatever assistance a sinner may receive from others in the way of repentance, in the last resort he must save himself by an act of his own will; he must himself cast off his sin: otherwise his repentance is illusory, a mere make-believe. Moreover, all true repentance implies that a man shall bear the consequences of his own sinful act so far at least as to hold himself, and not another, morally responsible for these consequences. He cannot shift the ultimate moral responsibility from himself to another. Others may help him bear the burden: but he cannot morally say to his helper: "the burden is yours, not mine"; nor can the other so take the burden upon himself as to relieve the sinner from working out his own salvation. The very concept of personal morality forbids such a course. How, then, can it be said that Christ in His own Person has atoned for the world's sin, and that our redemption is effected in and through His suffering and death? Is such vicarious atonement consistent with a true moral idea of life?

Now, it may be pointed out at once that in Catholic teaching Christ's atonement in no way relieves any man from the full moral responsibility for his own sinful acts nor from the necessity of making good, as far as he can, the evil he has done. The Divine Atonement is indeed a necessary pre-condition for the sinner's restoration to holiness of life and union with God: if Christ had not atoned for us, none could be saved. His atonement, moreover, has merited for us that divine grace which alone enables us to do our part in the work of our redemption. In taking the burden of our sin upon Himself He did in fact redeem us; our redemption is wrought in His suffering and death. And yet, none of us can be saved except we repent and have at least the will to make such reparation as we can for the sin committed. The moral responsibility for our own act, and consequently our duty to make reparation for the ill we have done, remains intact: and our co-operation with Christ in His atonement is as necessary to our salvation as is His redeeming work for us.

In fact, it was just this insistence of Catholic doctrine upon our moral responsibility for our own sinful acts and their consequences, within the divine scheme of redemption, which was at the root of the difference between the Catholic Church and the Protestant reformers. Luther's scheme of the Divine Atonement had no place for that active co-operation with Christ in our redemption, wherein Catholic teaching preserves intact in the fullest measure man's self-responsibility.

On the other hand, earlier heresies which have been taken again into our favour in recent years, have so insisted upon the necessity of every man working out his own redemption, as to destroy all notion of a vicarious divine redemption. Christ's atonement, instead of being regarded as the efficacious means of our redemption, is set forth rather as an encouraging example which we do well to follow. Our redemption, so it is said, is wrought in Christ as in a type of life set for our imitation: so far as such a life gives us encouragement in our own effort, Christ's redemptive work may be said to be an efficacious means of our redemption inasmuch as it inspires and moves us: but it is denied that our redemption is already wrought in Him and that the forgiveness of our sin and our consequent restoration to the life in God, is directly effected in Christ Himself, and through Christ is imparted to us, as St. Paul and the Catholic Church teaches.[1]

To a large extent the moral difficulty as it presents itself to the mind of many thinkers of the present day is due to the naturalistic interpretation of the Person of Christ. If Christ were merely a man, however holy, the doctrine of the Atonement, as declared in Catholic dogma, would, in its ultimate issues, be untenable: only as we accept the Catholic doctrine of the Personality of Christ can we admit the Catholic conception of the Atonement as the efficacious means of our redemption, in the fullest sense in which it is accepted by the Catholic mind.

But to some extent the difficulty arises from a defective psychology and a too superficial view of the phenomena connected with the idea of an atonement. Not infrequently when we speak of "an atonement" we limit our thought to the penalty which the wrong-doer has to suffer as a consequence of his wrong doing. A man is said to atone when he more or less voluntarily suffers for his sin. But atonement, at least in the Christian sense of the word, is something more than a voluntary acceptance of the penalty of one's misdeeds: it implies the thought of reconciliation with the injured party; and consequently the idea of forgiveness on the part of the injured. An atonement is complete only when the sinner has won forgiveness. That forgiveness may indeed be withheld; but if the sinner has done his part, the withholding of forgiveness is in Christian ethics a sin against the repentant sinner. But whether the forgiveness be given or withheld, a man is properly said to atone for his sin, only as he suffers for his sin in the desire for forgiveness. For atonement

[1] The theological student will recognize the similarity of idea in which much of modern opinion regarding the Atonement is related to the teaching of Abelard.

is essentially reconciliation with an injured party through repentance and suffering.

It will, however, be well at the outset to consider how this reconciliation between the wrongdoer and the injured party is really effected, if it is to be not merely an external reconciliation but a real moral reunion of severed lives. In the proper sense of the term, atonement has no place except as between persons. Atonement is not made to a law or idea, but to a person or society of persons; and it is dictated by the desire to re-enter into communion with those whose forgiveness is sought. We must keep this in mind if we are to understand what atonement signifies and the conditions under which it can be achieved. Moreover, an atonement connotes the idea of re-entry into fellowship with others on a moral basis. A man does not atone for a mere material injury. He may be asked to make compensation for the loss; but to ask him to make atonement for such injury would be a misuse of words. A man atones for moral wrongdoing and for the moral injury he has done another. In an atonement he seeks to put himself right morally that he may re-enter into the society of others in the acceptance with them of some moral ideal or law.

But no man can set himself morally right unless in the first place he acknowledges that he has done wrong, and is prepared to assume the responsibility both for his wrong act and for its consequences; nor unless in recognizing his responsibility he has the will to repair, as far as in him lies, the evil he has done. This acknowledgment of one's sin and the will to make due reparation are integral elements in repentance: where these are lacking a profession of sorrow for sin is either illusory or insincere. And on the sinner's part it is his complete repentance as included in the desire for reconciliation, which constitutes a true atonement.

But the concept of an atonement includes not merely the sinner's repentance but the injured one's forgiveness. The act of forgiveness itself implies an atonement made for the sinner in the mind or soul of the one who forgives. For where one's honour or moral consciousness is touched by the sinner's wrongdoing, there can be no true forgiveness, no true reconciliation or taking back of the wrongdoer into one's own life, unless he who forgives has first made an atonement on the sinner's behalf to his own honour or moral self. Ideally at least within the thought and affection of the injured one, the wrongdoer must be first reconstituted in the honour he has violated before one can forgive. In the pitying love which frequently forestalls the sinner's repentance, an atonement has already been made for him; since only as love for the sinner is united with shame and sorrow for his sin, can the injured one even contemplate reconciliation with the sinner without loss of honour or participation by consent in the sinner's sin.

Atonement on behalf of another is thus implicit in every act of moral forgiveness, and is in fact precedent to the act of forgiveness; yet this atonement in no true sense relieves the wrongdoer of the personal atonement implicit in his own necessary repentance. For just as the one who forgives must suffer, in his love for the wrongdoer, the shame of the wrongdoer's sin, and thus save his honour in his love; so also, because honour is sacred, he must demand of the wrongdoer a similar acknowledgment of sin and a true repentance of sin before an effective reconciliation can be completed.

Thus, in all true forgiveness and reconciliation where the honour of life has been violated, the love that seeks reconciliation must suffer the shame and sorrow of sin: on the part of the injured one this suffering love operates to save the sinner through pity; on the part of the wrongdoer, through repentance. In his pity—which is love suffering for another—the injured one is brought to the side of the wrongdoer in his shame and sorrow, and made a partner in the wrongdoer's burden of guilt; in his repentance the wrongdoer is brought to the feet of the injured one and received back into the pitying love. But it is in the common shame and sorrow for the sin, and in the mutual love bearing the burden as a common burden, that a new bond is forged and a new partnership of life is begun, through which the original bond and partnership in unsullied honour will eventually be restored as a bond and partnership in recovered honour. The new partnership begins in the sorrow of a mutual love for honour debased; it is consummated in the joy of a mutual love at honour restored.

But whether in sorrow or joy, who will hesitate to say that commonly the saving pity has the greater share? or who will hesitate to say that it is the pitying love which commonly saves the sinner, transforming remorse into genuine repentance? For the gravest moral offences are in their nature beyond the sinner's power to make good of himself. No man who has gravely violated another's trust can ever by his own unaided effort restore the broken friendship founded in that trust. An unfaithful husband can never of himself adequately repair the injury done to a pure and faithful love; there is an irreparableness about certain moral delinquencies, considered in relation to the wrongdoer's power to make restitution, which, when felt, tends to despair. Only the saving pity can bring hope into the midst of despair: only the partnership of the true and the untrue, of the pure and the impure, in a mutual love burdened with a common sorrow and shame for violated honour, can turn a fruitless remorse into a fruitful repentance, and reunite the severed lives in a bond honourable to both. Thus, for all true atonement there is needed repentance founded in the hope of forgiveness and, even yet more, a forgiveness fostering and upholding repentance.

So when the Catholic Church tells us that it is by the Divine Atonement we are saved; that unless Christ in His divine pity for us had suffered and died for us, there would have been no reconciliation between us and God; when, further, we are told that Christ's atoning life and death are the efficacious means of our reconciliation, though at the same time we, too, must make atonement in union with Christ—such teaching is in accord with the moral conception of atonement as we see it working for the salvation of the wrongdoer in the noblest and most effective examples of human forgiveness.

II

Three postulates are assumed in the Catholic doctrine of the Atonement: the divine honour in God's relationship with man must be vindicated and re-established before man can be reconciled with God; in the divine love alone lies the power to bring about this reconciliation and to make it effective in man's life; the repentance of the sinner is a necessary condition for his re-entry into the life with God. The Church insists that only as the moral demands implied in these three postulates are satisfied is the reconciliation between God and man effected.

It will be well to consider briefly these three postulates.

There is, first, the divine honour to be vindicated. To understand what this signifies we must remember that sin is not merely the violation of a law; it is the breaking of a bond, the violation of a trust: the breaking of the bond in which God designed to establish the life of His creatures in the truth and holiness of life which is in Himself; and the violation of the trust which He gave to man in giving him the power to know and will freely, thus enabling man to enter into partnership with God as a free agent, not by compulsion but by love. The heinousness of sin lies in the fact that man uses his knowledge and free will, God's best gifts to him, not to foster his destined life with God in holiness, but to break away from it and set up a rival worship of self against the worship he owes to God. By sin man not only violates the law of his own greater good, but he lays unholy hands upon the mutual relationship in which God and the creature stand to each other in the predestined higher life for which man was created. Thus, the very honour of God is touched in His relation with man, since sin is a betrayal of God's love for us. Hence the irreparability, on the part of the sinner, of the injury done by sin to the divine honour: for if the injury done to the pure and faithful human love is of its nature beyond the power of the wrongdoer ever adequately to repair if left to himself, infinitely more impossible must it be to make due reparation for a betrayal of the divine love. And yet adequate reparation must be made, if honour in the personal relation between God and man is not less dear and imperative than in the personal relations between men themselves.

God's honour must be vindicated. In any conceivable relationship between Himself and man the holiness of life must be re-established as the governing principle of that relationship; else God were not the infinitely holy and His relations with man would not be holy. Infinite as His love for His creature is, by the very necessity of His being, such love must acknowledge the holiness of life in which that love exists and must exact from the creature a similar acknowledgment before the relationship can be reconstituted. But in the very nature of the case such acknowledgment implies repentance and reparation once that holiness has been violated. It must be, too, an acknowledgment not only of the holiness of life but also of the sin whereby that holiness has been injured: and this dual acknowledgment must enter into the reconciliation both on the part of God and of the sinner. The sinner must acknowledge his sin in a true repentance; God, too, must acknowledge the sin in the pitying love which alone can effectually restore the broken bond. God's love, because it is established in holiness, cannot treat the sinner as though he had not sinned. It must confess to the sin and to the justice of the penalties which of moral necessity follow sin. In His very pity for the sinner God must uphold the law of holiness: so only even in His pity can God reconcile man to Himself. Otherwise His very pity would be a further betrayal of His holiness, and of the holiness in which man's own higher life is constituted. To debase by a weak acquiescence the honour or holiness of life, is no true love —either with God or man.

Yet as holiness is of the essence of God's life, so too is love; nor can we conceive of God except as exerting the whole power of His divine love towards a reconciliation with His sinful creature. And in regard to the sinner, God's love must of necessity be an atoning love: since only such love can truly uplift and save. It must be a love that can enter into the sinner's own life and take upon itself the burden of his guilt: a love which in its own inviolate holiness can yet associate with the sinner in his guilt, and journey with him the difficult way of repentance and final reconciliation in the holiness of life. Such power of atonement is inherent in all true love; and the nobler the love the more imperious is the instinct of atonement. The love that cannot stoop to the sinner in his guilt and live to raise him up, is in fact no true love at all but only a more or less ignoble self-love, whether it reveals itself in a cherished bitterness against the offender, or in the weaker form of putting the offender's guilt out of one's mind so that it may not disturb one's own peace or self-complacency. This meaner sort of love can have no place in the divine life. Yet many of the difficulties raised in regard to the Atonement have their origin in conceiving of the divine love as a love of this meaner sort. If God is Love, it is asked, how can He demand a suffering atonement as a condition of forgiveness? But it is just because He is the strong, perfect Love, that atonement through pity and repentance enters into the scheme of our redemption. All unreality must necessarily be abhorrent to Him, the Eternal Truth. He cannot weakly forget or "put things out of mind." But He can forgive though He cannot forget, because His love is such that it can reach to the very extremity of the pity which heals and restores.

And, in fact, it is in this pitying love of God, rooted as it is in His infinite holiness, that man's own return to holiness is made possible. Within the divine love, God in His infinite pity and man in his repentance are already reconciled in holiness before the external work of reconciliation in man's own life begins: else were the very idea of the forgiveness held out by God in the moment of man's sin, impossible to God; since it would be an insult to the holiness of the divine life. But for the very reason that within the divine love itself man is already reconciled with God in holiness, the divine will to forgive is operative in the world to bring man in his own actual voluntary life back into the way of holiness; since it is of the very nature of God that His will is creative of what He wills.

But since our reconciliation with God is a moral act, the reconciliation already existent within the divine love itself must have its counterpart within man's own voluntary life. The renewed partnership between God and man can become effective only as the sinner meets the atoning love of God with an atoning love of his own towards God: else were the renewed union lacking in the freedom and self-responsibility in which human nature was constituted at its creation, and man would be lowered in moral dignity. Man must atone in repentance as God atones in pity, if the renewed relationship between God and man is to be a free moral union, a union of love founded in holiness.

In the Catholic doctrine of the Atonement as it centres in Christ's redemption of our human nature, we shall see that these three demands of a reconciliation of the highest moral value, are set forth and satisfied. In Christ we shall see the divine love reconciling man with God in holiness without any derogation from man's free will and moral responsibility. We shall see the Divine Atonement as a drama of the divine forgiveness unfolding itself in the actual life of the God-Man, and set in our midst for our own acceptance.

III

The Divine Atonement, then, can only be rightly apprehended as we see in it a supreme act of the love of God towards man. "God so loved the world," says St. John, "as to give His only begotten Son, that whosoever believeth in Him, may not perish, but may have life everlasting" (John iii. 16). And it is only in the light of the divine love manifested in the mystery of our Lord's atoning life and death, and adumbrated in the noblest examples of Christian forgiveness, that the high moral significance of the Atonement becomes clear to us.

God loved the world and His love is shown in the redemption wrought for us by Jesus Christ.

Theoretically speaking, God might have brought about a reconciliation between us and Himself in other ways than that which He chose. He might have reconstituted us in some sort of blind obedience to the divine law without leaving us any freedom of choice between good and evil; but He could only have done so by taking from us our highest natural prerogative. Such a course is conceivable if we have regard merely to the fact that God is our Creator, and can make us what He will and set us higher or lower in the scale of created perfection than where we actually are by His own decree.

Or, again, granting that God willed to reconcile us to Himself without derogating from our human freedom, it were theoretically possible that the Divine Atonement should have been accomplished apart from the incarnate life of Christ. Christ need not, in other words, have become Man and suffered and died for us, that the way of reconciliation should be opened to us. In the divine pity as it exists eternally within the divine life the way to reconciliation is in fact opened to us, and conceivably that divine pity might so have operated in the world as to stir man to repentance in the hope of an eventful reconciliation, even though Christ had not come amongst us.

But all such theoretical considerations are of value to us only as they emphasize God's freedom in His dealings with man and elucidate the truth: "God so loved the world, that He sent His only begotten Son." For it is in its perfect freedom from any inherent necessity within the divine life that God's desire for reconciliation with man, and the means He chose to bring about this reconciliation, manifest the perfection of His love for us.

God has reconciled our human nature to Himself, not because we are necessary to the perfection of His own life; He has saved us by way of Christ's atoning life and death, not because in no other way could He re-establish His moral sovereignty over us: but He has saved us, because He loved us; and the way of our redemption and atonement has been dictated simply by His infinite love of man. First and last, Christ's atonement is the triumph of divine love over sin. And for this very reason, perhaps, the rational explanation of the Divine Atonement is strewn with so many pitfalls. Of all emotions and workings of the human soul, the emotion and activity of love are the most difficult to analyse logically in the light of a moral theory. Love, it is said, is a law unto itself; and the saying is true so far as love has a way of reconciling mercy and justice, which is perfectly convincing to the moral sense and yet baffling to the logical reason. The explanation lies in the fact that love is in some way as deep and simple as personality, and evades those partial aspects of life in which the logical reason is most easily at home. Logically unsound as it may appear to those who have not felt the imperious call of the great sacrifice, and difficult as it may be even to those who make the great sacrifice, to justify the act by argument, yet only the mean soul will fail to confess that the man who gives his life for another's good has in his death lived supremely. But the confession were indeed mere foolishness, did not such a death witness to man's moral consciousness of some reality of life from which the nobler sort of men cannot escape, however mysterious it may be to them. But if this nobler, self-sacrificing love vindicates itself so imperiously to our moral sense, how can we exclude it from the life of God? Is not His own life in its relation to His creation the very source of the moral law by which we spiritually live?[1]

So it is that all attempts to elucidate the dogma of the Atonement on grounds other than that of love have proved so inadequate and unconvincing: always the final argument has had to be: "thus God has shown His love for us and in His love has redeemed us."[2]

If it is asked why God redeemed us in one way rather than in another, the only answer must be that His love manifested itself in the way consistent with His own purpose in the world. That purpose as revealed in the Catholic Faith is the rehabilitation of human nature itself in its predestined holiness of life; not indeed as though man had not sinned, but by way of a reconstitution of his supernatural life out of the wreckage sin had wrought. In other words, God chose that man should be reconciled by the way of redemption, by the buying back of his wasted years in making good the evil he has done. Man's past life was not to be wiped out as though it had not been: the past itself must be made good in its effects. What man by his own will had shattered, by man's will must again be built up. Thus man's responsibility would remain intact, and his new life

[1] It might be argued that the way of personal sacrifice for another's guilt, such as is exhibited in the Catholic doctrine of the Atonement, accords with the nobler instinct of man in the process of his moral development, and that therefore the moral instinct demands what to us seems the more generous way of love, since otherwise God's love would be proved less generous than the highest human love. But we must remember that *our* moral life is formed in God's dealings with man: our moral sense is an effect of the law of life which God Himself implants in us. In God's choice of our actual redemption our own moral life is established. It is not we who condition God but God who conditions us. But for that very reason our own moral life in its spiritual tendencies elucidates God's dealings with us.

[2] Thus St. Bernard in the great controversy with Abelard, though he made use of the arguments drawn from legality, so common with many of the Fathers of the Church, fell back upon the simple argument of St. John that man is saved by an act of God's love and that the Atonement must be explained in terms of love. (On this question of the speculative attempts to explain the Atonement cf. J. Riviere, *The Doctrine of the Atonement*, Eng. Trans., by Luigi Cappadelta. London: Kegan Paul, 1909.)

would be in the most complete sense a restoration or reconstitution of the old life; so that in the end it might be said, no years had been lost but all were made good in man's attainment of his predestined goal.

But if the lost years are to be made good, if they are not merely to fall out of man's life, it can only be by voluntary acceptance of the consequences of our own acts, and setting ourselves to retrieve the evil we have done in spite of the handicap of the circumstances our own sin has created.

Now in the Catholic doctrine of the Atonement this making good by redeeming the lost years, is the basic principle of the divine scheme of our reconciliation. In one sense, it is true, mankind has to start its life over again, to make a new beginning, to enter into a new life with God. The life of sin is to give place to a life of divine grace. At the same time the new man is still the same man who sinned. He has still to prove good the same nature in which he was created, and in that nature—perfected indeed by grace but still the same nature—enter into his life with God; he must form again in holiness the very life he has deformed by sin. In his acceptance of the hard conditions which result from sin he will recognize and accept the true law of life as established in the divine will; in his endeavour to remedy the evil he has wrought, he will again bring his life into harmony with the eternal laws of truth and holiness: and in that endeavour the lost years will be made good and have their place in his eventual achievement of his higher spiritual life. The lost years will have taught him the inviolate sanctity of the divine law: in his confession of sin he will come into a knowledge of truth; in his endeavour to repair the evil he has done, his will will be again established in the law of obedience to the divine will: and thus in the end the lost years are regained and contribute to the sum of man's moral and spiritual achievement.

Yet experience tells us how hard, and at times how almost impossible, such a "regaining" of one's lost years is, if one is left to oneself. Just in so far as a man has lost grip of his moral and spiritual life and become entangled in the maze of difficulties where only a clear spiritual insight can avail to save—just so far the wrong-doer is helpless unless his life is in some way reconstituted for him by another: he needs more than mere guidance; the life in which he must walk must be in some way built up for him before he can walk in it. The prodigal who returned to his father's house could never have started life afresh unless his father's house had been opened to him and he had found the way to a more worthy life prepared for him: otherwise he would but have drifted helplessly from bad to worse. No moral admonitions would have availed if there had been no tangible supporting life within which he might start his own life anew. Nor would the father's pity have saved the son had not that pity brought the father into the prodigal's own misery and made him a co-partner in the son's endeavour to regain himself.

It was just such a complete moral and spiritual wreckage that sin wrought in the world when man first turned from the divine law and made to himself a law of self-pleasure. His world-life, cut off from its divine purpose, became morally and spiritually disorganized; his spiritual faculties became ineffective as his mind and heart were engrossed in the pleasures of the sense-world; left to himself he would but have drifted farther and farther away from the divine law of life without hope of recovery.

But God did not leave man to himself. In the very moment of man's sin, the divine pity manifested itself in the promise of the Redeemer to come: and in that promise the work of man's redemption was already begun.

To the Catholic mind the whole religious history of the world since, in so far as it witnesses to man's recovery of the desire for the supernatural life and to the fulfilment of this desire, is the story of the divine pity shepherding the lost sheep back to the divine sheepfold.

That the redemption was not straightway accomplished with the giving of the promise of the Redeemer, is due to the fact that in the divine scheme of atonement man must freely co-operate with the divine activity of God's saving pity. This free co-operation of man implies both a turning away from sin and a positive return to the holiness of life for which God designed our human nature. But before man can renounce his sin he must be conscious of it as a real evil, and it is this consciousness of sin as a real evil which is lacking to the sinner in his sin. Yet until a man realizes sin as the death of his own higher self and as a rebellion against the law of his true happiness, there is no true conversion of heart towards the higher life. To be "convinced of sin" as an evil is a necessary condition for a voluntary acceptance of the divine law of life, once sin has found a lodgment in the heart of man.

In the world-drama of history, the Catholic sees the saving pity of God brooding over a fallen world, permitting man in his rebellious self-will to learn by bitter experience the misery of sin, but at the same time meeting this growing "conviction of sin" with the promise of an eventual redemption planted in the heart of man. Further, as history proceeds the dawn of that redemption appears in the gradual revelation of the Christ-to-come to the people of Israel. This revelation is no mere adumbration of the world's yearning for a higher life, as is the religious life of men outside the prophetic nation; it is the direct action of God through supernaturally inspired prophets, making known to man the life of holiness from which the world had departed. Under the divine influence of that revelation Israel awakens to a concept of the diviner life of man as founded in obedience to the law of divine holiness; it realizes sin not merely as a world-evil pitiless in its judgments, but as a rebellion against the holiness of God, the true law of man's life; further, it recognizes that only in a return to holiness can the world get free from sin and its consequences. But this revelation in its gradual development is given not merely as an intellectual concept, but as a life to be lived; as a law set in the midst of the nation for its acceptance or rejection; and in its stages of development accommodated to the growing spiritual capacity of the nation to receive it: until at length "in the fullness of time" it is finally made manifest in the person of the Redeemer Himself.

Two things are to be noted in this divine scheme of the world's redemption: the first, that man's salvation implies a reconstruction of human life in obedience to the revealed law of God's holiness, a reconstruction in which man has to do his part; the second, that from the beginning God has entered into fellowship with man in man's struggling endeavour to apprehend the divine law and to fulfil it; God led Israel step by step along the difficult path of spiritual regeneration in the hope of the Christ-to-come.

Both these facts attain to their supreme and final expression in the life and mission of our Lord.

Christ is the Holy One foretold to the prophets, whose coming is to inaugurate the reign of holiness amongst men. In Him the life of holiness is made manifest in its purest and most absolute form so that all may see and learn. His Sacred Humanity is the living law and type of the new humanity to be formed in the holiness of God. But this life of holiness revealed in Christ is, in its immediate manifestation, the sublimation of our own life of endeavour to regain the life with God. Our Lord in coming amongst us did not take the form of the new spiritual humanity in the ultimate perfection of its regained life of holiness. Whilst on the one hand His earthly life was the perfect manifestation of the sacred union between God and man, in which lies man's ultimate happiness, yet on the other hand it was a manifestation of that union in the conditions—the lingering results of man's fall—which stand between us and the perfect possession of the life with God. His mission was at once to reveal to us that life of holiness in which man's supernatural life is constituted, and to break down the final barriers of sin which stand between man and his complete possession of the supernatural life. Therefore Christ took upon Himself the burden of our fallen nature, made Himself one with the world in its repentance, yet so as to reveal in His own life the positive law of holiness for which repentant man was seeking, and in His divine fellowship with man to become the beginning of a new humanity established in a supernatural life with God. It was in this fellowship with repentant man that Christ wrought our redemption and so finally opened to us the new life with God revealed in Himself: giving to those who received Him "the power to become sons of God."

That is the divine scheme of our redemption as it is revealed in the Catholic Faith: a scheme which, as we have pointed out, is reflected in the noblest examples of human pitying love which the world has known.

In Christ, God not only manifests the new life of holiness which will make us to share in the divine life, but He enters into an intimate, irrevocable partnership with repentant man in his endeavour to attain to his new life. The Christ-life of the Incarnate Word, which, as we shall see, is the principle and law of our final reconciliation with God, includes that victory of holiness over sin, of the will towards God over man's rebellious self-will, which is the necessary condition of our entrance into supernatural union with God. We can enter into that union only as we voluntarily cast sin aside in favour of the divine law of life. Of ourselves the task was impossible to us: it is made possible because of our divine Lord's fellowship with us in our endeavour, "Who deigned to share with us our human life, that we might become companions with Him in His divine life."[1]

[1] Cf. the prayer *Deus qui humanae substantiae* in the ordinary of the Mass in the Roman missal.

We need, in fact, go no farther to find a reason for the life of Christ on earth and for the humiliation, suffering, and death which it implied. Divine love brought Him into fellowship with us in our fallen humanity, that in and through His fellowship with us we might be enabled to regain ourselves and be restored to our life of voluntary partnership with God.

IV

We can only realize the significance of Christ's humiliation and death which figures so largely in the Catholic doctrine of the Atonement, as we apprehend that the purpose of Christ in His coming amongst us was to establish a new life wherein man might find his reconciliation with God: a life new, not only in the sense that it was to be founded in holiness as opposed to sin, but new, inasmuch as it implied conditions which would have had no place in a life of unsullied innocence. We should totally misinterpret the suffering life and death of our Lord if we regarded it merely as a penalty due to divine justice without reference to the purpose dictated by divine love. Christ suffered and died "for our sakes and for our salvation": had there been no salvation for us, Christ would not have died nor have come amongst us in our suffering humanity. Christ was not destined to death on the Cross as a consequence of God's anger, but as a consequence of the divine love working for our salvation. Christ suffered and died because in His fellowship with us He submitted Himself to the law ruling created life—a law which in its divine integrity results in our happiness, but which, when broken by man's rebellious will, can only result in misery to man. The disorder and consequent suffering which comes when the divine law of life is broken, is in truth a punishment constituted in the very nature of things. The breaking of a law of life naturally entails suffering and death. The punishment of sin is not the arbitrary punishment as of an avenging God, as one might gather from the oratorical declamations of some writers and preachers. Man by his sin in breaking the law brings upon himself the punishment of the broken law: he becomes his own executioner. It needed no new act on the part of God to avenge the law which man had violated. But a new act was needed to bring healing and the power of recovery into the punishment; and that new act was the Divine Atonement. Thus Christ's suffering and death so far from being the direct outcome of God's anger, would never have occurred had not "God so loved the world as to give His only begotten Son" for our redemption. In the long history of man's restoration to his higher life with God it is the spirit of divine love which "moves over the waters" and brings light into the darkness which is upon the face of the deep.

We shall do well to remember that the mystery of the Divine Atonement as it is manifested in the Scriptures, is not only the mystery of the remission of man's sin but even more the mystery of man's renovation in Grace with God: the home-coming of the prodigal and his embrace in the father's love; not his judgment. This truth is the constant burden of St. Paul's teaching. "Christ gave Himself for us, that He might redeem us from all iniquity, and might cleanse to Himself an acceptable people" (Titus ii. 14). "Who died for us, that we might live together with Him" (1 Thess. v. 10). "In Him it hath well pleased the Father that all fullness should dwell, and through Him to reconcile all things to Himself . . . to present you holy, unspotted and blameless before Him, if so you continue in the faith" (Col. i. 19–23). The emphasis is always on the new life which Christ has won for us by His humiliation and death, a life He shares with us, if so be we adhere to Him in the faith He has revealed to us. Punishment enters into the scheme because of the broken law: but in the Atonement punishment is no longer mere punishment; rather is it an expiation of love: and the expiation is already the beginning of a new life in which man is reconciled with God in holiness. The renewal of life in Christ is the central truth: "Christ died for us that we might live together with Him."

Hence the story of the Divine Atonement does not end with Calvary and the Cross: it continues in the truth of our Lord's Resurrection from the dead and His Ascension into heaven—His entrance into the plenitude of the new life He has gained for us; it has its further completion in the Pentecostal mystery of the world's renewal in the mystical Christ-life wrought through the indwelling of the Divine Spirit in "those who receive Him."

The distinctive feature, then, of the Catholic doctrine of the Atonement—and that upon which we must fix our attention—is that God's purpose in the Atonement, was to create a new life, in and through which man is restored to his supernatural union with God. This new life is set over against the old life of sin; yet not as something utterly disconnected from the old life, but as a renovation and restoration of our fallen nature in a new life of grace. In Scriptural language, it is the life of the "Kingdom of Heaven" as opposed to the life of "the kingdom of this world": the Kingdom of Heaven which has its actual beginning in our present life of trial and atonement, though its fulfilment is in the life everlasting.

Of this new life the incarnate life of our Lord Himself is the uniquely perfect manifestation, and at the same time the divine principle whence the new life is imparted to us. In Himself Christ has reconstituted our human nature in the law of divine holiness, and in His Sacred Humanity He has come amongst us as the creative life-force of the new Kingdom of God, and the living law in which the kingdom is constituted. "My sheep hear My voice; and I know them, and they follow Me: and I give them life everlasting" (John x. 27–29): "I am the door. By me, if any man enter in, he shall be saved, and he shall go in and go out, and shall find pastures." Christ Himself in His life amongst us is the manifested life of our human nature's reconciliation with God: in Him it is made manifest to us for our acceptance; in our fellowship with Him that life is imparted to us and we participate in it as in our own true life. The immediate purpose of the Divine Atonement was to create and manifest this life to men and to set it amongst us, that in our free and voluntary acceptance of it we might make it our own and so attain to salvation.

Analogous instances of this divine method of the world's redemption and salvation, are found in the lives of many of the spiritual regenerators of mankind. They are the "reformers" who do not merely preach the higher life, but who in their own very lives exhibit the truth they preach and moreover manifest in their own conduct of life the common way by which "the waiting people" may attain to the truth set before them. They attract the world by the power of the spirit which is in them and draw men to themselves by the vision of the truth as exhibited in themselves. But their practical influence is in proportion as they have felt the burden of adverse conditions which weigh upon their fellow-men, and themselves have fought out the battle of life which their fellow-men must needs fight to win through to the ultimate goal. Two classical instances at once present themselves to the student of history: in the non-Christian world, Sakyamuni, the father of Buddhism, and in the Christian world, St. Francis of Assisi. Both in their own spheres, were vital spiritual reformers, transforming a winter of spiritual discontent into a new spring. The Catholic sees, indeed, an infinite distance between them and the God-Man: but the point of comparison lies in the fact that they acted on the world for its spiritual uplifting, not primarily as preachers and law-givers, but as revealers of a new spiritual life embodied in themselves; a life sublime in its spiritual realism, yet such as men in their spiritual weakness and darkness could lay hold on for their own uplifting. They seemed to men to bring the higher life itself into the midst of this earth; and in the presence of this life men's souls were quickened to receive it. They did not merely point to the heavens above; in their fellowship with their fellow-men they seemed to bring heaven to earth.

It is in the bringing of heaven to earth—the earth of our suffering and struggle—that the Divine Atonement has its significance: *Qui propter nos homines et propter nostram salutem descendit de cœlis et incarnatus est.*

In His coming amongst us Christ, Himself the eternal Witness to the truth of God, came to witness to that truth as the divine Form of our human life in its predestined union with God, but He came to witness to it in the form of our human nature and amidst the conditions of our fallen nature. In His Sacred Humanity He made Himself the prototype of our redeemed humanity—"the first-born of the sons of God"; whilst at the same time in virtue of His divinity, this new life of ours which He made His own, became in Him the creative principle of the new life in us: "As many as received Him, He gave them power to be made sons of God."

Christ, then, in assuming our human nature, took to Himself those conditions of our own actual life in which we ourselves must regain our lost holiness of life, since in the plan of our redemption, only as He made our life His, could His life become ours. In the expressive language of St. Paul, "He emptied Himself taking to Himself the form of a servant being made in the likeness of men and in habit formed as a man" (Phil. ii. 7). St. Paul is evidently speaking here of fallen man; and this was the great humiliation of Christ to which He attributes our redemption: "He (Christ) humbled himself, becoming obedient unto death, even the death of the cross" (ibid. 8). It is in the humiliation of our present earthly life that Christ atones for our sin, a humiliation which culminated in His death on the cross. For let us remember our Lord's entire life on earth was included in His atonement; His death on the cross was but the final act whereby our redemption was wrought; the summing up in one supreme moment, of the life of witness and self-sacrifice which He lived on earth.

Now there were two ways in which our human nature has been humbled by sin and brought down from its destined high estate of union with God.

In the first place there is the moral taint which sin has left upon us, disposing us to evil. That was an effect of sin which Christ in His divine holiness could not take upon Himself. Nor, in fact, having regard to our redemption—and apart from the consideration of His divinity—could He have taken our sins upon Himself in this sense. For it is only in proportion as he himself is free from sin and from the taint of sin, that anyone can become a source of spiritual regeneration to others. The sinful may warn other sinners against evil and so contribute to their repentance; but only the good and morally blameless are potent to impart goodness. It is goodness which radiates goodness and has the power to save. Only in His own absolute holiness could Christ be the principle of the new life of holiness in which we can find reconciliation with God. His life must be the absolute antithesis of man's sinful life: the pure spring of that holiness in which alone we can be reconciled to God. Hence the argument of the Fathers of the Church that no man however perfect could have wrought our redemption but only the Incarnate God, is unanswerable, if we remember that our redemption is wrought through the life-giving grace of Christ's atoning life amongst us. In the scheme of our redemption only the All-Holy could redeem us.

But apart from the moral taint which actual sin has left in our human nature, there is the other consequence of sin which we may describe as a throwing back from the freedom of the spiritual life to a state of servitude to the sense-life. In itself this state of servitude is not sin; it is the natural penalty of sin, and it is the state in which all men more or less exist. The spiritual endeavour of man's life is to escape this servitude. In various ways this servitude of the spirit manifests itself and it is realized the more vividly the more we endeavour to regain our spiritual freedom. Both intellectually and volitionally we are held down by the tyranny of the sense-life over our spirit; in our separation from God, the divine law of holiness has become something external to ourselves and instead of being the law of our freedom it comes to us as a law of restraint upon our undisciplined nature. In the subjection of our spirit to the sense-world, too, we have fallen under Nature's own law of dissolution and change: death which should be the mere assumption of man from an imperfect beatitude into a perfect, has acquired the sting of mortality. Finally, in casting off the supremacy of divine truth and holiness in the conduct of life, man became a law unto himself and thus became subject to human law. Such are the universal conditions in which man finds himself as a consequence of sin; and through which he must retrace his steps towards the recovery of that spiritual freedom of the supernatural life to which God destined him. Such a retracing of the path of life must mean conflict and suffering, a life-long battle between the opposing forces of godliness on the one part and man's selfishness on the other part; between the spiritual aspiration which urges us on and the material world which holds us back.

It was in the acceptance of these conditions of our life as the conditions of His own earthly life, that Christ came amongst us. He took upon Himself our life of spiritual humiliation and suffering, but at the same time transformed these conditions of servitude into conditions of our restoration to the freedom of the children of God, through faith in God and obedience to the divine law.

We have here the great mystery of Christ's life on earth; for a mystery it must be until we ourselves enter into that perfect knowledge and understanding which comes with the full possession of the supernatural life. How could it be that the eternal Word of God, the eternal Witness to the divine truth, should in His earthly life walk by faith in His own clear truth? again, how could He Who is One with the Father in truth and love, yet in His human nature submit Himself to the divine will as to an external law outside Himself, even as the neophyte in the spiritual life must do? It is a mystery which in our present imperfect knowledge of God's truth, can never be explained beyond all cavil. Yet this we know: had He not lived the life of faith and obedience in which we must walk, His life had not been ours: whilst were He less than God, His life would not have been the life in which we are once and for all reconciled to God.

The intellectual difficulty however is lessened if we remember that faith is in no way contradictory of clear vision; nor is submission to the divine law as external to our own human will, in opposition to that perfect freedom in which the human will is no longer conscious of any motive of activity other than the fulfilment of the divine will. Faith as the knowledge of truth not yet fully understood, is true knowledge and a participation in the truth: voluntary obedience to the divine will as an external law, is too, a participation in the utterly free obedience which is of the essence of a perfect love. Thus between the faith in which our Lord lived His human life on earth and His divine self-consciousness of the truth of God, there was no intrinsic contradiction; nor between the perfect oneness of His divine will with the Father's will on the one hand and His earthly human obedience on the other. Nor again, from the moral point of view is there any intrinsic difficulty in our Lord's submission to this spiritual humiliation of our nature. For this faith and this obedience to the divine will in which we begin our ascending life of holiness, are themselves manifestations of holiness, even of the perfect divine holiness, though in a condition of imperfect spiritual freedom on the part of man.

Consequently there is no intrinsic contradiction in our Lord's submission to the humiliation of our nature in His own human life amongst us. If He could take our human nature at all, He could take it to Himself in any condition which does not violate the truth and sanctity of the divine life.

In Catholic doctrine this possibility is set forth as a realized fact. Christ did make Himself one with us in the imperfect spiritual conditions of our fallen nature: in His love of us He took upon Himself those consequences of our sin which are in themselves the vindication of the divine law of man's life. He Who as the eternal Word of God is the eternal expression of divine law, thus became Himself in His earthly life a witness to its supremacy even when man sets himself in opposition to it: since either for weal or woe our life is necessarily subject to the law in which God has constituted us. So it was that Christ submitted Himself to the infirmity of our fallen nature, to suffering and to death; so too He submitted Himself to the law of our spiritual renovation which begins in a voluntary submission of ourselves, intellectually and volitionally, to God as to the Higher Power whom it is our duty to obey.

It was in this submission of Himself, in which His human will was at one with His divine will, that Christ in His human life realized the perfection of holiness: for Christ was not less holy on earth than He is now in heaven. From the first moment of His incarnate existence His human life was perfectly at one with the holiness of God; His human activities were the simple human expression of the mind and will of God. He was, in a word, the All-Holy One between Whose human will and the divine will there was no antagonism, but perfect harmony; Whose thought was the reflex of eternal truth;

Whose whole being was a conscious worship of the Divine Life. The very essence of the Divine Atonement lies in the fact that in Christ's earthly life, His human will was perfectly obedient to the divine will and that His earthly life was a simple manifestation in human form of the holiness of God.

But it was a life of holiness lived under the conditions proper to man's repentant life—conditions which prevent the full enjoyment of man's spiritual freedom. It was this which constituted the "humiliation" of our Lord's life on earth; and, in His case, this humiliation was in the strictest sense a self-humiliation, since in the unique creation of His Sacred Humanity, in its effable union with His divinity, there was no inherent subjection to the conditions of our fallen nature. By reason of its own absolute holiness, His Sacred Humanity had a right to the enjoyment of the perfect "liberty of the sons of God," which in theological language is "the glory of heaven." But for our sakes, for the sake of His fellowship with us in our redemption, Christ voluntarily forwent this glory and subjected Himself to the conditions out of which we, in our free will, must rise to the glory of our supernatural life with God. He submitted Himself "because He Himself willed it," that He might reconcile us to God in fellowship with Himself. Voluntarily He took our life to Himself, that He might impart His life to us: that is the great truth of the Divine Atonement.

V

In such wise, then, are we reconciled to God through Christ—in a life of fellowship with Christ in the knowledge and love of God which He Himself reveals to us.[1] To the full possession of this life we attain only as we are freed from the consequences of sin; but even now we may possess it, though imperfectly, in the life of faith and of obedience to the divine will in which Christ lived with us whilst on His earthly mission.

But it may be remarked that so far we have but incidentally alluded to our Lord's death; and yet from the days of St. Paul, the Atonement in Christian teaching has been pre-eminently related to the death upon the Cross. "Christ died for our salvation" has been the Catholic formula in all the ages; and to His death the Christian people have turned as to the decisive factor in the redemption.

[1] As St. Paul says: "Doing the Truth in Love we may in all things grow up in Him who is the Head, Christ" (Eph. iv. 15).

It would certainly not be in keeping with Christian tradition did we regard the death of our Lord as in some sort an accident in the divine plan of the Atonement. Rather must it be said that in the divine plan, Christ's death at the hands of an unbelieving people was fore-ordained by God as the supreme act whereby our redemption was to be gained.

St. John, commenting upon the words of Caiphas addressed to the Council of the Jewish elders, "It is expedient that one man should die for the people and that the whole nation perish not," declares that Caiphas "spoke not of himself but being the high-priest of that year, he prophesied that Jesus should die for the nation, and not only for the nation, but to gather together in one the children of God who were dispersed" (John xi. 49–52). But indeed throughout the New Testament, Christ's death on the Cross is taken as the the fulfilment of prophecy, that is to say, as fore-ordained by God in His will to save mankind. And certainly in the Gospels there are evidences that our Lord not only foresaw His death but voluntarily accepted it as needful for the consummation of His mission. "I lay down my life for my sheep . . . therefore doth the Father love me, because I lay down my life that I may take it up again. No man taketh it from me, but I lay it down of myself and I have power to lay it down" (John x. 15–18).

In truth no exposition of the doctrine of the Atonement which tended to minimize the specific value of the death on Calvary, would adequately set forth that doctrine as it is enshrined in the Catholic faith. "Christ died for us . . . that we may live together with Him" (1 Thess. v. 10). His death opened the way to the world's restoration to its life in God, for through his death sin is remitted: "in Whom we have redemption through His blood, the remission of sins" (Col. i. 14; Eph. i. 7).

But this emphatic insistence on the death of our Lord as the cardinal factor in our redemption, does but bring out more clearly the distinctive character of Christ's atoning purpose. As we have already noticed, Christ came amongst us, not merely to give us an example, not merely to manifest to us the new life in and through which our salvation is achieved: He came—and this is the all-important doctrine—to win that new life for us who could not win it of ourselves: and to win it for us he sacrificed Himself. The note of self-sacrifice, as we have seen, runs through the whole of our Lord's earthly life: He sacrificed Himself for us in accepting the humiliating conditions of our fallen human life. But the sacrifice on Calvary has a specific character: the death on the Cross was in fact the result of Christ's conflict with the powers of evil in the world; it was the supreme act in His witnessing to the iniquity of sin against a world which in malice or ignorance would justify sin; the culmination of the inevitable struggle between the Truth of life which He came to reveal and vindicate, and "the powers of darkness" whose vested interests were opposed to that Truth. For Christ, we must remember, was not simply a teacher of Truth; He was the divine propagandist Whose mission was to dispossess the powers of evil of their domination over mankind. His purpose was a direct challenge to a world whose pleasure or interests lay in maintaining an order of things at variance with the divine law. Only in so far as men are freed from this tyranny, internal to themselves as well as external, can God's kingdom be established amongst us. The spell of sin must be broken—that spell which holds the human mind and heart in thrall like some unholy love: and the death on the Cross was God's chosen means to this end.

We are here brought up against what must be regarded as the most humiliating experience of human life—the servitude (for it is nothing else) of man's mind and heart to ideas and passions which militate against the higher spiritual life. We know its pervading tyranny not only in individual life, but in all forms of social life; and how it persistently works to discredit and bring to naught the moral idealism in which men seek to "better" the world. This servitude is as an enveloping atmosphere darkening the judgment and enervating the will in regard to the higher, spiritual truth of life: but it is an atmosphere sustained in the will to evil, in the deliberate ungodly selfishness of our fallen nature.

Moreover in this humiliating experience of man the most poignant element is the constantly recurring fact that those who break through this servitude and set themselves to free their fellow-men, accomplish their task only at the cost of personal suffering and, frequently, death for the cause they have at heart. The "legal murder" of John Brown was needed to stimulate the lagging conscience of the Northern States of America on the question of slavery; the persecution of the prophets of Israel kept alive the cause for which they pleaded; "the blood of the martyrs is the seed of the Church." So frequent has been this phenomenon in the history of the moral and spiritual progress of the world, that one might well be justified in regarding it as a law of the world's spiritual regeneration that "one man must die that the nation perish not." The death of the just man at the hands of those he would save, has ever been the one almost irresistible argument against the sophistry in which evil customs and unjust laws are entrenched: and the argument is the more convincing as men see in it the love of God or man spending itself for the world's good.

What primary life-laws are enshrouded in this phenomenon of the ultimate sacrifice, we have no space to discuss.[1] All we can point to here is that the death of Christ on the Cross is in keeping with this "law" of the world's spiritual regeneration. Christ died to break the bonds of our servitude to the powers of evil which hold the world in sin: and the breaking of those bonds is, as St. Paul says, "our redemption, the remission of sins." And as a matter of fact our Lord's death on the Cross has been throughout the Christian ages the breaking of the servitude of sin to countless multitudes who "in spirit and in truth" have believed in Him. From the apprehension of the mystery of the Cross they have come to realize consciously at once the enormity of sin and the compelling beauty of the divine holiness which sin rebels against. In permitting the carnal-mindedness of a sinful world, as embodied in the hatred of the Jewish rulers and in the indifference of Pilate, to wreak its unholy will upon Himself, our Lord in His supreme act of self-immolation has convicted our fallen nature of the essential unholiness in which its rebellious self-will is established; whilst in His submission to the Cross He has manifested the fundamental law by which alone this unholy self-will can be supplanted and our human nature reinstated in the holiness of God—the law of self-sacrifice in voluntary obedience to the will of our Father in heaven, whose will is our true life. But that law as it is manifested in the death on the Cross is transfigured in the Christian faith by a clear manifestation of the divine love working for the world's redemption. Our Lord's acceptance

[1] The attempt to explain the "justice" of the ultimate sacrifice of the Cross has given rise, as students of Church History know, to various speculative theories: but the only value of these theories, from a dogmatic point of view, is in their insistence that Christ did redeem us by His death and that His death was included in the divine scheme of our redemption. Speculation, it must be remembered, is not dogma; but merely a human attempt to explain the divinely revealed truth of the Catholic faith. For that reason we have felt under no obligation to deal in this essay with the many "theories" of the Atonement, which after all are but of secondary importance even to the theologian. The one thing that really matters in an exposition of Catholic teaching, is the dogmatic belief of the Church.

of His death at the hands of men is an act of His own will at one with the will of His Father in the divine love towards the world. Christ died because "God so loved the world as to send His only begotten Son" to redeem the world: and the obedience in which our redemption was gained, was our Lord's obedience to the saving love of God for man. In the divine scheme of the Atonement, as already remarked, man is reconciled with God in holiness, through a moral conviction and acceptance of the truth revealed in Christ. To convince the world of the iniquity of sin and thus bring man to a true voluntary repentance as the beginning of the new life of holiness was the direct purpose of our Lord's submission to the death on the Cross,—*Qui propter nos homines et propter nostram salutem descendit de cœlis.*

VI

It now remains to consider the relation between the two statements in which the Catholic doctrine of our redemption is summed up: Christ once and for all redeemed mankind and reconciled man with God; yet our salvation or damnation depends on our own will: Christ has saved us, yet it is for us to accept or refuse salvation.

We have already seen how in Catholic doctrine the purpose of our Lord's coming amongst us was to create a new life of holiness in which our human nature would find its reconciliation with God. That life was perfectly accomplished in the Sacred Humanity of Christ. In our Lord's life on earth it was accomplished under the conditions of our earthliness; in the life of the Sacred Humanity in heaven it is accomplished in the full freedom of the life eternal. But whether on earth or in heaven it is the same life of holiness, only under different conditions.

Christ came to reconcile the world with God: but the means whereby we are reconciled is that new life which He brought into the world in His own Person. Only as we enter into His life and become one with Him "in spirit and in truth" do we find our life with God.

But in Christ this new life exists not merely as a created spiritual activity, as it does in us when we receive it. In Him it is at the same time a creative activity, since He is both God and Man, the eternal Truth in and by Whom all created life is formed in the Image of God: His Sacred Humanity is the divinely chosen medium through which this creative activity works amongst men. Christ's own personal life is thus the life-giving principle in and by which the new life of men with God is formed. Hence it is *in* Christ that we are saved as in the very source of the new life which is our salvation; *by* Christ we are saved since only as He imparts to us the new life which is in Himself, can we do anything towards our salvation; *through* Christ we are saved, since union with Him in His life amongst us is the condition of our salvation. Thus His life with us in our human nature is in the strictest sense a creative life, of its own power forming us in the life which is His own. Hence St. Paul's analysis of the Christian life: "I live, now not I, but Christ liveth in me"; since whatever of saving grace there is in us, is from Christ the author of our new life with God.

Yet on our part, there is the necessary co-operation of our own active will with Christ if this new life is to become effective in us. By our own voluntary act we must take this new life to ourselves and make it our own: and in this world our co-operation with Christ is necessarily a co-operation with Christ in the work of our own and the world's redemption; for we, too, can enter into the freedom of our union with God only as Christ Himself in His Sacred Humanity entered into it—by the suffering path of our fallen existence illumined by our faith in God revealed to us in Christ, and by our willing obedience to the divine law. We ourselves have yet to make good, so far as it lies within our capacity, the evil wrought by sin in ourselves and in the world at large: we have yet to do our part in restoring the bond between God and man. Only, our endeavour is now upheld and made effective by the creative activity of Christ's own life amongst us. Our reconciliation with God is in fact a continuous act of partnership between Christ and ourselves: Christ sharing His life with us and in His divine power recreating our lives in the grace of His own life; we co-operating freely with that grace and thus making His life our own voluntary life.

Hence the Divine Atonement whereby the new life of holiness with God has been gained for us in Christ, is not a merely passing act in the history of man's reconciliation with God, but the divine "world-form" of our human nature's redemption and reconciliation. So long as the world lasts, Christ's atoning life and death give the law to man's supernatural regeneration. Only as we spiritually share in the life and death of Christ can we enter into everlasting union with God and attain to holiness of life. With Christ we must pass through the Red Sea which separates the life of sin from the Promised

Land of our freedom where sin no longer has any sway over us. With Christ we must suffer the consequences of sin as the just expression of the broken divine law of life; and at the same time work to restore that divine law within ourselves and the world around us, in that spirit of love towards God and man in which the new life is founded. For as an unholy selfishness or self-assertiveness is the root of all evil so (as our Lord has taught us) is the love of God and of man in relation to God, the root of all supernatural virtue and holiness. And it is as the symbol of that divine love, steadfast and triumphant amidst the uttermost iniquity of man's sin—the slaying of the God-Man—that the Cross has its healing power with those who turn to Christ for deliverance from the servitude of sin. That healing power lies first in the supreme witness of the Cross to God's own love for man; and then in the reconstructive power of that divine love within ourselves, as it becomes to us the law of our own life in our union with Christ our Redeemer.

VI

THE CHURCH AS THE MYSTICAL BODY OF CHRIST

BY

E. I. WATKIN

I

OF the two complementary truths, that man possesses an individual being, inalienable and incommunicable, and that he is by nature a member of a society, unable to attain complete self-expression except through membership of a society, each in turn has been over-emphasized or exaggerated, and its consequences drawn out, with too little regard to the complementary truth. The one extreme, the undue isolation of the individual from his necessary social environment, has received its obvious baptism under the name of individualism. For the other there is no recognized title forthcoming. It ought surely to be called socialism. That name has, however, been appropriated to an economic doctrine which, even if it be regarded as the economic expression of the general tendency of thought with which I am dealing, is not that tendency itself. I shall nevertheless make bold for the purposes of this essay to employ the term socialism to designate the opposite pole to individualism. It is evident that neither line of thought is ever found pure, without admixture or correction by its complement. Such an isolation would at once manifest its absurdity.

Nevertheless, there have been movements and groups, ecclesiastical and secular, theoretical and practical, as also particular historical periods, in which individualism or socialism have respectively dominated. Speaking broadly, Protestantism and the period from the sixteenth to the nineteenth century, particularly the latter epoch, have been dominated by individualism. In economics it appears as *laissez faire*, in politics as Whig liberalism, and in religion as the search for a purely individual salvation to be attained by the communion of the individual soul with God. A church and its social system of worship and sacraments were either denied or, at least, thrust far into the background of religious thought and practice. In the early nineteenth century this individualism had reached its height. The age that witnessed the triumph of Ricardian economics and the liberalism of Macaulay and the Reform Bill saw evangelicalism triumphant in the religious sphere. Of course there was a party of reaction and opposition, in religion the Catholic revival: but individualism was supreme. Throughout Catholic Europe indeed, the authority of the Church kept this individualism at bay; but despite the ultramontane movement, the Church was losing in the struggle.

To-day we are in the full tide of reaction against individualism, and, as in all reactions, the pendulum is swinging to the opposite extreme. In all directions the progress of scientific research is showing us how intimate is the dependence of the individual, even in his most apparently individual qualities, upon his social environment. Scientific sociology has revealed to us the enormous power of heredity and environment in creating the endowments and in moulding the very character of even the strongest personalities. Even the genius despite his powerful personality is the man who is most widely responsive to the intellectual, moral, and æsthetic forces of his age. A more scientific treatment of history has made us realize the enormous power of social forces—economic, political, religious—and the reality and strength of that strange social phenomenon termed by the Germans the *Zeitgeist*, in virtue of which the same ideas and desires spring up at the same period without any traceable connection in the most widely diverse groups and individuals. In the late war countless multitudes of individuals of most divergent characters and aims were swept to a common doom, and still larger numbers rushed to the unreasoned support of a common cause. Even the few who did reason matters out for themselves, starting from the most diverse judgments as to fundamental values and the nature of reality, usually arrived at the same conclusion according to their membership of one of the two opposing groups.

This has brought home even more forcibly the apparent dependence of the individual for his very individuality, his feeling, his thought, his will, on the social group. It is no matter for surprise if men are widely drawing the conclusion whether avowed and formulated, or held as a half-implicit under-belief, that man's individuality is an illusion; and that the so-called individual is but an impermanent cell in a wider social organism which is the true and abiding personality, a temporary organ and expression of a collective soul—whether the soul of humanity, or more widely a purely immanent deity of which humanity itself is but a member containing in its turn this multitude of apparently "individual" cells. Indeed, the biological fact that man's physical being consists of a multiplicity of cells, each possessed of a subordinate life of its own, lends the sanction of analogy to a view which treats the entire man as a similar cell in a group-life. This "socialism" is therefore natural enough, for it can bring to its support such an imposing muster of facts—facts which certainly do render impossible the individualism of our grandfathers.

But there are other facts which defy disproof. Each man is stubbornly conscious of an individual being peculiar to himself alone. We do resent and rightly resent any attempt to destroy or thwart our individual self-expression in the imaginary interest of a social group: we do on the contrary desire the happiness of a full self-realization. However much the genius may owe to society, it remains true that he renders to society a peculiar contribution which is the expression of his individuality. It remains true that in proportion to a man's intellectual and moral and æsthetic attainment, he feels himself less the blind tool of social or other forces external to himself, and more able to direct and use these forces for his own end. Indeed, this is the reason why the man of exceptional ability is inevitably more selfish than the undeveloped man, because more deeply self-conscious—unless and until he has learnt the lesson of that higher unselfishness which is a conscious self-realization through self-sacrifice.[1] Facts of this kind we cannot deny, and in view of such facts we cannot surrender ourselves to socialism.

Even less, however, can we return to individualism. Is there no other solution, no conception that will account alike for the facts that point to the pole of individualism, and the facts that point to the opposite pole of socialism. There is such a conception. It is the conception of solidarity. The scope of this essay forbids me any attempt to apply this conception of solidarity in any secular sphere. I can but briefly attempt to define its nature and to show it in the sphere of religion as the Catholic conception of the Church. According to the conception of solidarity, individuality[2] is real, permanent, incommunicable, inalienable, and involves a unitary consciousness and volition; but it is neither impenetrable,[3] nor self-contained, nor self-sufficient even for its own existence and still less for its own fulfilment. Society, on the other hand, though neither a unitary consciousness as is the individual, nor a being absorbing and

[1] We can trace this opposition between self-expression and self-sacrifice in the later tragedies of Ibsen who, however, for lack of religious belief could never find the solution.

[2] I am speaking here of *personal* individuality.

[3] Only God totally penetrates a soul, created spirits *as such* can only penetrate it partially.

annihilating into itself the individual consciousness or being, is nevertheless a real being constituted by the functional co-ordination of individuals in an organic whole, and involving in proportion to its intrinsic perfection a co-consciousness of individual consciousnesses and a co-volition of individual wills; and in proportion to its extrinsic perfection is self-contained and self-sufficient.

It follows, therefore, that the individual cannot even come into being except as a member of society, for in order to do this he needs immediately parents, mediately a social order to which these parents belong. Still less can he achieve the realization of his capacities, that is to say, the complete expression of his individuality, except as a member of society. Thus the self-realization of the individual is identical with the accomplishment of his function as a member of society. But society in turn, as it cannot exist apart from the individual, cannot be perfected except by the fullest and therefore the freest self-realization of these individuals, each in the fulfilment of his individual function. Hence, a society that demands the ultimate sacrifice of any individual either total, by the entire loss of his being, or partial by the non-fulfilment of any potentiality of that being, is to that degree an imperfect society.[1] On the other hand, an individual of whom any activity did not either mediately or immediately fulfil a function in the social organism is to that degree an imperfectly self-realized individual. Hence also any activity which while apparently a function of a lesser society, e.g. the State, is inimical to a greater society, e.g. humanity, is no true function of the lesser society.[2]

It is plain that the analogy of the physical body is most apt to figure this solidarity. The co-operation of all the members to the one end of life, the co-ordination of all the members under the direction of the brain by means of the nervous system, and the multiplicity of subordinate cell-lives under the control of the soul are physical "sacraments" of social solidarity.[3] The obvious differences

[1] In this world of course where no society can reach perfection such sacrifice is often necessary. No believer in another life can, however, regard it as ultimate. The law of a world where good is achieved by struggle with evil, must be one of sacrifice, the attainment of life through death.

[2] If, as we shall see, the Church is the perfect society of souls raised to the supernatural order, every right activity of its members is a function of the Church.

[3] In the metaphysical sphere individualism is represented by pluralism, socialism by monism, solidarity by theism. In the politico-economic organization individualism is represented by anarchy, socialism by the totalitarian state, solidarity by a co-operative organization in terms of function, a corporative society.

by which the human body seems to exemplify socialism rather than solidarity—namely, the unitary self-consciousness of the entire man, and the absolute subordination of the cell-lives to the life of the soul, as also the impermanence of their existence, are to be explained by the fact that the cell-lives are below that level of existence at which their complete and permanent individuality would have had worth, either for themselves or the whole of which they are parts; whereas the conscious life of the individual man has such an existence of such value that it must be unitary and permanent. If, however, this individual life is to be unitary and permanent, that very unity and permanence excludes a unitary self-consciousness in the society of which the individual is in turn a member. Analogies between a lower and a higher plane of existence can never be perfect, for the difference of plane must make a difference. But this being granted, the analogy of the body does present a most valuable analogy and "sacrament" of solidarity, and its value in this respect has only been increased by the discoveries of modern biology.

Having thus stated the conception of solidarity, I turn to consider its application in the religious sphere. There, as we might expect, we find it more perfectly exemplified than in the merely natural and human sphere. Our salvation, that is our attainment of that supernatural union with God which constitutes eternal life, is found to be effected through solidarity. We are not to be united with God as independent and unrelated units. Indeed, such a conception is ultimately self-contradictory since we could not be united with God without being by the very fact of that union united with all those other souls in union with Him. Our salvation is from beginning to end a progressive incorporation into a supernatural society of human souls. That society is the Church. This fundamental doctrine of Christianity may be said hardly to have developed in its exposition since the first preaching of the Apostles: it is in fact the fundamental doctrine of St. Paul as it is preserved to us in his Epistles. So fundamental is it, that as Père Prat points out, it is in a special sense his "gospel" to which he so frequently alludes, and he has explained it, particularly in the two captivity Epistles to the Ephesians and Colossians, with a clearness and precision that has left little to be added by future theological speculation. Let us therefore turn to this Pauline doctrine of our salvation by membership in the Church-society, as it is set before us by his greatest modern interpreter, Père Prat, S.J., in his *Theologie de St. Paul*.

To understand the Pauline doctrine of the Church, is to have apprehended the essence of Catholicism. Sacraments, hierarchy, veneration of saints, the function of Our Lady in the Christian economy, eschatology, bodily resurrection, ethics—all these, even to the doctrine of indulgences, flow naturally from the solidarity of the Church, as St. Paul taught it to his converts. Without this basic doctrine they are disconnected and meaningless, like parts of a building whose plan is untraced, or the organs of a plant whose functions in the life of that plant are not understood. In the light of this doctrine they are seen as the necessary parts of one harmonious edifice, as the mutually adapted organs of one life. For St. Paul the Church is one body. By this he means that it is a society of individual souls diverse in function, but moved and vivified by one common life-principle or soul, the Holy Spirit. In the human body all the members and even the cells are vivified and moved and directed by the one soul. It is true that the cells have their subordinate life; but whilst the body lives the cell-life is obedient to the soul-life and receptive of that life. The independent action of the cells leads only to the disintegration of the body. Thus all the members of the Christian society, are in proportion to their possession of sanctifying grace and to their obedience to it, vivified and moved by God through the indwelling of the Spirit in their souls. As a man advances in grace, the Spirit possesses, dominates, and fashions his soul with increasing fullness, until at the last when the work of sanctification is complete, his entire soul-life is moved and vivified by the Spirit. Then every soul-act is an act not only of the human agent, though it is always his human act, but at the same time an act of the Spirit received in his soul.[1]

This life of "Spirit-reception" St. Paul terms life or activity "in the Spirit," as opposed to the purely natural and human activity which he terms "in the flesh." It is plain that the incorporation of the bodily member or cell into the living body will be more complete in proportion to the completeness with which the life of a bodily member, or of a cell, is subordinated to the life of the animating soul and is informed by the soul's activity.[2] But it is also clear that

[1] Cf. 1 Cor. xii. 4–13, Rom. xii. 11 *et passim.*

[2] Since the Spirit is as God incapable of being related to any creature or forming part with it of any whole, the "information" of the Spirit is only analogous to that of the soul in the physical body. As I pointed out above, a difference of plane renders all analogies imperfect. As Scheeben explains, the Holy Spirit informs the soul not in the strict sense by inherence and confusion

to effect any change of relationship of the mutable creature to the immutable Deity such as man's life "in the Spirit" implies, a created gift of God to man is necessary. This gift is sanctifying grace which is a new quality added to the soul. The possession of this grace therefore involves participation in the Spirit-life of the mystical body, and consequently incorporation into that body. In the human body the soul's action is to a large extent mediated through the head, the seat of its chief organ, the brain. Thence is mediated through the nerves efferent and afferent, the conscious life of the body. So, too, in the mystical Church-body there is the Head through which the Spirit moves every limb and animates every cell. This Head is Jesus Christ the God-Man. Consequently, to be made a member of the Church is to be incorporated into the body of Christ. God, says, St. Paul, "gave Him (Jesus Christ) to be Head in every respect of the Church, which is His body, the complement (πλήρωμα) or Plenitude of Him who is fulfilling Himself wholly in all."[2] In this text the Church is treated as the complement of Christ in His representative character as the Head of a society, the society of redeemed mankind. Because the Church is one body with its divine-human Head, because it is thus the extension of His personal life, a continuation therefore of the incarnation of Godhead in humanity, St. Paul calls the entire Church-body, Head and members, by the name of Christ. As he uses the phrase "in the Spirit" to express the participation of Church members in the Spirit-soul of the body, similarly he uses the phrase "in Christ" to express their participation in the mystical Christ—the extension of the personal Christ—by incorporation in His body under Him the organic Head. Surely St. Paul could not have expressed the solidarity between the members of the Church and Christ more strongly than by using thus the very name of Christ or Christ Jesus, to denote the spiritual entity constituted by members and Head together. Hence the formula "in Christ" is substantially identical with " in the Spirit." To be in a body is substantially the same thing as being moved and vivified by the soul of that body.

As Pére Prat points out, this identification of the Church members with Christ was implied in the divine word spoken to St. Paul at his conversion: "Saul, Saul, why persecutest thou *Me*." This

in one nature "as the soul informs the body," but "by coherence and inhabitation" (*Dogmatik*, French Trans., Vol. III, pp. 632, 633).

[2] Eph. i. 22–23.

implication in its turn throws light on the deep significance, indeed the literal truth, of our Lord's words in the Gospel, "Forasmuch as ye have done it to the least of these my little ones, ye have done it unto *Me*." It explains also the apparent paradox of St. Paul's statement that he is making up what is wanting to the sufferings of Christ. In His natural body Christ had suffered enough, more than enough to redeem mankind, but in His mystical body His sufferings are yet incomplete, though a host of saints, from St. Paul to the present time, have been filling them up to the measure preordained by God.

It has already been pointed out that the process of sanctification, inasmuch as it signifies an ever closer incorporation into the body of the Church, is an ever more complete vivification of the soul's life by the Holy Spirit, the soul of that body. It is now evident that sanctification is also an ever closer union with, and direction by, the Head, Jesus Christ. For as the soul moves and directs the members of the body by the mediating instrumentality of the brain, so the indwelling action of the Spirit in souls is effected in the members of the Church-body through the Head, Christ. But, as we have seen, this "informing" by the Spirit is effected by a created sanctifying grace. Grace is therefore given us in Christ (the mystical Christ—the Head and members), and is derived from and through Christ (the personal Christ, the Head); it is, as theologians say, the grace of Christ. As the physical head through the brain unites the body by the co-ordination of all the functions of the members, so the Christhead of the mystical body is the principle of union in that body, since that union is the harmonious co-functioning of all the members in their common obedience to His will "unto the building up of the body of Christ . . . into a perfect man, unto the measure of the stature of the plenitude of Christ . . . who is the Head from whom all the body derives the harmony of its parts and its compactness (cohesion) throughout all the joints of its mass, each several part operating in its own sphere; whereby the whole body grows unto the building up of itself in charity" (Eph. iv. 12–16, cf. Col. ii. 19). Unlike the physical body, where a man by taking thought cannot add one cubit to his stature (since the vegetative life of the body though effected by the one soul, is not effected through the brain), the growth of the mystical body (not only the external growth which consists in the addition of new cells, but the internal growth which consists in the increasingly perfect incorporation of cells already partially and in principle incorporate) is effected from and through the Head, "from whom," as St. Paul says, "all the body through arteries and ligaments, being supplied and compacted, increaseth with the growth willed by God" (Col. ii. 19). Had St. Paul possessed our knowledge of the nervous system, the analogy could have been stated in more accurate and more striking biological terminology, but the analogy itself would only have been strengthened. In St. Paul's time nothing was known of the nerve system. Nor was anything known of the cell-life in the body. I may perhaps be permitted for the sake of clarity to use "member" for the classes of souls performing the same general function in the body, and therefore existing from the beginning of the Church, and "cell" for the individual soul, each added in turn, when each soul is raised to the supernatural life by its first incorporation into the body.[1]

When the process of sanctification and therefore of incorporation, is complete for each soul-cell, the soul will be wholly moved and filled by the Spirit, the Spirit of Jesus Christ the Head; and will at the same time be wholly directed by the Head in perfect union with Himself; as in a perfectly healthy natural body each member is wholly directed by, and in perfect union with, the brain. In this completed sanctification there can be no activity of that soul which is not a fulfilment of its function as a member, and therefore a fulfilment of the will of the divine Head. Every act of such a soul, interior or exterior alike, is then an act of the Head, an act of Christ; just as it is, as we saw above, an act of His Holy Spirit. Such a soul has fully the "sentiments of Christ Jesus" (Phil. ii.); His "dispositions," to use a term of more modern spirituality. It is perfect as Jesus is perfect, not by possessing His perfection, for the perfection of a member of a body cannot in the nature of things be the same as the perfection of its head, but by being a perfect cell, as He is the perfect Head; and by the perfect fulfilment of its function as a cell of the mystical body, as Jesus Christ perfectly fulfils His function of Headship. When all the members attain perfection (as all the saved must ultimately attain it) then the entire body will be perfect: for then the entire body will be wholly responsive to the Spirit-soul, will be wholly incorporated with Christ, its Head, and be expressive of, and wholly obedient to, His will. Then the whole body will be the

[1] As was pointed out above the analogy is incomplete in this point that only the members, not the individual cells, are in the natural body directly actuated through the brain, whereas each cell of the mystical Christ-body is actuated by the spiritual soul through union with the Head.

complete mystical extension of Christ; it will be one mystical Christ complete and perfect not only in its Head as it was from the Incarnation; or in the Head and partially in the members, as at present but complete and perfect in the Head and in all the members. This is the consummation desired by St. Paul when he speaks of "the building up of the body of Christ . . . the measure of the stature of the plenitude of Christ," that we "may grow up in all things into Him Who is the Head, Christ."[1]

This solidarity of the mystical body, down to its least cell, with the divine-human Head is the principle of redemption. The Atonement has been treated elsewhere. I need therefore only recall here that as physical solidarity with the first man involved us in his exclusion from the supernatural life, so the satisfaction rendered by the obedience of the God-Man even to death, offered a human glory to God that more than fulfilled the undue lack of that human glory caused by the sin of Adam. But this atonement could not be simply vicarious, something done by Christ for others. It was the satisfaction of Christ in His oneness with redeemed mankind, in fact as the Head of redeemed mankind.

But this solidarity has to be effected actually for every soul saved or set in the way of salvation. Hence the elevation of a soul to the supernatural life is necessarily the same act as that soul's incorporation into the body of Christ; and completed salvation is the completion of that incorporation and union. Hence sanctification in its inception, progress, and final consummation, is a union of the soul-cell with the Head in His work of redemption, and in particular in the two supreme achievements of Christ's redemptive work—the death on the cross and the resurrection. Thus for St. Paul regeneration is a burial into Christ's death and a resurrection in union with His (Rom. vi. 3–11, Col. iii. 1–4). For this regeneration is essentially the reception of the Spirit of Christ, of the Spirit that worked in Him unto His death and resurrection. The soul thus receives in principle the divine life supremely expressed in the life of Christ.

But as sanctification progresses this Spirit-life, still potential, must develop and express itself in action. This it does by crucifying our natural life, in so far as this excludes the life of the Spirit, and raising us ever more fully to the heavenly divine life of the risen Jesus, until at the last even our bodies are raised by it from physical death and so spiritualized that they become an adequate vehicle of the Spirit.

[1] Eph. iv. 12–15.

Hence the spiritual life—that is the life of grace—with its manifestations in the mystical life on earth, in the crucifixion of purgatory and in the risen life of heaven, is a participation in the mysteries of Christ's life, especially His death and resurrection; and this, not only by an organic unity with Him in these mysteries, but by their reproduction in us, by the working of His Spirit. This reproduction, however, is not an external copy but expresses itself in terms of our individual function in His body.

Protestant mysticism has laid stress on the reproduction of Christ's mysteries in our souls from His birth to His glorification.[1] So too, does Catholic mysticism, following St. Paul, when he says, "little children of whom I am in travail till Christ be formed in you." Nevertheless for the Catholic, Christ in the soul—the renewal of His mysteries in the soul—is secondary, and is overshadowed by the conception of the soul's participation in Christ's mysteries, the Pauline formula "in Christ." Certainly both aspects of sanctification, Christ in the soul and the soul in Christ, are aspects of one and the same process. But the Catholic stress on the second aspect has the advantage of avoiding a subtle danger of self-worship under the guise of the Christ within,[2] and of emphasizing the dependence, throughout the process of sanctification, of the individual on the Church-society. There is thus no danger of the soul coming to fancy itself a second Christ, called to some peculiar imitation of Christ or union with Him *in isolation* from the community: for it knows that the more perfectly Christ's mysteries are reproduced in itself, the more intimately is it incorporated as a member of His entire body; and that only in virtue of such membership are His mysteries thus shared and expressed. It is the whole body, not one cell or group of cells (e.g. a religious order or all the religious orders or even the clergy as a whole), that reproduces and continues and, in the sense explained above, completes the redeeming death and resurrection of Jesus. It is the Church in her entire history enacting continually the mystery-drama of Christ's life, death, and resurrection, in which all her members are actors. In that drama each has an appointed part whether prominent or subordinate, and the drama can be acted only by the co-operation of all the actors.

In the New Testament the analogy of the body as an expression

[1] See Rufus Jones's *Spiritual Reformers, passim*, also A. E. Waite, *Way of Divine Union*, Chap. VIII.

[2] Cf. G. K. Chesterton, *Orthodoxy*, 135–7.

of the supernatural solidarity of the Church of souls, is illustrated by other analogies. In St. John's Gospel we have the analogy of the vine and the branches; in the Epistle to the Ephesians and 1 Peter, that of the edifice of which Christ is the foundation and we are stones. This latter analogy gives us a wider outlook on the diversity of functions and the vastness of plan in the Church-society than does the analogy of the body. It also enables us to view sanctification as a progressive fitting of each soul into its place in the spiritual building, by the gradual and often painful cutting and polishing away of all that is opposed to that perfect incorporation. Then we have, also in the Ephesian Epistle, the analogy of marriage—the perfect marriage, monogamous, indissoluble, and sacramental, of Christianity. As the bride is one flesh with her husband, this analogy returns to that of the body. It emphasizes, however, the supremacy of the Head, His peculiar relationship of personal identity with God[1] and His loving self-donation. It also emphasizes the fact that the multitude of redeemed souls, though as we learn elsewhere each may be rightly called Christ's bride, are not many brides, but one bride—the one immaculate wife of the Lamb, seen by St. John in the Apocalypse, adorned for her espousals; yet also seen by him as a city: so that his symbol thus combines most intimately unity with multiplicity, and guards against religious individualism. These analogies are, however, subordinate to the central analogy of the body, and should be used to illustrate that primary analogy.

As I have pointed out elsewhere the law of progress is the increasing unification of an increasing multiplicity,—in other words an increasing differentiation of functional parts ever more intimately united in one organic whole. This is, however, the law of solidarity. It is also the law of the Church-body. When the Church-body is perfect as it is now in the Church triumphant, and will be wholly at the end of this world, there will be a perfect unity throughout the body. All the members will act under the one impulse of the Spirit-soul through the Christ-head. Therefore the action of each will never hinder the action of any other. There will be a harmony so complete as to amount to co-volition. Yet the activity of each soul will express the divine-human Will diversely from any other, in terms of its individual function which it, and it alone, can fulfil. The Godhead will thus be reflected in redeemed and supernaturalized humanity in a manifold variety of aspects, as light in all colours and

[1] Cf. 1 Cor. vii. on the respective relations of man and woman to Christ.

tints, as a jewel with a myriad facets. Yet it is the one light of the one God that shines in all. Hence, as St. Paul tells us, every soul has its own special gift, its *charism*; but all those *charisms* are the working of one and the self-same Spirit. Even Christ could not, apart from His mystical body, express this multiplicity of divine reflections in mankind—for it is of the nature of individuality to exclude the simultaneous possession of other individualities. Only the entire Christ, Head and body, can be the "one man" who is the completed human temple of the Spirit.[1]

The unity of the Church-body, the fact that the Church is "one man in Christ" to use St. Paul's words, does not therefore exclude internal multiplicity, but on the contrary requires that multiplicity; just as the unity of the human body does not exclude but rather necessitates a multiplicity whose extent and complexity have been revealed to us by the progress of biological research. But this unity does forbid that external multiplicity which opposes one part to another, and excludes one part from another.[2] In the body of Christ not only the individual difference between soul and soul is preserved, but even those differences, family, racial or national, between groups whose members are bound to each other by some common natural tie, and who possess certain common characters as members of that group. All are necessary as are all the diverse notes of a complex symphony. But there can be no exclusion or opposition of these individuals or groups, no assertion of one individual or group to the detriment of another. No gain by one individual or group is a loss to any other individual or group. Rather is the gain of one the common gain of all. It is in this sense that in Christ there is neither "Jew nor Greek, bond nor free, male nor female."[3] All walls of partition between souls or groups of souls, are destroyed; not by the abolition of difference, but by the abolition of mutual exclusion in a mutual inclusion in the one mystic Christ vivified and acting by the one Divine Spirit.

The consequences of this Church-solidarity extend, as was pointed

[1] In value it is true the humanity of Jesus is infinite—in virtue of the hypostatic union. But it surely cannot have the multiplicity in unity of redeemed mankind. Yet see Essay VI on "The Person of Christ," pp. 176 *seq.*

[2] The physical organism, of course, because it is physical, extended matter, forbids only opposition of part to part while retaining mutual exclusion. A spiritual organism permits an interpenetration of parts impossible on the material plane. Moreover, there is an interpenetration of mutual interaction and dependence even in the physical body.

[3] Gal. iv.

out above, to all spheres of theology and spiritual life. This "communion of saints" involves the mutual interaction of prayer and merit by which, *within the limits imposed by individual free will and responsibility*, the supernatural activity and value of one soul overflows to supply other souls who are united with it by a common participation of the Spirit. Leon Bloy speaks of "the perpetual miracle consisting in an infallible balance between human merits and demerits, a balance of such a character that the spiritually destitute are assisted by the wealthy, and the timid supplied by the bold." This takes place, he continues, "according to the ordinance, strangely unknown, of the affinity of souls. That motion of grace which saves me from a grave danger has possibly been determined by some act of love performed this morning or five hundred years ago by a man altogether obscure whose soul was in some wonderful correspondence with my own, and who receives thus his reward." In this world where the incorporation of members into Christ's body is imperfect, and where the life of the Spirit is only revealed to consciousness in a few holy souls, this communion of souls is also secret. When, however, the divine Spirit-life is fully manifest, as it is already in heaven, this solidarity of souls will also be manifest in all. Sharing the self-knowledge of God, in His unveiled self-union, souls will be, as in heaven they are now, co-conscious because God-conscious—co-conscious in the one God-consciousness. Of their co-volition in the divine will I have already spoken. Hence, it is impossible to be in communion with God without being in communion with the saints in one and the same union. Moreover, the fuller and more conscious the union with God, the more intimate and the more conscious is the co-union with the saints. All Protestant misconceptions of an interference of the saints between the soul and God are by this truth automatically destroyed. Man has a natural craving for communication with the departed for which spiritism seeks to provide a premature and harmful satisfaction, since on a purely natural plane a true satisfaction is impossible. By the communion of saints this craving receives a satisfaction supernatural and everlasting, and, when perfected, intimate and conscious.[1]

That there is a hierarchy of souls is evident from the very fact of diverse functions in one body. Though every function is indispens-

[1] It is surely plain that the doctrine of the treasury of merits and of indulgences is an application of this solidarity. In mystical experience and its theology, suffering for the sin of others is known as "mystical substitution."

able one must be more important than another. In the physical body the brain has necessarily a more important function than the toe. Therefore the holiest souls must possess a more important function than the less holy. Hence also follows the unique function of the holiest creature, the soul most filled of the Spirit because in closest union with the Head—our Blessed Lady. Theology sums up the function of Our Lady in the body of Christ when it terms her mediatress, in terms of the mystical body the neck through whom the vital influx derives from the Head to the members. Certainly this conception is absent from St. Paul and is the result of a later doctrinal development. But the reason for this absence is easy to discover. As the Epistle to the Colossians shows us, the early Christians were often slow to grasp the unique headship of Christ and in grave danger of co-ordinating with Him angelic mediators between themselves and God. Until the Headship of Christ had been firmly established in the consciousness of Christians, the doctrine of the neck could not have been stated without inevitable misunderstanding and abuse. But none the less St. Paul is the precursor of St. Bernard.[1]

In the sphere of morals we can see that an entire ethic issues inevitably from the principle of Church solidarity. This ethic is the one law of charity in its manifold applications—the supernatural love of all for God and Christ, implying, as its other aspect, the supernatural love of each for all. This love is due primarily to our supernatural neighbour, and secondarily to all men as potentially, at least, members of the supernatural Church-body.[2] This law, being the ethical aspect of the "unity-in-multiplicity" of Church solidarity, is a unity which contains and harmonizes all moral laws; and it works itself out in such a perfect fulfilment of all ethical duties that they are accomplished no longer by external submission to an external code but as the spontaneous activities of one love-life. In this sense the law is destroyed in Christ—as St. Paul tells us in several passages of daring force—but destroyed only by its more perfect, because interior, fulfilment. Since, however, in this life all souls in grace are not actuated wholly and at all times by the Spirit, and since they are often ignorant of what the law of love commands, external

[1] Though St. Bernard did not actually use the metaphor of the neck he uses the metaphor of the "channel" (aquaeludus) which means the same thing.

[2] We have, indeed, also duties to dumb animals both of justice and of love. Though animals are by their nature excluded from the supernatural, we should treat them well, and with St. Francis love them from supernatural love of the God Who made them.

precepts must still survive.[1] Nevertheless, as sanctification advances external obedience is more and more completely transcended by the interior activity and fulfilment of love, and in the consummation when ignorance and unsupernatural self-will are no more, love, the law of the Spirit working unimpeded in the members of His body, will be the one sole law—a law henceforth no law, because identical with the free life of the soul.

The ethic of the mystical body is also alone capable of reconciling self-realization with self-sacrifice. For in this body when a soul-cell has completely sacrificed self-will in its love of the divine will, it attains in this very renunciation to the full expression of its own individuality by the perfect performance of its function in the Church organism. For this functioning is the perfect fulfilment of its potentialities, its individual capacities and its character. Its self-sacrifice is thus its self-realization; since it is the attainment of a new unlimited life of participation in the divine life of God in the Church.

We are the witnesses to-day of premature attempts by communism and anarchism to abolish progressively at least, the right to property, the distinction of mine and thine. Such an abolition is chimerical, being on the natural plane impossible to human nature. But it is progressively accomplished on the supernatural plane by the supernatural solidarity of the Church-body. Although in this world the imperfection of that solidarity will always necessitate the social and ecclesiastical maintenance of property-right, such right will be continuously attenuated by Christian charity and by the voluntary communism of the religious life; and it will, as St. Augustine points out, entirely disappear in heaven. There, not even our internal activities will be our own in an *exclusive* sense, for they will be receptions of God's activity in us and, therefore, of an activity common to us all. Hence the act of one will be the act of all, while at the same time because it is an *individual* reception of the one divine Act, it will remain peculiarly each one's own. Thus in this divine solidarity there will be simultaneously achieved the end of property—namely, the free and full functioning of the individual—and the end of communism—the intimate co-operation and co-enjoyment of the entire society.

Let us now turn back to the description given above of the notion of solidarity—that mediating conception between individualism and

[1] These however derive their obligation from their fulfilment or service to the law of love.

socialism which would preserve the positive values of each while rejecting their mutual negations. It is evident how perfectly this concept of solidarity is fulfilled in the Church-body which I have been describing. In this body, individual personality with its supreme and incommunicable significance and worth—is maintained as real, permanent, incommunicable and inalienable. The individual soul never ceases to possess self-consciousness, not indeed the exclusive self-consciousness of the natural self, but an individual reception of the God-consciousness in which it must know itself in God as a distinct being from Him, and self-volition, not the self-actuated and exclusive will of the natural self, but an individual reception of the will of God.

On the other hand the individual is not impenetrable, since he is informed and filled and moved by God, and penetrated mediately by other souls in God. Nor is he self-contained, for he is incorporated as a functional member of a supernatural society, and enveloped—if I may use the term, steeped—in the Spirit of God. Nor is he self-sufficient: he is not self-sufficient for his being, for that being supernaturally as well as naturally is wholly dependent on God, nor is he self-sufficient for his fulfilment, for that fulfilment is, as we have seen, at once a reception of the Spirit of God which is the soul of the social organism, and a perfect incorporation into the Church-body, and a perfect functioning as a member of that body. At the same time we find in the Church a society which does not possess a unitary consciousness; which neither absorbs nor annihilates individual being or consciousness: in fact the Church derives from the individual differences of its members a manifold variety and exquisite harmony. Nevertheless, the Church is a society which, more completely and more perfectly than any other, both extensively and intensively, is an organic whole constituted by the functional co-ordination of individuals. Being in its consummation more intrinsically perfect than any other society, the Church attains, as we have seen, to a most intimate co-consciousness and co-volition of all its members. Being also in this consummation more extrinsically perfect than any other society, it is absolutely self-contained and self-sufficient, being independent of any external society—indeed of any being purely external, since God as Man is its organic Head, and as the Spirit, its informing Soul. Thus in the supernatural organism, whose cells are souls, whose Head is the God-Man, whose Soul the Divine Spirit, whose name is the Church, we have the most perfect expression of that solidarity which, between the exaggerations and mutual denials of individualism and socialism, alone answers to all the facts of human nature and fulfils all its needs, individual and social alike. For in this Church-body human nature is raised to that supernatural and eternal plane where it is united to God and filled with God, the only plane on which the problems arising out of man's individuality and sociality can be fully solved in the complete but harmonious, indeed identical, satisfaction of both.

II

If my essay ended here, no Catholic could feel that I had given a sufficient account of the Church. My account might perhaps satisfy the anti-ecclesiastical Protestant, but it could not be acceptable to a Catholic. For I have spoken only of an invisible Church of souls united by the purely spiritual bond of the Spirit and by union with an invisible Head, the glorified Christ. But to the Catholic this is only one aspect of the truth of the Church. For he is essentially a member of a visible body into which he is incorporated by a visible sacrament; and in this incorporation he is maintained by visible sacraments. This body, moreover, is possessed of an external and visible organization, a hierarchy of external government and teaching united under a visible head, the Pope. If we turn to St. Paul we find the same doctrine of a visible Church, though naturally its organization is still rudimentary. Indeed he never thinks of the invisible Church of which we have hitherto spoken, apart from a visible society; nor does he ever explicitly distinguish between them. For him the visible body is the invisible in its external aspect. This visible body is a divine foundation intended to contain and to unite all men. This visible Church is the temple and spouse of Christ—His mystical body, His "fulfilment," the body in which the Spirit dwells. The regeneration which is, as we saw, union with the redeeming mysteries of Christ, is identified with the sacrament of baptism, whose very symbolism of immersion and extraction represents the participation of the soul in Christ's death and resurrection. And in the Pastoral Epistles the visible aspect of the Church is in the foreground. It is her visible teaching authority exercised through an official hierarchy that makes her "the pillar and ground of the truth," the repressor of heresies; and it is her official ordination that confers the grace requisite for the exercise of the Order conferred.

That the invisible Church should thus be embodied in a visible society, is in harmony with the sacramental relationship which everywhere subsists between the material and the spiritual. Man, being in his very personality composite of soul and body, cannot live on a purely spiritual or a purely material plane, nor be conversant exclusively with pure spirits or with material objects. He must always find the spiritual in, through, and beyond the material plane, and must always embody—if only in the images formed by his imagination—spiritual realities in material forms. Man sees in material nature a spiritual reality in and beyond itself. In art he selects and presents natural forms as symbols of that immanent and transcendent spirit. Benedetto Croce has pointed out that æsthetic intuition is essentially an expression—if only an expression in an internal image. Nor can we think of the most abstract metaphysics or theology, without embodying our concepts in images drawn from the material world of space and time. Religion and its worship have never been able to dispense with the symbolisms of material images and rites. In the Incarnation God Himself is incarnate in a material body: for the end of this Incarnation is the redemption and sanctification, that is the supernaturalization, of the entire man, body as well as soul. And the body itself must finally share in the eternal life of divine Union, being made in the resurrection a perfect vehicle of the soul in its life of grace. It follows that the spiritual Church must also have an external visible embodiment on the physical plane. If the Head is incarnate, His body will also be incarnate, not merely in individual cells but as a body. For the extension of God Incarnate must itself be incarnate.

It may be objected that the Church in heaven is purely spiritual. To this I would reply that in the consummation its members will again be embodied, and that there will even be a physical environment for the resurrection-life of the Church. It is true that there will then be no official hierarchy or sacramental system. But there will be a visible hierarchy although of a more perfect kind. Then Jesus Christ will be the *visible* as well as the invisible head of the Church-body. Under Him there will be a hierarchy of dignity and, it may be, of function. But this hierarchy will immediately emanate from the spiritual worth and function of its members in the invisible soul-Church. It will therefore embody that invisible hierarchy more perfectly than can the visible hierarchy on earth, which, in the nature of things, cannot express the measure of sanctifying grace nor be dependent for its validity upon the measure in which its members are in possession of God. For example, a priest is not a priest because he is personally holier than a layman, but because of his sacramental function in the visible hierarchy. In heaven the sacraments certainly will have passed away, but they will have disappeared in a life in which all material things clearly and without alloy reflect the divine glory.

We have seen, therefore, *a priori*, that a Church of human beings must have a visible embodiment. We have also seen that this was the apostolic teaching. Unbiased study of the Gospels, and especially of the first, will show that the Apostles were only carrying out the will of Jesus Christ, Who instituted as a capital point of His work a visible Church.

Moreover, history witnesses to this necessity of a visible Church. No body of dissenters from Catholicism—however individualist in doctrine, however strongly insistent on the invisible Church as the only Church of God—have been able to dispense with some kind of visible society. Even the Quakers are a visible religious corporation with a definite organization and with an instrument of corporate action.[1] Such Protestants, however, maintain that this visible embodiment of the invisible Church, is of purely human and accidental institution and character. But this is to introduce a strange cleavage between the divine soul-Church and its purely human body. Such a cleavage, which is opposed to the analogy of the personal unity of body and soul, would constitute a most unnatural and inharmonious discontinuity, and would necessarily impede the action of the Spirit-soul on the visible plane. Hence, it is unlikely, *a priori*; and possesses no shadow of warrant in the inspired words of the New Testament. Moreover, if the invisible soul-Church must be expressed by an external society, it is surely plain that this must be one body, not many. For the mutual exclusion and opposition of many diverse corporations could not express that unity-in-multiplicity which we have seen to be the law of the invisible society. One soul does not inform more than one body, nor can one soul inspire a plurality of diverse and conflicting consciousnesses. The rare phenomenon of multiple personality is obviously pathological. Believers in one invisible Church expressed by a multitude of conflicting visible institutions with opposing beliefs and aims, must thus find the

[1] E.g. during the World War their general meeting *on behalf of the Quaker body* decided to oppose the press censorship. This is as much the action of a visible Church government as is the action of the Pope.

physical analogy of Christ's body in a condition of extreme psycho-physical disease and disintegration. Therefore, the one Lord and the one Spirit and the one mystical body demand one visible Church-body with one creed and one system of government and sacraments. Hence St. Paul, in the Ephesian Epistle, mingles together both unities, invisible and visible: "one Spirit," "one hope of your calling," "one Lord (Jesus Christ), one God and Father"; invisible principles of unity: "one faith" (that is, one creed), "one baptism"; visible principles of unity: "one body"—at once an invisible and a visible unity indistinguished.

Here, as elsewhere, St. Paul seems to teach a simple identity between the invisible and visible Church. Does it then follow that this simple identity is the actual relationship? Must we say that the Spirit-soul is operative only in those who are members of the one visible Church? Is the maxim *extra ecclesiam nulla salus* to be understood in its most obvious and literal sense without qualification of any kind? Certainly, if we had nothing but the bare letter of Scripture to guide us, it would be difficult to escape this conclusion, however distasteful. If the New Testament were placed before me, with no guidance for its interpretation other than itself, I should conclude that no one on earth could enjoy the supernatural life of grace-union with God, however invincible his ignorance of God's will in this regard, unless he were incorporated into the visible Church and continued in that visible membership. But, as we know, the Catholic Church does not teach this conclusion, a conclusion obviously belied by the multitudes of devout souls outside the visible Church, who have given such signs of supernatural life that if we were to deny them membership in the invisible Church, we should have no solid ground for finding the supernatural at work anywhere in the world.

If St. Paul nowhere makes any distinction between the invisible and the visible Church, it is because he is laying down the divine economy of salvation. According to this economy every regenerate soul is also a member of the visible Church. Hence, those souls who are members of the invisible Church, without embodying that membership in a membership of the visible Church, are in a position essentially false, a condition contrary to the divine plan, and it is only their implicit will to be members of the visible Church (if they knew that such was the will of God) that enables them to be in a state of salvation. It is not surprising that if the Apostles taught the divine plan by which one visible Church was to embody on earth the invisible Church, without weakening this essential doctrine by making explicit provision for an anomalous condition due to sin. Moreover, in the Apostolic age there had been no opportunity for the existence of large bodies of Christians brought up in good faith outside the Church. Those outside the Church were those who wilfully left the Church; and that, not when its truth had been obscured by worldliness and moral corruption in its members, but in the first days of Apostolic fervour.

There is, too, in the New Testament an evident reluctance to dwell on the unhappy case of those who, while remaining members of the visible Church, cut themselves off by mortal sin from possession of the Spirit and therefore from membership in the invisible Church. The actuation of the infant Church by the powerful life of the Spirit was such a mighty reality, that the resistance of some Christians to that divine life is but a shadow in the background.

But with the process of time, proportions are changed. It is only too obvious that, owing to the inevitable misuse of free will, the visible Church is not co-extensive with the invisible Church on earth; that it does not perfectly embody that Church on the earthly plane. Within the visible body there are numbers of dead cells—still, however, externally joined to the body, and therefore in a peculiarly advantageous position for reanimation by the Spirit-soul. Of the living cells the animation is for the most part very imperfect. The life of these cells is often not actuated by the Spirit beyond the minimal degree that keeps them from spiritual death. These facts, in turn, prevent the visible Church from appearing to the eyes of many as that visible temple of the Spirit, that obvious continuation of the personal Christ, animated in all its acts by His dispositions, which it would be, were the divine plan fully carried out. Hence vast numbers of Christ-loving souls fail to recognize the Church as His bride and His body, though prepared to join her at all cost, did they but recognize her as such. In face of these facts theology has been obliged to develop explicitly the distinction between the soul of the Church—the invisible Church-body of all souls who share in the supernatural life—and the body of the Church—the visible Church Catholic and Roman. In proportion to the healthiness of a body there is no need for any distinction between the acts of the body and the soul. Only in the case of disease is the perfect unity impaired, so that we must remark acts of the body that do not express the will of the soul, and volitions of the soul which the body refuses to execute. But sin, and an ignorance ultimately at least due to sin, are diseases which prevent adequate embodiment of the soul of the Church by the body of the Church. This sin is in the first place that of Catholics, in the second place that of those outside the Catholic body. For the attitude of unreasoning hostility towards the Church adopted by so many non-Catholics, cannot surely be acquitted of moral fault. In the Apostolic age the Church-body of Christ was relatively healthy. Hence the lack of harmony and of adequate expression between the visible body and the soul, was not conspicuous. About the time of the Greek schism, and again at the dawn of the Reformation, the condition of the Church was as unhealthy as, we hope, it is possible for it to be. Hence the growth of Christian bodies external to the one visible body of Christ, whose individual members are nevertheless incorporated into the mystical body of Christ by their inclusion in the soul of the Church.

It is a pathetic story to trace the attempts, often noble in aim[1] but so obviously misguided and impracticable, from Montanism down to the present day, to establish a visible body which should be the adequate expression of the invisible, the perfect vehicle of the soul-Church, a visible body composed exclusively of members of the invisible Church and co-extensive with them. Let us take one example out of all these—the foundation of the Family of Love in the sixteenth century by Henry Nicholas.[2] Impressed from childhood by the obvious failure of Catholics to manifest the life of the Spirit, that is to say by the inadequate embodiment of the invisible Church by the visible, and not receiving any proper instruction by Catholic teachers as to the true causes and remedies for this failure, he left the Church. He took this step, as I conjecture, in the good faith of sheer ignorance as to her true doctrine and the amount of actual sanctity, even at that sad epoch, to be found within her pale. He then founded a church of his own, the Family of Love, which was to be the adequate externalization of the supernatural order, the adequate embodiment of the invisible Church. A strange, sad delusion this of an ignorant enthusiastic soul; and typical of many similar errors! After some fifteen centuries human sin had rendered the Church founded by Jesus Christ so incompletely expressive of

[1] That is, if and when their founders were in good faith—which God alone can determine, we at best but conjecture.
[2] See Rufus Jones, *Studies in Mystical Religion.*

His Spirit, so inadequate a manifestation of His mystical body on the earth plane; and the church of Henry Nicholas was to be and to remain this adequate and complete expression of Christ! To-day the church of Nicholas is dead and wellnigh forgotten. But the visible Catholic Church, though unhappily still far from co-terminous with the invisible either extensively or intensively, has afforded fresh proof of her divine institution as the embodiment of that invisible Church, not only by a revival of the spiritual life in her body, but by her position and function to-day as the supreme home, focus, and teacher of supernatural religion. Though badly scarred by the assaults of modern naturalism, she is still living and fighting, while the non-Catholic bodies are lying prostrate and mortally wounded all around her.

It may seem strange language this that I have been speaking. How can the visible Church of God ever be the inadequate embodiment of the supernatural order on earth? This difficulty is due to a failure to distinguish between two aspects of the visible Church—the Church in her essential constitution and *de fide* doctrine, and the Church as a body of human and therefore more or less sinful and ignorant souls. In the former sense she can, of course, never be inadequate; in the latter she can. Had Nicholas and his like realized this distinction they would never have left the Church, or they would have returned to her fold.

It is clear, then, that the term "Church" when used of the visible body is susceptible of contradictory predicates according as the former or the latter aspect is intended. Thus we may say: the Church is infallible, the Church can err (for example in the case of Galileo); the Church is all-holy, the Church has sinned; the Church is indefectible, the Church has in a certain crisis failed. If for the Church you substitute her head the Pope, this distinction and its consequences will become more obvious. The Pope is infallible, Popes have made mistakes; the papacy is holy, but Popes can sin.

This doctrine of the soul and body of the Church and of their mutual relation, as it is taught in Catholic theology, saves us from the two opposed extremes of spirit-denying exclusiveness and undenominational indifferentism. We can recognize that, because the sin, both social and individual, of Catholics has prevented and does still prevent the visible Church from being the adequate home and vehicle of the invisible on earth, the action of the Spirit may be found even outside her bounds; and that the soul of the Church is therefore more extensive than the body. Nor shall we presume to limit the possible intensity of this action of the Spirit in individual souls outside the Church. We, shall, moreover realize that as the body exists for the soul and not vice versa, the visible Church is secondary, not primary; the means, not the end. It is the invisible Church for whose sake the visible exists. It is therefore only the invisible Church whose membership is absolutely and without qualification necessary, since incorporation into the invisible Church is the one and the same thing as supernatural union with God. At the same time we shall recognize that the ideal, the divine plan, is that the visible Church shall be coterminous with the invisible on earth, its adequate embodiment; and that this, therefore, is the goal for which we should strive.

It will also be evident that the visible Church is of necessity the one *corporate* embodiment of the invisible. No one therefore is free to remain for any reason whatsoever outside the visible body; for he is bound to fulfil the divine plan as far as he knows it, and to the utmost of his power. Moreover, we shall expect and discover that the fullest and most powerful action of the Spirit is exercised within, not without, the visible body which He formed for His inhabitation, and which, despite all disease and partial paralysis, lives by Him as its life-principle.

The relationship between the soul and body of the Church can, I think, be expressed by the figure of the sun and its light. The actual body of the sun—the focus of the sunlight—represents the visible Church; the light-rays extended from and beyond the solar body till they are gradually lost in the darkness and cold of space, represent the energy of the Spirit in souls outside the visible Church. If, in defiance of astronomy, for the sake of pictorial illustration we imagine the sun-spots on account of their dark appearance, to be unilluminated portions of the sun's mass, they will serve to represent the souls who are members of the visible Church only, in which case the disappearance of the sun-spot will symbolize the conversion and revivification of such sin-dead members. But in making use of this illustration we must not forget that while the extension of sunlight beyond the sun is natural, the lack of co-extension between the soul and body of the Church is unnatural and anomalous, the effect of sin. On the other hand, and it is a most consoling thought for a Catholic faced with the present divisions among Christians, a very large, perhaps the largest, portion of the members of Christ's mystical body has already passed beyond this division and disharmony and is united in the complete unity of a Church wholly one. In purgatory and in heaven the non-Catholics have escaped beyond the barriers which in earth have kept them from expressing their invisible communion by an external communion in the Catholic Church. In purgatory and in heaven the invisible is identical with the visible; and when at the resurrection the communion of saints receives again an external incorporation, it will be its co-extensive and adequate embodiment.

III

On the basis of this conception of the Church as Christ's mystical body, itself enbodied on earth in the visible society known to all as the Catholic and Roman Church, we can discuss three religious problems of peculiar emphasis at the present day. 1. The nature and synthesis of authority and liberty. 2. The nature of faith as assent to revealed dogma taught by the Church. 3. The possibility and limits of progress in religion. The limits of this essay will render any discussion of these problems very brief, far too brief for any pretence of adequate treatment; but in the light of the doctrine of the Church I hope at least to indicate the general lines of a solution.

1. *Liberty and Authority.*—The obvious distinction between *de fide* dogma and theological speculation is in itself sufficient to prove that the sphere of authority is not unlimited; that as in any state, even the most autocratic or bureaucratic, there is a sphere of anarchy—namely, a sphere in which the Government leaves its subjects a free self-direction—so in the Catholic Church there is a sphere in which action and thought are determined by the private judgment of individuals. We can, however, penetrate to a deeper standpoint than this external distinction of a sphere of authority and a sphere of liberty, to a standpoint from which authority, when exercised in its divinely appointed sphere, is seen not as a limitation of spiritual freedom but as the condition of that freedom. All life energizes according to law. In proportion to the absence of law there is an absence of life and the disintegration of decay and death. For my life is the fulfilment of the immanent law of my nature, the operation of my nature accomplishing its function in a wider economy. To do what I please, is often to prevent the free functioning of my life; it is often the distracting disintegration of my will among a multitude of desires. At best the absolute self-determination main-

tained by advanced thinkers, is a self-imprisonment which prevents my free self-realization (by the fulfilment of function) in a wider social whole. Self-determination thus turns out to be self-termination. In practice it usually means termination by some very limited group or by some very temporary and superficial phase of thought or sentiment. Liberty is therefore not freedom from law but freedom from a law external and hostile to the immanent law of the living organism. A plant or animal is free[1] when it grows and unfolds to the uttermost in accordance with the inner law of its own nature, unhindered and undeflected by any interference from without, inimical to that law. So does the spiritual organism of Christ's Church-body live and grow freely by perfect obedience to the immanent law of its nature, the will of the Divine Spirit. The only obstacle to the freedom of the Church will be any restraint on the action of the divine Will in the Church organism. But not only is the entire organism free when the law of its life is perfectly fulfilled, but each cell is free when it follows without impediment the subordinate law of its own particular function in the organism. A cell as such, a cell as an organic part of the entire organism, is not free when it works by itself in disintegration and corruption, but when it perfectly fulfils its function as a cell. Therefore a soul is perfectly free when its incorporation in the Church organism is so complete that it fulfils perfectly its function in this supernatural body; when it operates in entire freedom from the limitations of the natural self-will that would confine it within the limited life and sphere of the purely temporal. Moreover, since this inner law of the Church-body is the unlimited love-will which is identical with the infinite Godhead, perfect freedom for the soul is necessarily identical with perfect obedience to this immanent law of the Church-body, the "perfect law of liberty" which is the infinite Divine Spirit working through a human Head personally one with the unlimited Deity. To seek freedom not to belong to the human organism of the divine life, to exclude oneself by the bonds of nature and self-will from participation in the life of God from union with His unlimited action, and in that divine life from union with all human souls who are thus united to God, is a self-stultifying endeavour, a deliberate self-imprisonment. Thus in the mystical body of Christ, and there alone, liberty and obedience to authority are seen to be identical, two aspects

[1] Of course freedom below the human level is only analogous, for it is essentially limited by the lack of consciousness or of rationality.

of one indivisible life. If the visible Church were the perfect and adequate earthly embodiment of the invisible, wholly actuated by the Spirit, in perfect union with Christ, its Head, this simple identification would hold good here also, and there would be no need for any division of spheres between authority and private judgment. Since, however, the visible church is composed of souls not yet in perfect harmony with the working of the Divine Spirit by reason of human sin, nor wholly enlightened by the divine truth by reason of human ignorance, the identification between liberty and obedience to authority can only be partial. In so far as the Church rules and teaches by divine authority, the identification is complete even for the visible Church. Thus to submit private judgment to a *de fide* dogma is to liberate the understanding from the limits of natural ignorance by a participation in the divine truth, and to obey the moral law of the Church is to free the will from human limitation by a reception of the divine love. On the other hand the less certainty there is that any doctrine or moral teaching possesses divine authority, the more doubtful becomes this identification of freedom and obedience and the greater therefore the need for individual freedom of choice. The history of dogma confirms the identification of liberty and obedience in this divine sphere of ecclesiastical doctrine. For it shows that the defined dogmas, far from restricting the freedom of truth, have prevented the imprisonment of the mind by extreme and one-sided statements which would have excluded the complementary truths maintained by these definitions. A particular period or a particular body of men has apprehended some aspect or portion of truth so keenly that it has neglected or denied a complementary aspect or portion. The Church has intervened to maintain both. Moreover, the body of dogmatic truth is not a series of disconnected statements, but the unfolding and exposition of a supernatural economy—the economy of the supernatural union of mankind to God in the Incarnate Word and His extension, the Church. But it is in realizing the truth of this supernatural union that man attains to the freedom of his supernatural life. Therefore his intellectual freedom, in as far as it is attainable under the limitations of earthly life, is attained by the revelation of that supernatural economy to his intelligence, through the dogmatic system expounded and unfolded in the definitions of the Church.

2. *The Nature of Faith.*—We have been led on thus to the consideration of faith as being essentially no mere external acceptance

of dogma; for this acceptance is but the outer expression of the faith-act, is but the elevation and incorporation of our knowledge into the self-revelation of God in and through His mystical body. This elevation and incorporation is itself but the cognitive aspect of the elevation and incorporation of the soul into an organism informed by the Spirit of truth. We cannot, however, infer from this, that, as certain Protestant mystics have taught, the soul receives divine truth directly from the interior illumination of the Spirit. It is the divine will that the object of faith be received through the teaching voice of the external Church. For the one self-revelation of the Spirit-soul through Jesus the Head is embodied in one external utterance of the society as a whole. Moreover, this utterance can no more be delivered by the entire body than the entire physical body can speak. As the mouth in the physical body is the sole channel of utterance for the soul through the brain, so the Pope, and the episcopate when united with the Pope, is the one official teaching utterance of the Spirit through Christ. But it is the immediate illumination of the Spirit which enables each soul to believe the doctrine of the Church by that habit of supernatural faith which is, as I have explained elsewhere,[1] a participation of God's self-knowledge. Moreover, as incorporation in the body and in the life of the Spirit increases, so does faith become less and less an external acceptance of dogmas, and is increasingly an interior personal apprehension of the truth contained in these dogmas. For example the ordinary Catholic believes there is a Trinity in the Godhead only because the Church so instructs him. The soul in the highest degree of mystical union often perceives this same truth by an immediate though veiled intuition. Such faith is no longer an unseeing apprehension of revelation. The participation of God's self-knowledge has become manifest in a personal though obscure vision of divine truth. Finally, in heaven all need for external dogmatic teaching has passed away. God's self-knowledge is shared without veil by every soul: faith has vanished into sight.

3. *Progress in Religion.*—The final problem to which I would apply the doctrine of the mystical Church-body is that of progress in religion. The present epoch enamoured of progress and dominated by the concept of evolution, would fain see no other category operative in any sphere of human experience. All is becoming, nowhere is there rest. Religion, too, must be an endless progress, an

[1] In my *Introduction to the Philosophy of Mysticism.*

evolution with no final term. There can, therefore, be no body of truth immutable and eternal, revealed once for all. An *a priori* condemnation is passed on positive historic revelation; the religion of Christ is regarded as self-condemned because it claims a static reality. That this is a one-sided exaggeration would surely require little argument, if only men would consider facts without bias. In every sphere there must be the static as well as the dynamic element, continuity and identity as well as flux. Otherwise personal identity would be impossible; and despite Bertrand Russell, I must persist in regarding my own identity as a self-evident truth. There are many truths of natural science established once for all, to remain equally true for the men of a thousand years hence as they are for us. On the other hand it is also true that nowhere do we find pure rest. Though my individual entity persists, the states of my soul and the very atoms of my body are in constant change. As science progresses, established truths are better understood, placed in a wider context, and often modified in their presentation. To take one instance, though the atom remains a physical reality, a true constituent of matter, it is now known not to be atomic. We should therefore expect to find in the religious sphere also this union of change and permanence. Nor are we disappointed. In theology the essential revelation remains, revealed once for all, unalterable, equally valid for all time to come. But its exposition gradually develops. In the physical body man's specific nature, his fundamental anatomy and physiology remain fixed from the outset. The new-born babe grows to manhood, but his physical character does not essentially alter. The changes that do occur are but the complete unfolding of that nature, the development of what was predetermined and potentially present in the infant. Moreover, while the embryo develops new members, the child is born with the whole of its members complete.[1] So it is with the Church-body. Its life is but the unfolding and development of a fixed nature—determined by its creative Spirit. This fact must therefore be true of the cognitive aspect of Church life, its theology. After a series of partial revelations corresponding to the stages of embryonic growth in the human body, Christ's body, the Catholic Church, was born at Pentecost with her essential character now complete, and her revealed doctrine entire so that no further revelation from without is henceforward necessary. But as the human child without addition of new members to his physical

[1] I speak generally of all the important and characteristic members.

system, develops that system of members; so the Church continuously develops her revelation by drawing out its implicit consequences to meet the successive needs of each generation. Fr. Tyrrell criticized this Newmanic conception of doctrinal development in his *Between Scylla and Charybdis*, urging that in this form it was unknown to the primitive Fathers, since even the development taught by Vincent of Lerins was but a stage on the way to the doctrine as expounded by Newman. Though he exaggerates the ignorance of doctrinal development in the primitive Church, we may admit a measure of truth in his contention. But Fr. Tyrrell merely proves that the theory of doctrinal development is itself a development. Indeed he traces its gradual and logical development in the course of his attack. Why should not the doctrine of development develop as much as any other doctrine? Indeed, since the development of doctrine is obviously secondary to the body of doctrine developed, it would naturally not develop till this body of doctrine had itself developed: there would be a development of doctrine before there was a doctrine of development. Perhaps this is a digression. But it seems to me that the doctrine of the mystical body vindicates the doctrine of development against the superficially damaging attack of Fr. Tyrrell.[1] This doctrine has enabled us to reconcile the fixity of revealed truth—which is of the very essence of a revelation, indeed of any absolute truth—with the progress which is the law of every kind of life.

It also permits us to deal with the wider problem of the nature and extent of religious progress. A comparison of the New Testament, or of primitive Christianity, with the present condition of religion, is enough to convince us that there has not been a continuous religious progress. The primitive Church conquered; the modern Church for the last seven hundred years has been almost continuously losing. The primitive Church was a united brotherhood; the modern Church, while retaining the unity essential to its existence, can hardly be said to exhibit that unity of heart which the external communion should express and produce. In all probability there are proportionally fewer dead members amongst those who make up the visible body of Christ than there were in the Middle Ages; yet perhaps there was never a larger number of living members of the soul of the Church who failed to express and complete that membership by a membership of the visible body. But there is no sphere of being in

[1] I do not mean that Fr. Tyrrell was superficial. Whatever his many errors, that cannot be fairly said. But in his critique of development he is superficial.

which continuous progress is the rule. Even in physical science, where we should expect a continuous building up of truth on truth, there have been long periods of inertia. Biological evolution presents us with numerous instances of arrested development and even of degeneration. The history of civilization does indeed display a progress. This progress, however as Prof. F. Petrie and in another form Mr. Dawson have shown in some striking diagrams, is a progress consisting in every sphere of a series of fluctuations backward and forward. It has been in fact a series of tides advancing and receding. The tide of religion was advancing from the period of Augustus to the period of Augustine. It has been receding since 1300—though the recessive movement met with a considerable check in the late sixteenth and seventeenth centuries and a much slighter check in the Catholic revival of the early nineteenth century. But in every sphere the high-water mark reached by each tide is higher than that attained by its predecessor. I believe we are now past the Augustan nadir, and that religion is beginning to advance once more. To-day as of old under the Roman empire we witness a confusion of diverse religions and religiosities, fantastic sects and superficial superstitions. But they are all signs that the tide has begun to turn. We may hope that, as it seems to be God's plan to manifest even in this world of time the first fruits of that regenerated humanity whose full revelation is reserved for eternity, He is about to manifest His mystical body of redeemed souls, His supernatural kingdom, even on this earth-plane with a fullness and perfection never seen in the past history of the Church.

But whether or no this expectation be well founded, this progress is after all of secondary value. The doctrine of the mystical Church-body shows that there is a progress of primary and everlasting value —the continuous growth of the perfect body of Christ by the continuous entrance of new souls into the life everlasting. There they are building up continuously the heavenly Jerusalem, our mother, the Lamb's stainless bride, of which the earthly Sion, the visible Church, is but the place of education and of training, a suburb built of temporary dwellings. In this glorified body progress and present attainment are united; progress, by the continuous addition of new cells; present attainment because the Head is there already and the neck and so many fair members. Even though, as Scripture seems to warn us, the fullest manifestation of the mystical Christ on earth will be followed by a final apostasy, the mystical body of Christ abides there behind the veils of time and death. The final parousia will be thus the conclusion of a long process, the unveiling of a Christ-figure which is being carved through all these ages of historical achievement. It will be sudden, as sudden as the appearance of a plant shoot above the soil, or a child's birth from the hidden life of the womb. But there will be no break of continuity in the life of the supernatural organism thus revealed in its completion. The concept of progress, the progress of a divine kingdom gradually built up in time, for whose making all human history and all human endeavour possess significance and value is thus shown to be one with the concept, often mistakenly opposed to it by philosophers of religion or history—the concept of a heavenly kingdom appearing suddenly from without. The struggle of good against evil, of grace against sin has its permanent worth, is a real struggle, whose fruit will be revealed at the final consummation. But the divine kingdom, though as yet unrevealed because as yet incomplete, is a present reality at once immanent in the earth-life and transcendent in heaven. The one Christ-Head and members ensouled by the Spirit, is at once an accomplished reality and an incomplete growth, still growing to the end of time. In the mystical body of Christ we have a being at once eternal and temporal, perfect and imperfect, present and future, this-worldly and other-worldly; a value transcending all earthly values, abiding when they perish, and eminently containing them all—yet a value which does not destroy earthly values, but enhances them by giving them permanent value as means to the realization and unfolding of itself. If such an all-embracing, all-reconciling reality be the need of human thought and endeavour—especially of religious thought and endeavour—it is here; the Christ, the God-Man, continued and manifested in His mystical body. Thus is the mystic Christ the universal Reconciler. Christ in His mystical body reconciles all things in Himself—not only as St. Paul teaches us, all classes, all races and both sexes; but all things in heaven and earth—matter and spirit, nature and supernature, individual personality and society, self-realization and self-sacrifice, liberty and authority, the universal and the particular, multiplicity and unity, change and rest, progress and present value, becoming and being, history and eternity.

VII
THE SACRAMENTAL SYSTEM

BY

C. C. MARTINDALE, S.J.

NO one who has even the slightest acquaintance with the Catholic Church is unaware that her worship is ringed about with ceremonies, and that she makes use of what are known as Sacraments. The Confessional, in fact, creates, for many, the worst of stumbling-blocks; and it has become a proverb in our language to say that "what matters is the Mass."

It is wished here to describe the Sacramental System of the Church, in its logical connection with the rest of her creed and practice.

I

Those who have read this book thus far will have ascertained that the Catholic Church teaches this at least:

God, unique, infinite, and eternal, lives necessarily His unshared, incomparable Life.

Man, utterly dependent and limited, created by God, is born, grows, fades and dies, though his soul persists after the falling to pieces of his body, and is indestructible.

God has willed, however, that to this Man should be offered a life of Super-Nature, which, without destroying his manhood, should unite it with God, Source of all that is, in a real and vital manner, transcending all the claims and possibilities of unaided human nature.

The free acceptance of this gift and its consequences are what God desires for every human soul.

This sublimation, and this unification, might no doubt have been accomplished by God through some simple declaration of His offer, met, on man's side, by an equally simple act of consciousness and will. Or in many other ways, known to God's all-inclusive wisdom, His plan might have been accomplished.

An earlier chapter has, however, made it clear that He willed that this supernatural uniting of man's soul to God should be effected and also symbolized by the Incarnation. The Eternal Son of God united to Himself a human nature, so that thereby one Person, the God-Man, was formed; and He chose that each human individual should, by incorporation with the Word-made-Flesh, enter into a true fellowship with the very life of God, and be "made partakers in His divinity Who in our humanity did not disdain to share."

Now those, even, who expect that on the whole a man's self-will be reflected in his work, and still more those who are accustomed to seek and discover an exquisite logic, enchainment, and vital continuity in God's plan, will not be astonished to find this self-same principle consistently at work throughout the whole process of the supernaturalizing of man—namely, that the spiritual is mated with and works in and through the material. Neither extreme is scorned or left neglected. In the one Person of Jesus Christ, the divine and the human were inseparably united; henceforward, all of His action, all His achievement, will be "incarnational." Spiritual results will not normally be brought about independently of matter. God will work for man through man, and save him, not in defiance of the flesh, but in and through the flesh.

Throughout, then, the following pages you must attend to one great aim: the implanting, developing and, if necessary, restoring a superhuman life in man; and to one general method: the mating and the co-operation of the material and the spiritual. The whole of the Church's sacramental system is concerned with this; and it is from this point of view precisely that I would wish to examine it.

For it would be fascinating, no doubt, to indicate the pre-history, so to speak, of the Sacraments; and to show, both from pagan and Jewish cults, how resolutely men refused to believe their intercourse with God was to be merely mental, and how they tried to strike out formulæ and ritual transactions which should both symbolize the preternatural assistance of which they most felt themselves in need, and through which in some way or other this might reach them. But of the "initiations" into "mysteries," Eleusinian or other, we have here no space to speak. Suffice it to say that research has traced, in this matter, a sort of spiral. It used to be held by most non-Catholics that the Christian Sacraments were accretions, late—if not mediæval—developments of the primitive faith and practice. More intimate acquaintance with both pagan and Christian antiquity, revealed early Christianity to be so fully "sacramentalized," and pagan worship to be so unexpectedly sublime in some of the aspirations which here and there put a soul into its ceremonies, that it became the fashion to say that the Church borrowed not her ritual alone, but her very Sacraments, from that Greek or Asiatic or

Egyptian world with which she believed herself to be in mortal conflict.

A yet fuller erudition has shown that the conflict indeed was there, and the disunion radical. The Christians were almost savagely aloof from what they believed to be so bad. This alienation, this "hate for the human race" as popular opinion fancied it must be, was in fact responsible for much of their persecution. But the evidence for the sacramental life of the Early Church has remained. At most, St. Paul (very discreetly), and a Clement of Alexandria (more boldly) would consent to illustrate, by a use of pagan formulæ or "mystic" theories, the faith they held and taught.

Early Christianity, then, had its sacraments and ritual, and did not borrow these either from Judaism or pagandom.

It would, too, be of interest to discuss the evidence from *Acts* or Gospels for the shape the Sacraments had, and the place they took, in the earliest Church of all: in what precise sense it was Christ Himself Who instituted them, and how much liberty He left to His Church in the crystallizing of their "customs" or in the method of their administration. The Catholic Faith teaches that all the Sacraments she uses—other than which there are none—were instituted by Christ Himself: in consequence, they were neither the invention of the Apostles, nor the gradual creation of the Christian community.

A historical survey of exceptional interest might, too, be made, showing the gradual fixing of the doctrine concerning them, and what led up to the exact comprehension of their nature and consequent definition of their number. Attention here would be directed to the writings of St. Cyril of Jerusalem, perhaps, and of St. Chrysostom, more than to those of others, in the East; and to St. Augustine, in his period, most certainly, in the West. Without his work on this department of theology, the thirteenth century itself might have failed in one of its greatest achievements. For in that wonderful century, and its eve, the sacramental aspect of Christianity was realized as never, perhaps, before. Far from perceiving only the surface of things, those sensitive and penetrating minds were convinced that what is most real is precisely what is most hidden, because most spiritual. For many, things had but little value except in so far as they could be symbolical; "allegory" was now applied, not only as of old at Alexandria, to the Scriptures, but to every detail of cathedral, every gesture and robe of priest, every occupation, you may say, of life which could be interpreted at better than its face value. Small wonder, then, that the theology of the Christian "mysteries" *par excellence* was then elaborated; small wonder, too, that when the "humanity" of religion, the gracious Manhood of our Lord, the Motherhood of Mary, were appealing more and more to the Christian heart, the indescribable condescensions of God, as sacramentally made manifest, should be better than before appreciated. All life was offered to the Christian as, should he choose, a Communion in holy things.

Finally, under stress of Protestant denials, the doctrine was reiterated and exactly defined by the Council of Trent; and recalled when "Modernist" hypotheses endangered it.

Much, too, might be written concerning their proper ministers; and the theology of their action in the soul—to which, it will be seen, they not only represent, but convey God's grace and "cause" it; and of the due share of the soul in ensuring their effect. Something of this will indeed be said below; but to treat any of this in detail would be alien, we recall, to the scope of this book of essays, which is to present Catholic dogma massively and as a coherent whole, and not, say, as historically guaranteed, nor yet as philosophically true or false, nor again in any so exhaustive a manner as to satisfy the reasonable requirements of an expert theologian.

We wish then to assign to the Sacraments their place in this great general scheme of man's supernatural salvation; and at most to deprecate certain attitudes of mind which may cause a student of Catholicism to feel antipathetic to their existence and their use; and to say a little concerning those natural, and thereupon honourable, instincts common to all men and existent, therefore, in our own age and race, which are recognized and sanctioned, welcomed and perfected by the Sacramental system.

II

The whole of St. John's Gospel has for theme the Supernatural Life.

"These things were written that you might believe
That Jesus Christ is the Son of God
And that, believing,
You might have Life in His name."

And the history of the beginning and nourishing and safeguarding of that life displays, as it develops, a close analogy with that of the natural life.

(i)

It begins by *birth*.

Our Lord assures the aged Nicodemus that unless a man be "born again" he cannot "enter the kingdom of heaven." Now the word we translate "again" may equally well mean, and does here also mean, "from above." In St. John these challenging ambiguities are constant. Christ's interlocutor fastens consistently on the more material of the two meanings offered, and has to be led from the plane of "earthly things" to that of "heavenly." Nicodemus, with smiling incredulity, asks how a man, being old, can re-enter his mother's womb, and so a second time be born. Christ reasserts that, to enter the Kingdom of God, man must be re-born.

Of his natural parents, man is born into his co-natural kingdom of the earth; but that which is born of flesh, stays flesh. To inherit the spiritual world intended for him, he must be born, too, of the Spirit. Indeed, it "stands to reason"—we "must not marvel," says our Lord —that what remains but "natural," earthly, flesh, is out of all proportion by the very law of its existence with what is supernatural, heavenly, spirit. If indeed man enters such a kingdom he cannot *but* have been re-born.

How, then, are sons of men to be made God's children?

A sigh, a hope, a prayer, might indeed have been sufficient. And indeed, when nothing more is possible, such is indeed enough. The Baptism of Desire, like the Martyr's Baptism of Blood, opens the gates of heaven to souls who (through guiltless ignorance or other valid cause) cannot attain to that of water. But, just as we do not "marvel" that a birth of Spirit is required before a man can enter on the spiritual life, so we are not astonished, after all that we have said, that the Incarnate Son of God willed that it should be linked to, and accomplished through, a material transaction. Christ ordained that water should be poured, and a formula of words pronounced; and whosoever, man or woman, Catholic, heretic, or pagan, so pours the water and so speaks the words, meaning to do what Christ intended, does indeed "baptize" and cause the supernatural life to spring up within the soul. Perhaps because of the unique necessity of this Sacrament to all who know of it—for, unless a man be *living*, clearly no fruits of life can come from Him—Christ willed, and the Church has taught, that to "administer" this Sacrament is open to anyone, provided he does not alter its substance nor exclude the *will to baptize*, whatever baptism may be. And for the same reason, doubtless, the Church recognized at once that it was still Christ's will that little children should be suffered to come to Him, and are to be baptized, and that even in those whose wits do not seem capable of coping with the natural life of men, the germ of the supernatural may yet take root.[1]

It is this infusion of supernatural life, or sanctifying grace, which brings this Sacrament into direct connection with the fact and doctrine of Original Sin. For that, it will be remembered, is the deprivation of grace and supernature. It is patent that the infusion of life does away with death, and of supernatural life, with the death of supernature. Therefore not only does Baptism annul the "original sin," or gracelessness, of the recipient, but also any other cause of death—actual sin, that is—which he may have within him; unless, indeed, he *will* to retain it, and until such time as he alters that will. Hence noble symbolisms have been detected in the rite: the Sacrament as an Ablution, and sin—whether Original Sin viewed positively as a stain, or the blood and mire with which personal "falls," or sin-wounds, may have defiled the soul—is thereby washed away; it is, too, as St. Paul loved to contemplate it, a Burial, inasmuch as the old life, which, relatively to the new, is but as death, is itself dead and done with. Beneath the covering waters Adam's son plunges, and as Adam's son is drowned. He re-emerges as a God's son; incorporate with Christ, and a living member of His Body, which is the Church. And the earlier Christians loved too to regard it as God's Seal, set indelibly upon the brow of those who were marked, henceforward, as His own: a "character," as we now say, is stamped upon them; they can never be un-baptized. Should they slay the life within them, yet are they Christians, though dead Christians; and it is not re-baptism that will restore them, but a different Sacrament. All Baptism is only, and once and for all, into Christ's Church—"one Lord, one Faith, one Baptism"; one birth admits us into the natural life, and later "birthdays" are but anniversaries: once only, too, can a man be re-born spiritually; and once so re-born, he can never be unborn.

[1] Less and less objection should be taken to the Catholic baptism of children or the weak-witted, in proportion as modern psychotherapy proves how very deep and active is the sub-consciousness of those who, like children or seeming "idiots," have their superficial consciousness very undeveloped or ill-controlled. Yet this consideration is by no means exhaustive; and, at the same time, Catholics are forbidden to administer baptism recklessly; as, for example, to one to whom there is no likelihood of giving a Catholic upbringing.

(ii)

Now in the history of natural life, adolescence marks a crisis. At fourteen, some one said, all boys go a little mad. Anyhow, at a certain moment comes a significant change; growth ceases to be equable; vitality experiences a shock; real perils are run. Food, exercise, mental occupation ought all of them to obtain renewed attention and modification. This crisis of body and mind, if happily weathered, sets the grown boy or girl into a world where new modes of consciousness, new capabilities and responsibilities of work, duty of new efforts and recognition of new privileges are to be found.

In the development of the spiritual life a certain corresponding crisis may occur, demanding a spiritual reinforcement from the Source of life. Perhaps the very existence of this Sacrament proves that some such crisis really happens. At any rate a moment does arrive when the child can take fuller consciousness of its spiritual life too, though this need not, and probably does not, coincide with physical adolescence, and, in fact, normally well precedes it. The child may now be asked to begin to profess and if need be to suffer and fight for that faith which he has already held, indeed, but as children do hold such things, unreflectingly and incorporate with his general equipment.

To cope with this crisis comes the Sacrament of Confirmation, of Reinforcement, or of Establishment. Such is its essential power, that with it even an infant may legitimately have its baptism reinforced; and again, even the grown man, baptized perhaps late in life, will not disdain a new invigoration of his spiritual life, however fully he may have realized the fact of his new birth. Nor indeed, in his case, does it lack a special value, and should therefore be not over-long delayed: when the first shock of that new birth is over, a certain spiritual reaction and fatigue, a sort of apathy and distaste, may not infrequently be experienced, from which he must be rescued.

Oil, for the early Christian, symbolized strength: with it athletes were anointed, and grew lithe and supple for the wrestling ring or for boxing. Oil, therefore, was no unfit symbol and vehicle for the new infusion of a spiritual strength and for the direct preparation of a Christian warfare. So strongly was this felt in the Middle Ages, that the connection between the ritual of Confirmation and that of the consecration of a new Knight, is clear and very striking.

With a holy oil, then, the candidate is anointed; and upon him the bishop's hands are laid, and a formula is spoken. And nothing less than a new inhabitation of God's Holy Spirit is granted to him, as, in that Gospel of the Holy Ghost, the *Acts*, we constantly see happening; and this child of earth, already re-born God's son, and incorporate with Christ, is thus admitted into a yet closer communion with all the Blessed Trinity.

As adolescence comes only once, so too can Confirmation be administered only once. It, too, places upon the soul a character or stamp. It is, at the beginning of the deliberate and chosen Christian life, a new sealing of the soul as God's.

(iii)

Another great crisis in any human history occurs when a man or woman resolves permanently to join to his own, or her own, another human life. This is done by the contract of marriage. Even on the natural plane that contract is already quite good and valid, provided, of course, no condition be attached to it which would vitiate its substance, such as (to quote a decree of Gregory IX, about A.D. 1230) that the married couple shall prevent child-bearing, or that the wife shall yield her place to a richer or nobler partner, should such a one, after a while, be found; or shall profit by "marriage" to sell herself to others.[1] The modern form of such an invalidating condition occurs in the "experimental marriage," of which most people will have encountered several instances: "Let us try one another for a year: then, if things go well, we'll carry on with our connection." That is not, and never was, a marriage. The resolve to avoid offspring rarely takes, I dare say, a form nowadays which actually invalidates the marriage: but I may as well say, here, definitely and once for all, that the Catholic Church forbids positively and always the *prevention* of the natural consequences of a marriage. Abstinence may be in certain cases licit, desirable, or a duty; but positive interference, never any of these things. It defies nature, and even *a priori* may thus be recognized as an attack upon society; and we are certain that sociology—all modern prophets notwithstanding—protests against it. Conditions of life are nowadays appalling; but Catholics will never be dislodged from their position that they do demand that marriage should not be tampered with, but that the economic framework of society itself must be corrected; and Catholics will never cease to labour for this end. If a married man and woman have heroically to control themselves,

[1] These considerations admit of fuller elucidation here impossible.

or to resign themselves to bringing up several children with fewer advantages than one or two might have, and to sacrifice motor-cars to morality, their martyrdom lies at the door of the unscrupulous plutocrat, who himself will be too selfish to have more children than they have, or can have, save the illegitimate ones whose existence he will probably have forgotten; and not at the door of Christian ethics. Physiology itself declares, what the Catholic faith does, that pleasure is, however natural, utterly subordinate, in the association of man and woman, and that life must not be tampered with.

In Christian marriage the contract still holds good, and forms, precisely, the material co-efficient in a Sacrament. Through it, precisely, God's grace flows, and no better example can be found of the truth that the supernatural does not eliminate or destroy the natural, but preserve and reinforce it. A new life, even on the natural plane, has been begun when the two lives of man and woman, else separate, thus interweave; and from this interweaving, unless in some way nature be stultified, is to spring the new life of the child, so that, as again and again we need to-day to emphasize, the complete human unit is formed: for humanity does not exhaust itself in monads, nor yet in pairs, but in the earthly trinity of father, mother, child. Not this, assuredly, will God neglect. He raises the contract to the plane of Sacrament; and not only the man and the woman join themselves each to each, but God joins them, and on their clasped hands rests His own. So utterly is it their affair and God's, that, notice, in Catholic marriage, it is not the priest who is the minister, but the man and woman. Though the Church, as guardian of all holy things and Sacraments in particular, can lay down laws to regulate the manner of their administration, and, in the interests precisely of the safety of marriage itself, does indeed exact that normally the contract be entered upon, by her children, in the presence of the priest, yet he but witnesses and blesses the union; he does not create it.

Here would, then, be the place, were we entering into details, for a discussion of the "impediments" which may exist in the way of this marriage or of that. Some are diriment, and invalidate the attempted contract; some "impede" it merely, and render it illicit, but leave it valid. And here, too, might be explained the Church's method of "dispensing" with such impediments as are not, by Christ's law, absolute.

Now in all good human things, if they be compared to God, His nature or His action, that element of good which we discern and use for the comparison exists but secondarily and derivatively. Thus, if we compare human paternity with God, and call God "Father," it is true that the word and even the notion are gathered first by us from our human experience, but the thing itself exists first and supereminently in the infinite perfection of God, so that St. Paul speaks truth when he says that "after Him all paternity on earth is named."

Hence marriage, when it is spoken of by St. Paul in splendid comparison with the nature of Christ and His relation to the Church, is not the standard by which we estimate that nature and that relation, but (if the comparison be valid) is something which aspires towards what Christ is or does, and is its true self in proportion as it approximates thereto. He must not be judged by it: but we gain light concerning it by what we know of Him.

What, then, is this mystery in Christ to which marriage must endeavour to assimilate itself, and which Christian marriage does indeed necessarily resemble?

Nothing less than the union in Himself, as in one Person, of the two natures, divine and human; and again, of Himself with each and every soul with whom He, by grace, is wedded. His Church is true Spouse, consisting assuredly of human men and women, yet "coming down from Heaven," and God's Throne, since it is precisely by God's grace in them that their full unification is accomplished. The union of two lives, then, which marriage is, is something so high and splendid, that to nothing can it be worthily compared save to the transcendent mystery which is the very essence of the Christian revelation.[1]

Hence, as the Son of God took flesh, never to lay it down, and wedded to Himself His faithful Church, never to be disloyal; so in the human counterpart this, too, must be reflected. Christian marriage can be but of one with one, and can never be dissolved: for Catholics, no divorce. Not only marriage ought not, but for its own sake and true nature, cannot be allowed, even by God, to sink so far away from its divine exemplar. And at the root of the Catholic doctrine of purity lies not only Nature, which is defied by solitary sin or by wandering associated sin, but that supernatural marriage of Christ and the inmost soul, which must needs be truthfully reflected even in behaviour. What is *spiritually true*, ought to express itself truthfully, and hold good on every level of existence.

[1] I have already hinted that the Trinity itself is expressed, in terms of humanity, through the social *unit* of father, mother, child.

Let it not then be said that the Catholic Church thinks slightingly of marriage. In no religion or philosophy which history has ever known, has there been a conception of marriage even approaching, for loftiness and loveliness, for intimacy and transcendence, that to which through every variation of social theory and practice she adheres.

(iv)

There is another way of employing life, besides the inauguration of the family and home out of which human society is normally constructed. Even the scientific, military, philosophic expert may feel called upon to give up these. But there are those who realize too, the vocation to separate themselves from the ordinary stream of life, and to consecrate themselves unsharedly to the direct service of God. Such are priests. To them, for reasons partly ascetical or mystical, to which allusion is made elsewhere, partly quite practical and political, to which we need not allude at all, marriage is by Catholic discipline forbidden. But we will say this much at any rate; such souls need to be, more than others, in close union with the God whom they professedly serve and represent. Not aloof then is the merciful God from the hour in which His servant definitely takes on himself so terrible a task. Ordination is not just a recognition, nor a setting aside of the man for a great absorbing duty. It is a Sacrament; it, too, gives a "character" and makes a man "priest for ever," never to be unpriested; and, through the material rites, and the words of the ordaining bishop, grace flows which helps the man to live true to that priesthood to which the Sacrament has raised him. Of bishops, the special function is to ordain, and normally to confirm; of priests, to offer Mass and to absolve, and to administer the Sacrament of which I speak of next: and Episcopate and Priesthood and Diaconate are of divine institution.

(v)

Such then are the Sacraments which belong, we may say, to the crises of spiritual birth, adolescence, and maturity. One more great crisis awaits each human life; the hour when the physical coefficient in man's complex unity is exhausted, disintegrates, and dies, and the soul passes into its truer (yet not wholly true) existence, consciousness, and sphere. Upon death, too, then, the Sacraments attend.

The Last Anointing places upon the failing senses that oil which besides the strengthening which in Confirmation it symbolized, and the kingly consecration which it imparted to the ordinand, meant, too, a Healing and Refreshment. In Extreme Unction, there is given by God not only new peace of soul, cleansing from sin and the effects of sin, and spiritual strength to cope with the temptations peculiar to that *action of death* which, if none other, each man must do alone, but even, if God so wills, new health of body even.

Along with this Anointing is given the last of those Communions which are spoken of below, *Viaticum*, as the Church tenderly has named it, the "journey-money," which ensures to a man a safe and easy transit to his new world. Perhaps of all the Sacraments, this is that in which grace acts most visibly. Within palace or garret, of which alike at that hour the walls falter and fade as the reality of Eternal Life beats through them, in hospital or convent cell or upon battle-field, the spectacle of this gracious Sacrament and its effects have provoked, time and time again, the accustomed cry: "*That* is the religion to die in!"[1]

(vi)

It may well be said, however, that human life does not consist of crises; and, if the parallel we have used is truthfully to be pursued, so neither should the spiritual. And indeed it does not. There are two Sacraments remaining, which work on behalf of the daily needs of the supernatural life, namely, its purification from all germs of death, and its constant nourishment and increasing.

The fourth and fifth Essays in this collection have spoken of Sin.

[1] I may be allowed to illustrate this, without intruding my own experience, by two incidents of which I have had knowledge. During the World War of 1914–1918 a British Catholic chaplain and a Protestant officer were lifting a dying German, whose rosary, round his neck, betokened him a Catholic. The priest knew no German; the officer spoke it well. The dying boy wished to make his confession, and implored the *officer* to hear it and translate it. He insisted, though the priest declared that no such method need be taken. Having then thus confessed and absolved him, he gave him the Last Sacraments, aided by the officer, down whose face the tears were pouring. In that hour of radiant death, the young man begged to be made a Catholic. "Come back with me," said the priest, "and I will give you what instruction I can." "No," said he, "I can never believe better than I do, after what I have seen. Who knows how long I've got? Receive me now." The priest did so, and the lad was killed next day.

Again, a priest recognized, one night, the voices of some of his own men, wounded and in agony in No Man's Land, and unable, for the while, to be carried in. He crawled out to them, and voice after voice was silenced. "Give me some of that drug, padre," said an officer when he returned, "which you use to stupefy your men." It was no drug, but Absolution, Communion, and the Holy Oil, which the priest had given; and the pain was drowned in the spiritual peace.

Sin is the deliberate violation of God's known law: and strictly speaking, only that violation which is so grave as to cause the death of the supernatural life of grace is to be called sin. However, that name, too, is given to what falls well short of this, and does no more than weaken the soul's grace-life, or make it sick. Thus besides "mortal" sin, there is "venial." The body may be weakened or made sick by lack of proper nourishment or by wound, and yet not die; or it may be slain by complete starvation or by poison or by a deadly blow.

This distinction is not only important in view of the Sacrament we are here speaking of, but in itself. For we have met those who, by declaring (rather like the Stoics) that *all* wrongdoing is grave and "mortal," bind intolerable burdens on themselves and others; and many more, of course, who profess that there is no such thing as "mortal" sin, that all ignorance of the law is, at the moment, "invincible," or that there is no law; that wrongdoing, is but a regrettable mistake, or a "social error," and what not. Hereby real laxity is introduced. However, this is not the place to pursue these considerations.

We have here to ask what method, if any, has been found, for the restoration of the sick soul to health, or the dead soul, to life? Again, a look to God, a tear or prayer, might have sufficed. And so indeed, in a certain sense, it may. The moment that, under the impulse of God's grace, the soul "repents," and renews in itself the love of that God whom it has defied—a love that is not a lie, nor still subordinates its object, God, to that other love which led to sin; a love, that is, which not only *prefers* the all-perfect and all-satisfying God to all else, but *rejects* all else in so far as it offends Him and for His sake—at that moment the sin is forgiven and the grace returns. But involved in that new act of chosen obedience to God's loving law, is the resolution to fulfil also His detailed ordinances when the chance reaches me, and I shall seek, according to His decree, absolution from the Priest to whom he has given orders to receive my confession, and pronounce my freeing from my sin. In a line, then: if, after sin, I by God's grace can be sorry for my sin from a motive of "perfect love for God"—and that is less hard than you might guess—and resolve to use this Sacrament when I can, my sin is forthwith forgiven. But I will here add, that such is God's mercy, that, should I be unable to be sorry in this way, and have, not what is called "contrition," but "attrition," or imperfect sorrow of heart and detestation of sin arising from the spectacle of its hatefulness as such, or from the fear of God's punishments, I am in a state which predisposes me to love and to grace, and this, coupled with the use of the Sacrament, will win me my forgiveness.

But this Sacrament! This intrusion of a man into a transaction which surely must remain utterly personal between me and God!

Well, once more, just as God, had He chosen, might have restored the world to life without the intervention of the Man Jesus Christ, the Second Adam, so might Christ have chosen to fulfil His work directly, without human co-operation, without permitting men to share in His activity; He might have kept all His favours wholly in His own hands, and have had contempt for all essentially lower agency. Not such is the gentleness and delicacy of His heart. Not thus *exclusive* is He who willed to share our nature. Throughout, He associates men to Himself; these priests whom He calls in, to co-operate, are not just eminent among *humans*; He gives them a divine work to do; and they can do it, because through them and in them it is Himself who acts. The priest, assuredly, absolves; for *in* him, Christ absolves. The priest's hands, sick themselves, perhaps, yet become healing hands: not he is it who ever can *forgive*; not against him the offence, not his the redeeming merit, not he is source of grace. But caught up is he into an ordained fellowship with Christ Redeemer and Grace-giver, so that Christ bids him *use* that power which He delegated in the words: "Whose sins soever you remit, they are remitted unto them; and whosoever you retain, they are retained."

When, therefore, the Catholic is conscious that he has gravely sinned, he must repent. He must be sorry—I do not say *feel* sorry: emotion is not always under our control; and, strangely enough, in our human complex the feeling may exist without the fact—he must *be* sorry that he has offended God, Who is his Sovereign Lord, Who has been so good to him; Whose Son died on the Cross in grievous pain for him; and Who inflicts upon a rebellious soul the most terrible of all punishments, namely, a separation, temporary or eternal, from Himself. Further, he must resolve that, with God's help, he will not sin again: that is no *guarantee* that sin he will not in the future—man remains man; habits are there, likings are there, temptations will be there, and nature is ever weak. Indeed, he may foresee that with his temperament and history, and in the circumstances where he perforce will find himself, he is, humanly speaking, certain to sin again. But such resolution as is his, he brings to God, and offers it to Him, and asks His grace. The future shall be a co-operation: the poor percentage of his own efforts is what the man offers; the rich response from God makes up the necessary whole; and should he continue so to ask—and most assuredly to receive—even human weakness can ascend "from strength to strength"; keep always the soul's health; die, even, in the body, "rather than commit another mortal sin." With these, then, in his soul, contrition and resolution, he presents himself to the priest, confesses, and is absolved.

I will here briefly add that the priest gives us, after Confession, what is called a "penance," usually some short prayer. We know perfectly that no natural work of ours, however good, bears any proportion to what is supernatural. But we have already seen how, by grace, Christ and we are united and His life circulates in ours. Therefore from His merits, which we vitally appropriate, our good deeds, including those of "penance" or satisfaction, derive their value; it is a sacramental value, and works in with His to merit for us, truly, remission of our punishment, and increase of grace.

Since this is a statement of Catholic doctrine, and not even a defence of it, still less a discussion of the "natural" advantages of our religious practice, I will merely allude to the great light which modern mind-medicine is throwing on the evils of "repression," and the grave neuroses, even, into which a memory thrust back into the subconscious, and festering between the folds of a crumpled soul, may issue. As an Anglican clergyman said ruefully to me: "We shall *all* have to be setting up confessionals, or every one will be off to Harley Street to buy new souls." It is true that the average man tries to forget, at once, the deeds which make him feel ashamed; yet those who most of all, perhaps, would feel panic-struck at the thought of "confessing" to a priest, boast most easily, in smoking-room or mess, of the ill-deeds that give them "glory." Well, the confessional is instituted directly for a supernatural end; and the priest's work there is not, primarily, "spiritual direction." But just as he is there as "judge," and must normally first know the sins before he can pronounce their remission or retention, so, too, he is a physician, to heal the past, and a counsellor, to give assistance for the future. Hence while the confessional ensures a man not just pushing a sin away, unrepented, into precarious forgetfulness, but healthily pricks the abscess, and extracts the venom, so, too, an experienced confessor will know well how to discriminate the necessary from the advisable, and this, from the harmful. He will not even permit statements unwisely detailed, and calculated to inflame the imaginative memory; he will always guide the thought and aspiration to a more wholesome freer future; he will know just how far to allow the statement of venial sins, or the restatement of old forgiven sins; he will guard against scruples and frivolity alike, an easy-going disregard of past experience, or an anxious present, or a feverish exaltation and presumptuous security. He will guide the flow of grace, that the cleansing of the old may ever issue into the creation of the new. Morbidity! It is sometimes dreamed that the study of sin, in the confessional, must make a priest grow morbid, and that he becomes an expert in the pathology alone of the soul. Yet one hour, I believe, in that consecrated clinic, is likely to teach a priest more of the richness, the latent beauty, the truthfulness, the humble effort, the divine and lovely secrets of humanity, than a year spent in contemplation of life's evident successes.

(vii)

But again, life thrives not merely by successive healings. It needs its appropriate daily food. For the body, material meat and drink; for the mind, instruction, ideas. For the supernatural life, what appropriate food may be found? We are forced to answer in terms of that life itself. But that life is Christ's life: divine life communicated to man in so far as man can receive it. For that, what adequate reinforcement can exist, what that is not essentially weaker and poorer, useless, in short, as nourishment, save Itself? Idle to seek further. "He that eateth Me, it is *he* that shall live by Me." The soul *must* feed on Christ, if it is to live by Christ. And the Bread which Christ gives, is His Flesh; His must be the blood infused into the soul's arteries.

"If ye eat not the Flesh of the Son of Man, and do not drink His Blood, you have not Life in you. He who doth eat My Flesh and doth drink My Blood hath Life Eternal. . . . For My Flesh is a true food, and My Blood true drink. He who doth eat My Flesh and who doth drink My Blood, in Me remaineth, and I in him" (John vi. 53–6). And here, again, by some yearning aspiration, by hunger itself for Christ, the soul might have been allowed adequately to feed on Him. And indeed, here once more, if it does not know, or cannot carry out, Christ's completed plan, by such desire it can make its Spiritual Communion. But He Who in one Person was true God-Man, decreed that in body, soul, and spirit, we should make *full* personal Communion. The Catholic Faith declares that the bread He broke and the wine He offered, became, at His word and by His will, His Self, His Body and His Blood, His Soul and His Divinity, and that in no metaphor or symbol merely He gave them to His children that in these they should feed upon that life which is no symbol merely and no metaphor.

Linked with this doctrine, is, of course, its theology, and entwined with this theology, a philosophy. Thus in the technical language than which none is better for the expressing the knowledge we have of this great fact, we are bidden to say that the Real Presence of Christ in the Eucharist is effected by a *transubstantiation* of the elements, and into the dogma this word has altogether entered: lest we should imagine that in some way bread and wine remain upon our altars and are by us received. No; the appearances of bread and wine remain, but under the appearances, not only during the Mass, not only when we receive them, howsoever divided be those appearances or wheresoever placed, Christ is truly present and He only.

On this food, then, we are bound to feed. Lest we omit it altogether through lack of spiritual appetite, the Church decrees that we shall receive it once a year at least: frequent or even daily Communion she whole-heartedly encourages, unless experiment makes clear that, for this individual or that, such frequency be not profitable. To innocent children, too, provided (as the present discipline of the Church has ruled) they can, in the measure of their intelligence, distinguish between this Food and common bread, this heavenly nourishment is offered. To one only class of men access is forbidden: those in mortal sin. For in them, the life is dead. A corpse cannot be nourished, and Communion is life's *food.* Let but that life once more exist, then can the soul assimilate the food of immortality. *Then* grace increases, virtues flower forth, sin's shadows melt and, the pledge of glory is made ours.[1]

[1] In a note I may allude to the Catholic discipline, which exists in most parts of the Church, that the laity should receive Communion under the form of Bread only. Herein they are not defrauded. The reasons for this rule are partly practical (as, the difficulty of obtaining and transporting enough wine in, say, missionary districts; or, the danger of irreverence by spilling and the like), and partly historical (it is clear that in the early Church the *manner* of administering the Eucharist differed much in different places and circumstances); but these two sorts of reasons would not suffice without the theological one, namely, that Christ cannot be divided. Where He is at all, He is wholly. By the force of the consecrating words, no doubt, it is the Body which becomes present under the appearance of the bread, and the Blood beneath that of wine, but "by concomitance," as they say, the whole of the indivisible Christ is made present under both. So he who receives either, receives all.

We have mentioned the Mass. Not in a paragraph can we adequately describe, even, that central act of Christian worship. But Christ's Real Presence is upon our altars not merely for our feeling, but for Sacrifice, and from the beginning the Church has recognized in the Mass the fulfilment of Malachi's prophecy (i. 11) that in every place should be offered to God a "clean oblation."

For what is the eternal work of Christ, save to offer to God on our behalf the most perfect worship? Upon the Cross the expression of this His self-offering was consummated, so that God willed to attach the redemptive value of His life particularly to His death. But of that redemption this book has spoken elsewhere. In, then, the true Sacrifice of the Mass that perfect Sacrifice of the Cross is continually represented and applied; it *is* that Sacrifice, and no new one, as if the Cross were insufficient: it is no new Victim, for Christ is offered; no new priest, for He offers His own Self; no new Recipient of the Sacrifice is dreamt of, for it is God, and only God, to whom it rises. Nor is the object of that Sacrifice a different one: ever Christ gives Himself in Adoration, in Thanksgiving, in Propitiation, in Intercession. Nor are they for whom He offers different, they are the world of souls; souls still fighting for salvation, and souls not yet purified nor fit for heaven, but in purgatory. Only in hell the intercessory value of that offering is powerless only in heaven it is no more needed.

And notice that by *will* even the sinner can join in the priest's work. But once a man is joined, by community of life, with Christ, he is supernaturally associated to Christ's work, and co-operates, in that sense, in Redemption, and, by rightly "hearing Mass," enters into the whole sacrificial work of Christ. Small wonder, then, that the Mass is the very heart of Christian worship and energy, and that the Church insists no Sunday nor Holy Day should pass, without her children exercising their supreme and Christ-like office, even though they be not priests in the full sense, nor impersonate Christ in effecting that Sacrifice in whose offering they join.

Such, then, is the sacramental law of Christ for this world of space and time. It should be remembered, though, that in *substantial fact* the whole life of a Christian, in whom grace is, is one long Holy Communion. Christ lives in him ever; it is less truly he who lives, than Christ. But, since our eternal life is in us co-ordinated with our year-and-day existence, Christ has ruled that at intervals our inner Communion should be, as it were, agglomerated, externalized, and concentrated in an act. That the character of our human consciousness, our memory, our *real appropriation* of the inner timeless reality demands this, who does not see? It is hard for the soul to live in continuous actual utilization or even awareness of what is so utterly secret and unseen. But these our recurrent Communions, though they increase our life, yet in a sense do not affix to a moment of time and a point in space, that which is unextended and durable within us. When, freed from that space and time, we pass into our proper eternalized existence, and are "in heaven," there will be no need more of summoning altar-rails and the flaky descent of the Host upon our tongue; the temporal expression and readministration of the eternal Fact will be no more necessary for us in that beatific Vision and that completed Union.

III

To my mind the intricate simplicity of the Sacramental system should appeal to anyone who loves and understands human nature, who is not supercilious with regard to its humbler instincts and hours of earthliness, and who knows how from the very lowest of its state rise pure jets of love and aspiration towards God. There are those, however, to whom it is distasteful.

(i)

They may, in some manner, feel it to be materialistic. They will, should they be survivors from the Evangelical period, use the old formula that they want nothing between themselves and their Saviour. I feel little but gratitude for the old Evangelicism. It uttered a noble protest against the formalism of its day. Strong and lovable was the "character" it could produce: truly spiritual its creed and worship often was. But first, we use the Sacraments not merely because we want them, but because they are put there. We have and use them, because of that Authority in "hearing" which we believe we are "hearing" Christ. But anyhow, not separation is what Sacraments and priest occasion. A bridge does not push the river's banks asunder; the ether does not hold the sun away from us; without it, we should not know his rays; nor without air, his heat. But better than bridge, or undulating air, are Sacraments. It is, in a sense, true that, for the Christian soul, there *is* no river; or, we have crossed it, and stand upon Christ's shore. And not distant is our Light; in our own heart the Morning Star is shining—save, it is true, we have cleft anew the chasm, and put out the Light. For all that, this life, as we still perforce must live it, is made up of banks and bridges. Between each individual is an unfathomable gulf. Even words must disguise the thought they would fain express; even our thoughts misstate at least in part our truest and most real consciousness. All social life is intertwined by human "sacraments," in so far as what they hold, they hide; what they bring, they veil. The clasping of the hands—a kiss—we do not chafe at them, or should not. A kiss may be a poor way of expressing, and indeed conveying, love; even, by a kiss we may betray. Yet true lovers do not feel their kiss *divides* them, comes between them, or caricatures, because it is physical and external, the spiritual, inner love. All lovers wish to express what in their hearts they feel; the most loyal, after separation during which for lack of expression their love has indeed not faltered, yet are glad, no sooner do they meet, to return to more than the mere intercommunion of their minds. The Sacraments are the kiss of God, where-through He not only pours out on us the richness of His love, but satisfies the hungers of our sense and thought as well as our soul. And if it be urged that God, precisely, is the only one who needs no such thing as sense, or even reason-satisfaction, nor anything external, well, that is amply true. But not such are we. Love is reciprocal. It is not all upon God's side. It must reveal itself to *us* who are not only spirit, and must from us, from our whole self, receive a full response. But if it be further urged that our communion with our God *ought*, on our side, to be wholly spiritual; that our reciprocation *ought* to be so "mystical" and discarnate as to require no external expression, and indeed (truthfully viewed) admits of none, but is immediate, wholly interior, sightless, soundless, imageless—well, that again cannot be simply so. It is true all nature is inadequate to God. No sense, no thought exhausts Him. But we have resolutely to resist the doctrine that sense and thought are somehow bad, and ought to be eliminated. The chasm between that doctrine and the Catholic, though narrow (at first seeming) as a hair, is infinite in depth. See St. John of the Cross! who ever went further than did he, in his doctrine of *transcending* the best in sense, or thought, feeling or will? Yet with horror would he have sprung back from any teaching which suggested that Sacraments should be spurned. Moreover, human nature never *ought* to do what it *can* not. And it *can* not dispense with what is after all part of it. There are those who try to believe that they know nothing save their thoughts: that will is not free. Life at every turn confutes them. So with the rest. At every turn we enact what we most deeply feel. The artist is not base, when he summons colour and sound for the stammering forth of his unutterable dream. The dream and the business, the spirit and the flesh, who are we to forbid their wedlock, or rebuke all nature's God when He desires that with Him all nature should co-operate? Colour and scent and music; pure elements, like water, oil; bread or wine; men like ourselves, our Words and thoughts and actions, He gathers up, and *harmonizes* into His service. The oil, the wine, the man, cannot assuredly violate the Spirit; but the Spirit, which uses them, exalts and dignifies these humble things. *O admirabile commercium!* Our world God made, and into it He came; our flesh to Himself He wedded; pride were in us intolerable, should we insist that through the spirit only we could communicate with Him. Not then by stripping off, but by the holding of the hem of whatever robe God wears, shall we best reach to union with Him who is the All in all.

For completeness we should add that a more modern mind might judge Sacrament to be denounced as "magical." This is to misunderstand either the notion of Sacrament, or that of magic. "Sacrament," we have explained. God freely wills to exert His power through certain natural objects or actions, used with sufficient intelligence by those who, in response to His command, wish to enter into super-natural communion with Him. "Magic" is used (in accurate definition) as the coercing of God through natural forces. God refuses rain: the medicine-man tosses water in the air: rain is forced to fall. A fire is lit; the sun is spell-bound into shining. Magic, thus scientifically circumscribed, is the exact opposite of religion, which involves a relation of complete *dependence* on the Ultimate. And certainly, at each point, such "magic" marks a complete antithesis to the sacramental practice. And if "magic" be used with popular looseness to mean merely the production, by some sort of super-man, of results automatically following upon actions or words which bear no intrinsic relation to them, as though I wave a wand and a boundary-stone is shifted, or set up my enemy's effigy to melt and he, at a distance, wastes away and dies—that, too, is utterly opposed, at every point, to the idea and action of a Sacrament. There is, in the use of them, nothing automatic—neither their matter, nor their form, nor their minister, have any intrinsic power. The power is God's. God acts, and chooses to act in certain ways, through certain vehicles. The minister co-operates as bidden or permitted; the recipient profits, not automatically, but in accord with intention and intelligence. On my head the water may be poured, and with it, the words be spoken; but if the minister does not intend to christen me, or I intend not to be baptized, baptized I am not. True, God can act freely. He can give grace if He choose, to infants, or to the ignorant or all-but idiot. Receptivity for grace is not to be measured by artistic or by intellectual powers. But three wills must always, in this matter of the Sacraments, co-operate, God's, the minister's, and the recipient's. The mechanical and coercive element, inseparable from magic, is, by the very nature of a Sacrament, excluded.

Finally, let no one think that there is here any harsh doctrine such as that *only* through the Sacraments God can or does give grace. Our teaching is that those who know about the Sacraments, and can obtain them, are bound to respect God's covenant, and to make use of them. But even to them, in a thousand other ways, grace can find access; prayer, aspiration, any action done by a soul in union with Jesus Christ, is a means of grace. And God's grace takes *initiatives*: we could not even pray, nor do those actions, nor come at all to Christ, unless the Father "draw" us. And as for those who do not know of, or cannot reach the Sacraments, or, like the Anglicans, use rites that are (save Baptism) no Sacraments, still in a thousand ways God can impart to them His favours. He is free: *one* way is covenanted: it we must use, once we know of it. "We know," wrote St. Augustine, "that invisible sanctification has been present and profitable to some without the visible Sacraments; but not, for that, may the visible Sacrament be scorned; for the scorner of the visible can never in any wise invisibly be sanctified."

The Sacraments, then, are not only a work of God, but reveal the method of His working, and teach us, by imitating it, to sacramentalize the world. We are taught to seek for the true meaning and value of all that is, not on its surface, but within. We must not fantastically *allegorize* Nature, but we must expect to find God present and working in it. Hence joy; hence love; hence freedom in a world become God's robe; in all things we may reach Him; nothing must be scorned, for it clothes Him; nor shall we ever dare to disdain it, as being *but* His robe; for the robe is *His*. Thus the whole world finds meaning; and as no static vision merely of a Faith but as co-operative and dynamic.

And for patron in our effort to lay hold on this, I would invoke St. Francis, in whom, more visibly perhaps than in any other, even in his radiant century, did both nature and super-nature reach exultant union, till in no part of his most lovely earth did he fail to find a yet more lovely heaven.

VIII

LIFE AFTER DEATH

BY

C. C. MARTINDALE, S.J.

THE last clause of the Christian Creed is "Life Everlasting." And that Catholics believe in the survival of the soul cannot be unknown to anybody. Those, however, who have carefully read these Essays will not be slow to surmise that for us "everlasting life" means more that just "duration," and that we have a deeper doctrine concerning the soul's destiny than that it outlasts the body, or even that it is immortal.

However, it is of this that I shall write first, and of the map, in so far as it may be constructed, of that world into which, when the body dies, the soul passes. After that, the deeper implications of this survival will have to be set forth, in function of those main ideas which have guided, so far, the authors of this volume.

I

(i)

It is, I dare say, impossible to discover a race which in some shape or another does not recoil from a belief that physical death marks the end of a man's history. I am not concerned with the form in which his survival is conceived or described; nor to deny that the merest minimum of attenuated "life" may be all that this tribe or that, at this period of the race's history or that, was willing to assign to him. Nor am I in any way alluding to the sort of world which the ghosts, or again the "true selves" of the "dead" may be fancied to inhabit. All I would urge is, that it comes natural to the man to feel sure that the death of his body is not the death of *him*. This belief is scarcely less universal and ineradicable than the belief in God. I do not for a moment admit the sufficiency of the hypotheses which have been invented to account for this belief in God; save indeed the theistic hypothesis, which, as an earlier Essay has shown, is more than a hypothesis, though even as such it covers more facts and explains them better than do those of animism, magic, and the like. Nor yet do I believe, though it were easier to believe, in the adequacy of dreams, hallucinations, hereditary transmissions, nor even the general will-to-live, as explanations of the origin of the belief that I somehow survive my seeming finish. It is true, for example, that the dead appear to the survivor in dreams, as Patroklos to Achilles in the *Iliad*; but not only do such narratives, or those even about our contemporary "primitive" folk, take us nowhere really near to "primitive" man and his experiences, but all the psychological bias of the evidence is towards the conclusion that because, say, the Greeks believed in the survival of the soul, they thought it could petition for what it needed through dreams or otherwise, and not that, because they dreamt, they concluded it could survive. It is true again that in India, for example, there is a strong belief in the solidarity of the family, and in the substantial continuity of its generations; but not that gave rise to the belief that the soul survived the body, but, if to anything, to the idea of transmigration, which, later, was "philosophized" and linked up with ethics, as in Buddhist, even Brahmin, thought you now observe it. Moreover, if you attend to the indignant resentment with which primitive folk regard the approach of death, that is not because they do not foresee survival, but because they expect a particular *sort* of survival, namely, a shadowy, unsubstantial, halved life, so that the Greeks again could speak of the phantom or wraith in which "the wits are not," weak ghosts, flitting through a filmy sort of world, and capable of being galvanized into attention, consciousness, and speech, by the drinking of hot blood in which the "life" still was, though all the while the "man himself" lay a corpse upon the earth or in it. But whatsoever its destiny or dwelling, the "soul" indubitably "survived."

I am not offering this universal belief, which indeed it is scarcely worth while to illustrate, as a proof that the soul subsists after the body's death; though I might be allowed to say that we who on the whole *trust* human nature, and are for ever arguing that what is "natural" is right, would be singularly perverse were we to urge that humanity is an incurable *malade imaginaire* on these two points exactly, that God exists, and that the soul survives. Far more likely is it, and experience bears it out, that for one who thinks he has real reasons for asserting that they do not, there are very many more who say so because it would be awkward enough for them to suppose there were a God or an after-life; and very many too who, though they think they disbelieve in the existence of God or of immortality, are in fact unable to believe in some definite view of God, or in some sort of immortality, and so deny the whole. Moreover, it is the few, whom we may call half-cultured, or the hyper-cultured, who try positively to stand on the rickety pinnacle, as of atheism, so of complete extinction; and on the whole, if you watch carefully, you will find they do not keep their foothold there, but continually plunge off into the waves of superstitions that lap round them, fears of ghosts, of retribution, spiritualisms, fortune tellings, and the like; and climb back dripping; or at least are so wrapped in the mist of agnosticism that they do not see where in fact their feet are placed, albeit their head strives to hold itself high in a rarefied ether they were never meant to breathe. So you may go so far as to say that it is obvious nature does not *mean* us to do without the ideas of God or of survival, and that in vain you may try to pitchfork these notions out. *Tamen usque recurrent.*

Ordinary Catholic philosophy goes farther than this, however, and considers that there are valid intellectual proofs, as of the existence of God, so of the existence, survival, and indestructibility of the human soul.

(ii)

Some of the latter, indeed, to be cogent, imply the former, and a "formed" belief in the "character" and "attributes" of God; here, I mean, that He is infinitely powerful and just, and Creator of the world and of men. Now we observe in ourselves an ineradicable desire that justice should be done. Therefore we believe that this belongs to our nature and was "put there" by our Creator. But in this world we observe an outrageous travesty of justice. Men die, unjustly successful, or unjustly unsuccessful. Were their existence to be confined, then, to this world, we might without pessimism say that *on the whole* our desire for justice was derided. Therefore in another phase of existence it must be satisfied.

Again, our conscience incites us to much that has no correlative "reward" in this scheme of things and can have none; and yet, not only do we require our own interior recognition that we have been right, but we are justified in desiring that this should be acknowledged. For we are social, and should not divorce ourselves from the approbation of our fellows, not think lightly of their blame. Martyrs may die serene in the conviction that God knows what was in the heart; yet, somehow, somewhere, their innocence should be acknowledged. Else, evil triumphs "socially." So, a perfected "society," in which we and our true selves, built of our actions, survive and are recognized by our fellow-men, is morally exacted.

These considerations, which seem to be perfectly valid once you have the belief in God which earlier Essays have shown to be that of Catholics, none the less do presuppose that belief. Neither do they prove immortality, but only a morally *sufficient* after-death.

There exist, however, arguments drawn from the consideration of the soul as the vital principle of man. They observe that *a* vital principle is needed, in the case of all observable living things, to hold together into a living unit the chemicals which are in sort identical with what composes units that do not live; and in particular, a special principle would seem necessary to unite into a human being those elements which as such we share with the rest of material existence. Matter, as such, has no tendency to be "body" rather than anything else. Moreover, in the case of man, this principle is seen to be something strictly "spiritual," for it can do what matter cannot possibly be conceived as doing; for example, reflect, form universal concepts, abstract ideas; and it can *will.* Now such a substance cannot, it may be shown, consist of parts, as matter does; yet only by disintegrating into its parts, can a "unit" of matter cease to be itself; this fate, therefore, cannot befall the soul. That which has no parts, cannot be reduced to parts, whether by pressure from without or by explosion from within. Therefore the reflecting, recollecting, reasoning, willing soul cannot cease to exist, save by the abrogation of that sustaining will of God which alone accounts for the existence and continuance of any contingent thing. This consideration, if it be admitted, proves that the soul not only survives, but does so for ever, unless God wills its annihilation. But it does not in any way, as yet, decide what sort of existence such a soul enjoys once it is separated from the matter which it animated; though certain of its consequences can be pursued along that road.

A line of thought which appeals strongly to some, is that indicated by the soul's appetite and aptitude for the infinite (the mathematical infinite, that is; not strictly, perhaps, the theological); its intolerance, at least, for boundaries; its indefinite capacity for *more*. You cannot imagine yourself being unable or undesirous to have more; and to *will* what you know, or else its opposite, more and more. And thus in reality to *exist more*. It is true that life expresses itself on the whole in work, and that we work mostly through our bodies; yet ever is it mind and will which work; bodily action, bulk, the measurable by inches and ponderable by ounces, is not what is *most* real; that strikes us first, no doubt, and most sharply; but it remains that what we think and will *is* our self; into our self it is worked up; we do not merely *have* thoughts and choices suspended on us like so many necklaces. We *are* our thoughts and will; our physical actions express them and transmit them, but are not they. Therefore it would seem to be of the soul's nature to tend to become able to achieve communion with all that is; and that, not as though a superficial, extensive consciousness were in any way sufficient, but intensively, and more and more assimilatively of the very inmost of existence. But were this life all, the soul, as thus envisaged, would all along be cheated.

It would take much space to follow out any such line of thought, and to safeguard it from misapprehensions, to avoid entanglement in metaphors which are apt to keep us in the realm of the fantastic. But I have wished (as this book keeps recalling to its readers) not to *prove* Catholic dogma, but to display it, having prefixed just enough to show that there is that in nature to which it corresponds and to anticipate, therefore, that kind of instinctive horror with which so many approach the unknown areas of our Faith.

II

(i)

Students have by now become accustomed to exact that, in the departments of folk-lore and worship, an "adjacent anthropology" be first of all devised, and that not just anything be offered in illustration, nor the cults of Madagascar, say, be brought forthwith into connection with Mexico, nor Palestine with Peru.

So, though I do not intend to give any kind of complete view of Hebrew beliefs as to the soul's nature, destiny, or dwelling, we ought to know, at least roughly, among what beliefs Christianity grew up. It is Christian eschatology that we are outlining: there was no homogeneous authoritative Jewish doctrine: even a "summary" is difficult to make: many documents would have to be separately reviewed.

It is ample if we are clear that, except for the late sect of the Sadducees, a Hellenizing group, and quite out of the main current of Hebrew belief, there never was a time when the Israelites thought that human nature consisted exclusively of the flesh; and the idea of the soul and its hereafter became, in fact, all the way more definite and consistent.

It might be discussed whether the Hebrews believed that three vital coefficients met in man, of which one, clearly enough, was "body"; while the other two, which many people like to translate "life" and "soul," or "soul" and "spirit," were regarded as somehow distinct; or else, as a selfsame thing, but viewed, now in itself, and again as giving life to the man. That is not the point; and anyhow the Hebrew race was not metaphysical, and took an almost entirely ethical view of what concerned the soul. The point is, that something which went to make up "man" was not extinguished by physical death. Indeed, its destined habitat had some sort of a geography and *mise-en-scene*, and the conditions of the soul therein could reach imagination.

It must be frankly stated that Hebrew belief, as to all this, was but slightly, if at all, differentiated at the first from the main ideas of the Semitic world, and in particular from those of the Mesopotamian background of their history.

Vaguely associating the soul with the tomb of the body (rather as we, in spite of ourselves, and half in defiance of our creed, still feel churchyards to be uncanny after dark), they conceived it as subsisting in the gloom and dust of cavernous "Sheol," not experiencing reward or punishment, seemingly unconscious, and unable even to praise, any more, its God. The extreme melancholy, confusion, and relative unreality of this place and state brood dismally over the whole Book of Job. Yet, in the very heart of that anxious poem, struck out by stress precisely of the unjust conditions of the years of Earth, and by the natural human demand for some recognition over and above that of conscience, is a flash of exultant certainty. Job cries that the sufferer indeed may die, but that he *knows* his Vindicator lives, and that after all human judges have said their say, *He* will stand up and have the last word against them, and "I shall see God, whom I, yes, I shall see, and my eyes behold."[1]

A declaration like Daniel's (xii. 2–3) is different: "Many of those

[1] Job xix. 25–7. I select from these verses no more than what is useful here; and do not ask, e.g. whether Job says that "from," i.e. away from; without, "his flesh," he shall see God, or, "from his flesh," i.e. from within it, as I watch plain "from" hill, or indeed, as now I see things. In either case, the assertion that he will be personally aware of God and of God's public verdict, is definite. Even if he says: "and after my skin hath been thus struck off, *yet even so*, even without my flesh, I shall see God; God, not as a stranger, but on my side": even if he says that his Vindicator shall stand up *upon* that very dust into which his body shall have fallen, to close the debate in his favour —yet the declaration of a surviving conscious spirit is complete and firm. Perhaps more than that is included in Job's words; but there at least is that. It is a comprehensive moral problem that he is envisaging; and its adequate solution demands that the innocent accused, as well as his accusers, shall be aware of his final rehabilitation, even if this occur after the body's death.

that sleep in the dust of the earth, shall awake; some unto life everlasting, and others unto reproach, to see it always.

"But they that are learned shall shine as the brightness of the firmament: and they that instruct many to justice, as stars for all eternity."

While the action of Judas Machabees displays the belief of his time issuing into action and cult:

Making a gathering, he sent 12,000 drachms of silver to Jerusalem for sacrifice to be offered for the sins of the dead, thinking well and religiously concerning the resurrection (for if he had not hoped that they that were slain should rise again, it would have seemed superfluous and vain to pray for the dead), and because he considered that they who had fallen asleep with godliness, had great grace laid up for them.

It is therefore a holy and wholesome thought to pray for the dead, that they may be loosed from sins.

It was then in function of the national moral consciousness, sanctioned throughout by God, that Jewish religion in this point, too, developed. There were many hesitations, no doubt, and tentative, inchoate plannings out of the religious field and its horizon; but certain tendencies define themselves. A kingdom was to come, which should be at once the triumph of the Chosen People and of Righteousness. The whole nation should share in it; those, too, therefore, who had died before its coming. Just as the outlook wavered as regarded the Heathen, who were foreseen as destroyed, or subjugated, or again converted, so, too, it was not clear whether the wicked themselves were destined to immortality or annihilation. But in the interim the individual soul itself was increasingly felt to be in a state not of sleep merely, but of reward or punishment; and the prospect of a Kingdom which should at least in part be on the earth, with Jerusalem for its centre, involved not merely a spiritual survival of the soul, but some sort of resurrection of the flesh. "I know that he shall rise again at the Last Day," said Martha of her brother. Even, during that interspace, souls might be helped by prayer, and this prayer were neither "holy" nor "pious," but futile, were there no such resurrection (2 Macc. xii. 39–46). By the period of Apocalyptic literature (quite roughly, the last B.C. century, and of course after that), there was no substantial element in what makes up the Christian eschatology—apart from the personal share in it by Christ, though the person of the Messiah was well involved in this picture of the Judgment—which may not be found in some document or other expressive of Jewish beliefs.

But there was not much of homogeneous in all this, and no generally accepted consistent scheme. It might have been impossible to find any one Jew who would assert a theory or belief about the future life with the clear consciousness of its forming part of the national creed, that you would find entertained by a Catholic as to the faith of the Church.

However, it is clear that when our Lord began to preach, no one (save the Sadducees) dreamt of denying the survival of the soul, and all agreed that the Righteous would share in the ever more spiritually conceived triumph and glory and an everlasting reward of the Kingdom, and that the wicked would be punished; and most, perhaps, would have held that prayer for the predestined was a holy and availing practice.

(ii)

Our Lord in His preaching sought, we may dare affirm to administer at the outset the minimum of shock. And, throughout, He purified and developed what he found, and did not contradict it. Like the Baptist, He began with Repentance and the Coming of the Kingdom. Nor did He then or later announce any new or startling eschatology. He did not contradict any substantial article in the belief, which He found about the other world, nor repudiate the practice of praying for departed souls, but even spoke of sins to be "forgiven," not in this world alone, but "in the next."

It was in function, then, of the past history of His people that our Lord first of all proclaimed that doctrine of which the implications were to prove so sublime. Even He made use of the pictorial phraseology of the past; He spoke, not rarely, in "Apocalyptic dialect" and described, for example, the heathen as "sitting down" to God's celestial feast together with the patriarchs.

That He announced man's spiritual destiny in terms of reward and punishment, no one attempts to deny. Fully "juridical" is His scheme. "The Judge shall sit and the books shall be opened and it shall be rendered to every man according to his works." "Come, ye blessed of My Father; receive the Kingdom." "Depart, ye cursed, into the everlasting fire prepared for the devil and his angels." Strict was the correspondence between that fate and this life. "Inasmuch as ye have done it. . . . Inasmuch as ye have done it not." "Fear ye not them that kill the body, and are not able to kill the soul: but rather fear him that can destroy both soul and body into hell" (Matt. x. 28). "Father, those that Thou hast given Me, I will that where I am there they also may be with Me, that they may see the glory which Thou gavest Me" (John xvii. 24).

Into the metaphysics of eternity, it is true, He does not go; nor would His hearers have had minds even remotely prepared to receive any such instruction. Not prepared were they, even, as they should have been, to receive His moral doctrine.[1]

It is, however, mainly in the Gospel and Epistles of St. John that the deeper values of this doctrine of the soul's survival and judgment and reward are to be looked for. On these I touch below.

(iii)

As for St. Paul, it is clear that our Resurrection is the very first consequence of our union with Christ. As we are co-crucified and co-buried with Him, so are we bound to rise, too, and reign with Him, because from the dead He rose and dies no more. That is the whole essence of his argument in 1 Cor. xv. If Christ be not risen, then neither do *we* rise; there is no hereafter; we may live out this earth-life as best we can; if we spend it in a series of sacrifices for the sake of a future which is never to be ours, we are "of all men most miserable," having lost this world, and having no chance to gain another. "But now *is* Christ risen from the dead," the first-fruits, only, of those who must needs sleep in death. Rightly then is our earth-life so orientated towards eternity, that even now our way of living should be "in heaven."

What is deepest of all in St. Paul, I again reserve to allude to later on. Here I will but say that none is more relentless than he in emphasizing, too, the juridical aspect of death and judgment and destiny. "It is appointed to all men once to die, and after that the judgment." "The Lord Jesus shall be revealed from heaven in a flame of fire, yielding vengeance to them who know not God, and who obey not the Gospel of our Lord Jesus Christ; who shall suffer eternal punishment in destruction, from the face of the Lord" (2 Thess. i. 7–9) (literally, shall pay as penalty eternal destruction).

[1] Notice, that whatever He says of celestial felicity, He says too of damnation. I say this to anticipate criticism based on the Greek ἀιώνιος, which some would translate not "everlasting," but "long-enduring," æonian. What it means as applied to woe, it must mean applied to bliss; and it remains that the content of that elastic word must be judged from the contexts, and is not absolute.

"The smoke of their torments shall go up for ever and ever" (Apoc. xiv. 11; cf. xix. 3, xx. 10).

On the other hand, those who "die in the Lord" shall be for ever with Him; and I need do no more than recall those judgment scenes of the Apocalypse, with their terrible and exultant imagery, and their declaration of an eternity of weal or woe for the saved or unrepentant soul.

III

I will now outline the Church's doctrine on this subject.

Each man's soul is created by God, and is immortal, and will in fact exist for ever.

Those who are baptized and die without grave personal unrepented sin, and with all "venial" sin forgiven, and all debts paid, go forthwith to heaven and enjoy for ever the supernatural vision of and union with God, and their consequences.

Those who die without grace and with grave personal sin unrepented, go forthwith to hell, where they are eternally deprived of the vision of God, and suffer, too, that penalty of sense which Christ, and the Church after Him, describe as fire.

Those who die in a state of grace, but with venial sin unrepented or with their debt of temporal punishment unpaid, are detained in purgatory till such time as they are perfectly fit to enter the presence of God. In purgatory they are assisted by our prayers and in particular by the Sacrifice of the Mass.

At the Consummation we shall all of us rise again with our own bodies, to glory or to destruction.

(i)

I wish to approach this grave subject very slowly, and emphasizing certain principles, and eliminating, on the way, certain difficulties which arise from the disregard of them.

There is a *sort* of objection which, in itself, must be allowed no weight, but which bulks large in popular imagination, because, precisely, from the imagination it arises.

The simplest example is afforded by the catch-phrases, that white robes, golden crowns, and palms form no alluring prospect; and that "if heaven is like that," we don't want it. This naive materialistic "difficulty" is not common among educated folks, but others, essentially similar, are. Such are, that in heaven there will be nothing left to do: nothing to fight for; nothing to become. But with action, effort, and growth, is linked, in our present condition, most of our happier experiences. Only the lazy, or the very tired, like "peace," that is, "inertia." Or again, that no one could spend eternity even in praising God. This implies not only a confusion of thought which suggests that what we like now is effort, fight, growth *as such*, and not rather the victory, or at least the expression of strength, that is, of personality and life involved in each moment of these; but, a similar reflection into the future life, by means of imagination, of what we are accustomed to in this. We still picture it containing a very sublimated, purified edition of what we judge to be good behaviour here; heaven is visioned as the supremest form of church-going, and the never-ending praise of God as, after all, the recitation of some interminable psalter.

No one may scorn imagery, if only because we simply cannot avoid it. Imagination accompanies the most abstract of ideas: when we think "circle," we half see *a* circle; when we think "whiteness," we see, flickering, *something white*, or even the ghostly letters of that word. We should not therefore rebuke those who describe, or have described, what "eye hath not seen nor ear heard nor hath it entered into the heart of man to conceive," in terms of colour, music, and thought (for thoughts themselves are images); and some imagery has grown consecrated by long use, or because of its author's dignity, or for the sake of its intrinsic beauty Biblical imagery has always the first two claims, and often the third, on our respect; yet it is true that despite the extraordinary sublimity of most of the Apocalyptic imagery, for example, some of it has grown alien, and even distasteful, to modern feeling; such are those "four Beings full of eyes within and without," around God's throne; such, for a different reason, the Woman crying out in the pains of childbirth; such, even, we may reverently say, Christ's traditional portrayal of heaven as a celestial banquet. Where the imagery helps no more, we may lay it aside, even if it be His; and we *must always* transcend it, in search for the imaged Truth.

Probably, however, modern instinct recoils less from the pictured happiness of Heaven, than from the fiery scenes of Hell.

Are, then, Catholics free to declare that hell's "fire" like heaven's palms and crowns, is *mere* imagery, and that to it nothing physical corresponds? No one supposes Catholics to mean, when speaking of it, "fire of coals," as they say; do we therefore imply that it indicates a mental suffering *only*? No. Theologians would declare that to be unsafe and rash; and say that it is, technically, "certain" that lost souls are affected by some agent, physical, it would seem, and other than themselves. Doubtless the problem is somewhat falsified by our tendency to regard "fire" as a kind of separate thing, and not rather as a form of energy acting through matter. Unless, then, we are prepared to assert that in no way whatsoever can a soul be brought into vital contact with matter in whatsoever state, we cannot deny all *meaning* to the phrase that "fire" torments them. Yet observe, it *is* the soul which suffers. When, below, something will be said about the "resurrection" of the body, the image of "bodies of fire" will be found to be far from valueless in this connection.[1]

A careful course must then here be steered. Without *some* imagery you may succeed in so weakening your notions of heaven and hell that they come to represent nothing whatsoever. Yet, as I said, no sense-images, nor really thought-imagery, are in any way adequate to the spiritual fact, and *materialism* is not a reproach which ever can be brought against the Catholic dogma. But never, assuredly, will Catholics consent to discard the words Christ used, nor to dilute the terrible reality of His revelation, for the sake of modern nerves.

(ii)

However, most men would indignantly deny that their dislike for the doctrine of hell was in the last resort an affair of nerves, and a sensitive abhorrence of suffering as such. What they resent is the whole idea of such appalling punishment, and definitely, that it should be called "eternal." In fact, this singular phenomenon is seen. The revolt against Catholic dogma, out of which issued the Protestant sects, included a contemptuous denial of purgatory, but insisted fiercely upon hell: nowadays, those who believe in after-

[1] We should not under-stress, nor over-stress, the Biblical use of "fire." To start with, it is well embedded in general Apocalyptic dialect, and that is largely "pictorial." And once, at any rate, when our Lord uses it, He couples this unquenched "fire" with the "undying worm"; and whether or no this image be based on the burnings of dead bodies, or refuse, or of Moloch sacrifices, said by some to have taken place in the Valley of Hinnom, whence the name Gehenna, it remains that the "worm" is plainly metaphorical, so that the "fire" in this sentence of parallel members, should be taken so, too, *rather than* "literally." Similarly, when *Genesis* shows us God first moulding a clay figure, and then "breathing in" a soul through its nostrils, and so making man, we should act arbitrarily in regarding the statue as "real" when the "breathing" is clearly metaphorical; for God does not breathe, nor is the soul His breath.

death suffering at all, insist that it shall be purely purgatorial, and it is hell they will have none of. And the ground they take is moral, involving the whole character of human life on the one side, and our very conception of God upon the other; there is nothing in humanity, they would urge, to which hell could be proportionate: punishment which is not medicinal, is in itself immoral; God's justice no less than His mercy, His power equally with His love, are affronted if we conceive of Him as creating, or allowing "hell."

Modern minds are not the first to have felt, poignantly, this problem.

The Scriptures indeed and the earliest Church leave us in no doubt as to the doctrine of hell as Catholics now teach it having been an integral part of the aboriginal Christian creed.[1] It is, perhaps, Clement of Alexandria who first displays an inclination to suggest that the pains of hell may be "instructive," and therefore, presumably, not endless. But it was the speculative allegorist Origen who introduced a momentary hesitation into Catholic thought by his adaptation of the "circle" theory of existence which should bring about the "restitution" of all things. He influenced Gregory of Nazianzus, Jerome, Athanasius even; Gregory of Nyssa, I think, especially; but neither did these writers settle down into a belief contrary to the Catholic dogma; and despite his enormous influence, he was consistently condemned, sometimes by name, by Catholic authority. Catholic tradition does, however, admit that the sufferings of hell are not the same for all, even as the sins of all are not the same.

But none of this truly touches the moral problem. Where, however, that problem coincides with the whole mystery of evil, and how a good God could create a world in which sin and sorrow might find place, we must perforce refer the reader to the chapter which deals professedly with that. Here, I would only touch upon this subject in so far as it concerns *eternal* condemnation and the final loss of the soul.

Well, then, however great a sinner, a man cannot deserve *that.*

[1] Nothing can be based on the New Testament word κόλασις, "punishment." Not even in Classical Greek is the word always used of "educational" or "medicinal" punishment; and in N.T. Greek παίδευσις serves usually for that. And in those very myths of Plato and others, by the help of which rather later Christian writers are thought by some to have coloured their eschatology, and in which *most* souls undoubtedly were "educationally" punished, there was always a residue of the "incurable."

He doesn't know what he is doing: he is too weak to carry through the good he knows: there is not *malice* enough in the world to warrant hell. Wherefore God cannot be just, and send a man there; cannot be powerful and wise, if He fail to invent, and neglect to create, a world in which nothing shall make hell possible; cannot be merciful, if He punish *at all* from "vengeance"; cannot be loving, if He can support, in His eternal bliss, the knowledge that souls are damned; cannot be God at all, if He thus makes a world, and fail to make it a "success." Even the loss of one soul were failure.

Such is the grave and cumulative indictment against a God who sends a soul to hell.

We must state first that it is not revealed how many souls, or what proportion, are lost. Most Catholics would say that we know that Judas is; yet, for the human race, we have no knowledge of numbers or proportions; but that angels are "lost," we know; and if even one "soul" be lost, the problem stands. Our perspective may be shifted, but the fact remains.

Next, it is clear that Catholic dogma equally implies, that *if* a man be condemned, he deserved to be. The moment we can truly say, he did not know, or he could not help his sin . . . God has said that well first; and if we can see reasons for mercy that are true reasons and not unjust excuses, God sees many more. Sins of passion —well, "weakness" does go far to account for them: sins of pride, ignorance makes them possible. But never shall we permit ourselves to say that man *can never* do better than he does, or know more than he does. Some culpability survives. But is it enough? is it incurable? Well, for all that is not *quite* enough, that is only *just* rectified, purgatory exists. Even that most appalling thing to see— the man whose role in life seems simply to be putrefactive; who seems, passionlessly, to choose just to corrupt innocence—he must *know* it to be corruption; and it must be innocence—well, even of these I have now and again asked myself whether this be not due to a desire for power grown tyrannical in a man who has become so morally shrunken as to know he cannot exercise power for betterment, but can, by spoiling; and so just spoils, less for love of the spiritual decay he causes, than for love of the sense of *causing something*—and indeed, something so very vital and hence so great. The sin may be different from what it seems, and its excuse, if any, where we do not seek for it. The capability of good—perhaps of great good—may still be there. Easier is this realized in those who seem to be lustful irremediably. The power of worshipping true beauty, the capacity for true love is there, or may be, yet the torrential personality is diverted and hurled out upon the parody, the idol. And perhaps by the tiniest shift of bias, this out-streaming self may be redirected to the true, and the soul saved; for all the while it was seeking, in the distorted caricature, the pure loveliness which it was, in truth, desiring. If we then can guess that, much more can God have knowledge of it; and it grows wholly clear, that, however much *God* may perchance in justice pronounce sentence on a soul, *we never may*.

Ignorant, then, are they of human nature, and of God, who deride death-bed conversions, as though they must needs be insincere. Who knows what astounding shiftings of the personality may not, at that unique moment, and in unplumbed depths of the self, take place —nay, even, one would say, *must* take place in the all but discarnate soul, or have the chance of taking place? Foolish are they who sneer at the anxious effort of the Church, and her eager giving of the Sacraments even to the seemingly unconscious, or to the hardened sinner if but there be *some* symptom that his will has become susceptible of their effects; or even, it may be, short of that, you may almost *suppose* that in the interior soul that divine mysterious recognition and embrace is happening, which by no exterior symptom can express itself.

Here, then, you must remember that the Forgiveness of Sins is an article of our Creed. Here is no arbitrary condemnation in mid-life; no fatal mechanistic series; no Karma, even. There is only one complete, irreversible soul-suicide, the act of dying with the will rebellious against God's. After all, man is limited. The soul, I said, has an appetite for the infinite; yet not infinite is the soul. It is conceivable that the soul may so pour itself out into an act of knowledge, that it can do no more; it has *become* its knowledge; it is its own act; time exists no more for it. So, too, it is conceivable that a soul may, as it were, exhaust itself in an act of will: it has fully expressed itself in its choice; it *is* that will, then; the soul may *make itself* what is opposed to God. That gigantic act may indeed occur; it *is* an evil self; it is its own worst hell.

But this carries us beyond the juridical aspect of the problem on which these "moral" difficulties are based. From the side of man they disappear if it be recalled that man, if he finds himself "in hell," has *put himself* there. No Calvinist predestination is ours. "This is the will of God, your sanctification." "God wills that all men should be saved." Who dare say that Judas, who betrayed, sinned worse than Peter, who denied? But Judas despaired; Peter yielded to the sweet solicitation of God's grace. There is the difference.

And on God's side we have to recall that in Him all is one—mercy, justice, power, love. Only our limited, inexhaustive, analysing intellect sets these "attributes" as it were one against the other. He *cannot* defeat His mercy by His justice, nor justice by mercy; both are knowledge: in all He is being true to Himself; His action is His Self; He alone *is*, in the full sense, His Self. No deviation from the True Right is possible, on His part, without His ceasing to be God. This we *know* unerringly. Of the moral aspect of what we know we judge; and in human verdicts is room for almost every error.

As I said, the heart of this problem, in all save the one point of eternity, lies elsewhere, and coincides with the wider "difficulty" of evil. Yet this may be suggested: God, we are bound to say, *could* have created a world where there was no temptation, or where souls should have been so deluged with "grace" that they would never have yielded to temptation. In fact, in heaven, angels and saved souls are free, yet "cannot" sin. However, from our end of the series, I say that men *want* an effort and a hazardous one, at that. If they knew that, however slack they were, they yet were *certain* ultimately to succeed, by some *relatively coercive* help, then all elasticity, all spring of action would be gone, for many if not for each. The walls of God's City are high, and the moat deep. Yet even so we demand the escalade, and would resent a crane. "I *can* slip, I know; I can even try to plunge . . . yet never shall I fail to reach the battlements. . . ." No: I must be free to fail. There will be hours, no doubt, when I feel myself so weary or so perverse that I shall then call on God to "save me in spite of myself." I cry with St. Augustine, than whom none has better fathomed the deficiencies of human nature, his own to start with: "*Nostras etiam rebelles ad te compelle voluntates*:" "Even when our wills rebel, Lord, our wills to Thee compel." But we shall have *chosen* that uncoercive violence. We are still supplying the bare minimum of effort.

Is there not here, perhaps, a "false problem"? I mean, one of which the solution would depend on our adequate knowledge of two facts of each of which we know but part. If we try to "reconcile" them, we may be using for that purpose precisely those parts in which the element of reconciliation does not reside. Any reconciliation so effected, would necessarily be illusory and false. Now this problem of God's having created such a world, "despite" His knowledge that man could and would, in it, misuse his opportunities and nature, concerns two liberties and their interaction; ours and God's. But not even our own liberty can we truly analyse. Of it we have a direct intuition which is basic and cannot be cast aside. Deny it, and every step forward in life denies your own denial. But it eludes adequate analysis. Still less is the liberty of God to be grasped by human intellect. It is in our liberty we most resemble God; and continue—baffling paradox—so to resemble Him precisely when and because we freely defy Him. Here, then, is our human freedom mysterious enough; and there, divine Freedom, a full mystery. False is the problem that arises for us from a contradiction between two terms neither of which we fully understand, and indeed between those elements in them precisely, which are those we do not understand. It may then be said that so terribly does God *respect* this transcendent fact of liberty, even this participated liberty of ours, that His esteem for it outstrips (to put it humanly) His desire even for our happiness, and thus, even a world where liberty has been misused is not a failure.

Another less poignant moral problem before I pass on. "Heaven is itself immoral." To do right for reward's sake, is wrong. No. That is nonsense. Right *should* be rewarded. Effort implies *life*, and creates a claim for more life. That increase of life is effort's fitting—you may say necessary—reward. By acting rightly, I exist better, and have a greater capacity for good. Good *should*, then, come to me. Else there is disproportion. I should, then, *desire* this; seek for more life; earn it; resent the injustice which refuses it. Thus does society itself develop. I am right, then, to act, positively, *in view* of it. But I may, too, act disinterestedly; do that which shall bring me reward, yet not *for* that; regretting it, even, in the human area, lest the prospect spoil my "pure intention"; even, lest I be thought to have worked for "pay" alone. Yet not for that should the reward *not* reach me. I may act, for parent or friend, just for their sake, indignant, bewildered, at mention of "return." Yet reciprocated love, at least, is due. Even if I choose to act, serve, love, *in secret*, none the less a singular sweetness, a consciousness of betterment ensues. I *am* the better: I *am* more "man." The increase of my life, unasked, unsought, has happened. (So with pleasure: I need not act for pleasure, or may subordinate it; but on every increase of well-*being* attends its "pleasure," and I could only discard that, by destroying life.)

But when the result of my good actions is the increase of my share in God's life, I may act as disinterestedly as I please, but I cannot regret or refuse even the result, and in fact must seek it, for He is life. Christ came to give that "more abundant life" which I by instinct crave. It is my will to do His will: but His will is my salvation. My true self is my saved self: I *am* my heaven. Suicidal arrogance, to reject this; futility, to elude it; true self-realization, *because* true self-tradition; achievement, *because* sacrifice; renunciation is a function of desire. I want to love God: therefore, to be united with Him; therefore, "to be in heaven."

(iii)

Before passing on to that which most of all I want to say, I would recall that error arises not only from a misapplication of our imagination, and from many a false problem suggested by moral judgment insufficiently co-ordinated and valued as exhaustive, but from this fact, that whatever I know of God is known "analogically,"[1] and that my thought can never comprehend Him. What I know of God is, or can be, true as far as it goes, with that limited truth which is proper to human ideas, even the most abstract and irresistible. But I can never state, with adequate truth, anything at all about God. All in Him is independent, self-existing, infinite; all my ideas even, when most "refined" and purified, are drawn from the dependent and the finite, and are held by me as such. Therefore my human mind as such can never know God as He is; nor in any possible contingency, *comprehend* Him; and whenever I think even about finite things, not only I do not fully understand them in themselves, but am driven, when I think of them in their relation to God, to make statements in which I forthwith see an element of falsity is at least suggested, and I must at once deny it. Thus, if my bias is towards the otherness, the self-contained unithood of the Universe, I feel myself driven to think of God as "outside" it, and Himself as having an "exterior": if I lean towards the contemplation of God's infinity, and of His total presence everywhere, I all but fall into pantheism. If I reflect that all things stand in relation to Him, I seem to make Him finite as they are; if I perceive that He is in no relation to them, they on their side fade and seem to become nothing.

[1] See pp. 58 *seq.*

Let me illustrate this—the illustration is imperfect—by Art. The artist draws a charcoal sketch. "That is my friend." "Your friend?" "His image." "But it is just black and white—an outline—flat." "Yes; but, made with these materials, that is his image; *he*; he looks out through it. . . ." The artist colours it; makes, if you will, a statue, and tints that. Even though all should be enraptured over the portrait, or the statue, they will not take it for the adequately imaged person; indeed, that which in the statue or portrait really "lives" is the spirit of the artist; or rather the spirit of his friend, as caught *across* the flesh and eyes and hair, as met and welcomed and "mated" by the spirit of the artist, and committed to the paint or the marble. For notice, what the true artist *sees* is not merely—is least of all—the coloured surfaces, the curves, the bulks; not even their interrelation, the *whole* they conspire to form; but most of all what St. Thomas would have called the *splendor formae*, which does not mean the loveliness of shape, but the *eradiation* of that inner vital principle which gives intelligibility to the whole, which gives the thing its selfhood; nay, that which the shapes and colours may disguise, which would be lost by mere photography, by *copying*; which flashes forth perhaps for the artist only, so that he may have to rearrange, reconstruct, apparently even to deform the physical elements, for the sake of Truth and Being. Even the artist may will to see in his "subject" only the spiritual element of design: hence the vagaries of many modern artists; or only, perhaps, the *idea* suggested; hence the strange paintings of another modern school. Not that the artist ought to *excogitate* the idea from the offered material: he should *see* it, and paint truthfully to what he has seen; still less should he compose an idea of Nature, in, so to say, his studio, and then proceed to alter what he observes in favour of what he thinks. That is as academic an extreme as sheer reproduction. But he needs vision, and the vision of the true artist is of the True.

Consider, too, our efforts to conceive, and to express, what is multiple and yet one. In the human body are vast numbers of live cells: think of them as such, and you cannot count them up. Each is itself. And yet they form one body, one *living* body; they must not be so thought of, that is, as many, each complete: they have no sense, separately; they are meant to meet in that higher unity, and make one thing. Yet what a strain to keep those two ideas, multiplicity and unity, simultaneously in the mind: how hard to correlate them; how impossible to express both of them together; how seemingly contradictory are they, if we express them separately. So of the unity "composed" of soul and body. The Man is one whole; yet soul is not body, nor body, soul. So of a social unit, like the state. So of a most multiple unit, like the Church.

What we must do is to state each part of the truth as perfectly as may be, continually safeguarding ourselves from misapprehension even within our own minds, lest we be taken, or take ourselves to be stating the whole elusive truth. In matters of dogma we have the Church's guidance: "You must say this, you must say that; both are true, neither is exhaustively true; the way of reconciliation not you can fully see; *seen* reconciliation, in itself, is unneeded; but the results of the twofold mystery are yours to use and to enjoy. God is One, God is Three. Jesus is God, and He is Man. You are many; in Him you are one. The whole Trinity is wholly in you; but not you are It." We shall dutifully meditate these terrible mysteries, guided by God Himself; but not with *them* shall we quarrel, nor deny their truth, since not even human "mysteries," which we see to be true, can we analyse without destroying them. In fine, only the Infinite can comprehend itself.

IV

Holding this in mind, I would ask you to consider the following view of a soul's destiny. In it, I no longer use the "juridical" framework for our thoughts, but what I may call the vital and cosmic aspect of the matter, and after a while, this aspect super-naturalized and raised to the plane of which this book has consistently treated.[1]

(i)

Consider the soul, for the moment, apart from any idea of grace and the supernatural.

Separated from the body it passes into a mode of being where it operates along of its intrinsic powers, without communication from the senses. New problems at once arise—how it can know material things at all; how it can know this individual from that; what, and in what "shape," it can remember, what indeed is its principle of

[1] To make this transition is somewhat as though I were to pass from considering the Unity of the Church from the governmental point of view, to observing it as owing to its inner law of life, its proper cohesive social bond, in the long run, once more, super-natural. Both these bonds, outer and inner, are real, and operate in function of one another. Similarly the juridical aspect of heaven, hell, purgatory is legitimate, inevitable, traditional and authoritative. Yet it is inexhaustive and analogical.

distinction which keeps to it its own individuality. We know into what straits the greatest philosophers have been driven when contemplating this. The solutions to these problems do not concern us here; and never can we *imagine* at all its way of being and of operating, precisely *because* they are wholly super-sense, whereas on sense our imagination is entirely dependent.

But what is clear is that the soul keeps its own intrinsic power of knowing and of willing, and that in the way co-naturally suited to itself; it is *better* off for the contemplation of universal ideas,[1] and it is altogether rid of the innumerable distractions and illusions and the fragmentariness of the physical universe, and of the narrowings and contrasts and crippled reflections and refractions which the senses imposed upon it. Therefore, if the soul be not in some way injured and half dead, it exults to unite itself precisely to that which made such difficulty for it when it was in the body. It can do what Plato longed to do, and dispense with the imperfect twangings of the strings, and be aware of the essential music; it is no more at the mercy of things *always a little* wrong, and can contemplate the True Beauty; it is emancipated from that which so clothes the Truth as to make it always to some degree a lie, and can fly like an arrow to the undiminished Reality.

Therefore it grows *cosmic*. It enters into true spiritual communion with what it has loved and loves, but has been separated from so terribly by a thousand barriers of the flesh—for, love as I may, guess intuitively as I may the beloved's thoughts, yet can I not see through eyes that are not mine, think through another's brain: the chasm between individuals is unbridged, unplumbed, and doubly so when they are spirit-flesh, and the senses sunder the souls; and so true is this, that, unless a *spiritual* barrier exist, far closer already may the communion be between two, of whom one still lives this earth-life, while the other has passed out of it, nearer, that is, on that other's side, if not on mine. Physical death, then, separates indeed the bodies of two friends, but the one who has "died" on his side, at any rate, may be spiritually "nearer" and more intimately operative than ever before.[2] Most intimate, then, were such a soul's com-

[1] I do not discuss "how" or "where."

[2] I set to one side the problem of telepathy, and also of "direct intuition." I believe that two souls may, even though "in the flesh," interact directly, though this may not be normal, and is not to be relied on, nor be used as argument. I wish, however, to write a line on spiritualism. It professes to prove, and to describe in a measure, the other world. Also, to put us in contact with souls who have passed over, and thus to comfort mourners. I will briefly

munion with each soul it loves; different its knowledge, more unitive a thousand times its love. Different, too, its union with the society of souls, now that it can know differently precisely what unites, i.e. the vital, social, unitive link; instead of, as here, the material coefficient first and sharpest, which is what divides. Different, too, its knowledge of all that is most intimate and super-sensual in nature's self; more complete its communion with all that too; more universal in scope; more penetrative and from within. Cosmic has this soul grown, or may grow; and so precisely has human intelligence fastened on this glory of its future, that the Church itself has had more than once to condemn the exaggeration of that truth, the concentration on one aspect of it only, and to assert that there is not but one World-Soul, one Cosmic Being.

For individuality survives. There is no question of the soul's being *absorbed* into anything whatsoever. What is spiritual has no parts, and is not capable of emitting emanations, throwing off sparks, falling into fragments which shall be re-collected and identified. It is, really, the indolence of the East which, concentrating on the undoubted truth of the Unity into which are to be harmonized all differences, finds a quick way out of the problem by saying that, ultimately, the differences *cease to be*. The practical West, on the

state that those who admit the doctrines expressed in this book need no proof of the survival of the soul or of the existence of the world of souls; nor yet any information of its spiritual topography. Spiritualism can tell them nothing new about the other world, just as it has never told, so far, anything of scientific, literary, social, artistic, or religious value about this. Further, the element of fraud in its practice has always been very great; much of the remainder of its phenomena seem all-but demonstrably due to the legitimate, yet very rare, operation of psychic laws; some, further, of the reduced remainder, to the unwholesome operation of such laws—the silencing of thought and will, in a seance, must almost be *assumed* to induce a psychic dislocation, in which the soul may work, but work awry; and this would account for the "rickety" state as I would describe it—short indeed of lunacy or sheer moral breakdown in most cases—to which those who practise spiritualism usually seem reduced; finally, a residue of experiences I quite admit to be, more probably than not, due to spiritual agencies. But, since spiritualists, who *ex hypothesi* believe *in* spirits, cannot and do not deny the possibility of the existence of evil spirits, those who expose themselves naked to *any* spiritual agency, do so to the evil too (I do not insist on this, that automatic writing continually reveals blasphemy and obscenity uncharacteristic of the normal writer: the super-consciousness is, so to say "anæsthetized," and the subconsciousness, full of what has been *repressed* into it, surges up and disgorges it. To this the psycho-therapeutists must attend). Finally, there is absolute impossibility of knowing with *what* spirit you hold converse—quite apart from the usual method of that converse: enquirer, medium, control, communicating spirit. What if an incident be alluded of which you only, and your dead friend, had cognizance? You only and he *of living men* had cognizance. Myriads of spirits may have been present at that incident; any of these can be author of the allusion!

whole, observes the differences, and does not trouble to speculate on the mode of their unification. Each side sacrifices part of the truth in order to *see* the solution of the problem, or to shoulder aside, in the interests of action or of peace, all problem whatsoever. Catholic philosophy—for we have not been saying this *as* part of our faith, but of a philosophy: it is part of a philosophy a Catholic may hold, and in keeping thoroughly with that philosophy which underlies Catholic theology—well, our philosophy keeps firm hold on both truths, and insists on a unification by way of organized individualities, as in the human body, so in society; and so, at least in tendency, in the Universe. Therefore, in the most cosmic unification, individuality survives.

(ii)

But what builds up personality most of all? The will. What, then, if the will have been egoist, separatist, a Pharisee of a will? The very soul has received into itself a bias towards self-isolation. What, then, becomes of such a soul, when it reaches a world in which its whole business is unification, self-harmonization with the Universe? It must be, one would say, on a psychic rack. All the *will* built up of years of choices, sets away from what alone it is fitted for. *At last*, one can conceive it as slowly submitting to the right "twist," the corrective influence, the painful, gradual process of adaptation, of correlation; the dislocated self must be reset. Such were—in this rationalizing, speculative scheme—its co-natural purgatory. An illustration may make clearer what I mean by the possibility of man's sinking from level to level, and dwindling all the while in personality. Most of us will have met persons progressively victims to drink, drugs, or sex. Horizon after horizon becomes curtained off; field after field of action prohibited; wish after wish, hope, effort, will, extinguished. The world has become drink, or the opium dream. "I live for that. . . . There's nothing else." When *that* becomes impossible, even the lower "harmony," the "peace" of drunkenness or of drug or of afterlust itself becomes impossible. Nothing remains save a sort of *self-conscious nothing*; an affinity for life, and no life livable. Suicide is the escape attempted, unless a rescue be effected, and the long agonizing process of the soul's reconstruction, readaptation, reassociation with the world. Like God's action, indeed, is that of men who can attempt that work for a soul so all-but "lost."

Can we imagine, however, a soul, so rooted in its egoism, so proudly resolved on isolation, that no conspiring forces could achieve its reunion with the society of the Cosmos? Alas! why not? We can conceive a mind so sunk from level to level of existence, as to be disassociated once and for all from the higher levels it has sacrificed. Again and again nature is not mechanical, where souls are being spoken of. There is nothing that shall *force* it back on to a higher plane in the great organism. Nature is manifold in planes, in levels of existence. I see no reason in the essence of things why such a soul should not have willed itself into existence on some lower level, and there survive—by its own chosen law of *being*—as but the meanest element in the Totality, even *out* of all vital union with that Universe. Such were its hell.

Let us leave aside this pitiable possibility. Let us conceive the soul to have succeeded according to its nature. Two affinities belong to it. It has been, nay, it has *made* man. That was what it was meant for. It was not an angel; why should it ever be? As pure spirit, its existence were something alien to its history: in a sense, it suffers wrong until it has reconstituted the unity which ever was its function. Reason can never prove that, "naturally," a soul should end its triumph by reconstituting, together with matter, a human whole, the unit *man*; yet that were conceivable as fitting and to be desired. Man is not *mean*: from the completed Universe, *man* should not be eliminated. There would be loss, were there no eyes to *see* the colours of the clouds, prismatic spray, the curving clematis, the iris and the rose. Not for no hearing should the waves fall in music, the leaves whisper in the woods, and the lark tremble into song. Not into irresponsive emptiness should the warm earth exhale her fragrance, and the spring its sweetness. Even should all this cease, as cease for this our globe it ultimately shall, yet shall the Universe not fail to hold and to exhibit its myriad challenge to the senses. Pity were it, should no soul be able, from its place in that vast unity, to have joy in all these things, and render thanks.

For, at the opposite extreme, the soul knows God. How should it not? Though even so, it see Him not "face to face," but know Him in His image that is Nature, yet all, as I said, that is most true and real, universal and alive in that Nature, it knows; all that is most perfectly proportionate to pure intelligence, it knows, and all of it, it loves. Straight, then, to the source of Being it ascends; straight to that which gives intelligibility to all else; straight to the Fountain of all good, the Origin of all participated truth and beauty. Indescribable event! To this God, dimly descried through sense, during its earth-life, hazily, hazardously guessed across the confused and confusing shadow-play of things, hesitatingly adhered to amid the distracting loves that clutch and cajole it, to Him the soul at last sets steadily; and from end to end of all that is, exerts its essential energy. Such is its heaven.[1]

(iii)

Now I will ask you to recall the whole scheme of Catholic supernatural dogma as in this book it has been set out: for what has here been said is, I repeat, a picture of the possible futures open to the soul's co-natural powers.

"Now *these* are but the outskirts of His ways, and how small a whisper do we hear of Him" (Job xxvi. 14).

Beyond the tale of Nature we have learnt how God created man, and created him with a life in him which was supernatural—and how (who knows?) man may have had a consciousness of that, not the full consciousness, no doubt, of "heaven," but a consciousness far outstripping ours of "universal" things, so that he may as it were have seen the unity of the human race in himself, and known fully what he did in defying the condition upon which he held that super-

[1] Such, therefore, is the heaven of the unbaptized yet innocent. A child, dying unbaptized, passes into natural happiness, surpassing, as we may well believe, all that earth offers of delight. Of supernatural happiness it knows nothing; for that its nature clamours not at all; to that it does not strain. Let not, then, the Catholic faith be accused of cruelty towards such. Enviable were they to us, for their assured possession of the treasure that is theirs, were it not that we now know that to us is offered a happiness transcending even theirs. But in the yet richer harmony than what we have described, they are in their place. I will add that two lines of thought are licit to a Catholic regarding the pagan who dies unbaptized. It may be supposed that very little explicit knowledge is required for a pagan to have the "confused idea" of *deus remunerator*, a God who "rewards." Such an one can, therefore, sin, but also repent, and he may be presumed to desire implicitly to believe all ascertainable truth, and to do all that may be commanded. This may be all that is asked of him, and millions may save themselves, even super-naturally, this way, provided their "faith," however undeveloped, be *fides stricte dicta*, and drawn from "revelation," though how, we know not. But to some thinkers this seems to cheapen the super-natural. They prefer to think that many pagans are assimilated in spiritual and moral things to children and pass into a natural happiness such as I have indicated: technically they are "in hell," but they are far from suffering. They do not know of the unowed, super-natural happiness others have been offered, and have won. Their *nature* is fulfilled. This hypothesis, with its limitations, was elaborated, e.g. by Fr. Joseph Rickaby, S.J. I mention it to show that Catholic thinkers are not unaware of the grave difficulty which this part of their faith occasions for many, especially nowadays. I would refer such readers to Fr. Rickaby's *In an Indian Abbey*, especially pp. 47–61; 80–83.

natural life. However that may be, defy it he did, and the conditional favour was withdrawn; and we in him, along of social solidarity, lost it likewise, and are born and have had our human history upon the "natural" plane merely. Or so should we have had it, were it not for Christ, for God's having taken human nature up so as to form with it one Person, into Himself incorporating all such of our race as should freely choose, and having chosen, persevere. Of this our Head, then, the Church is the Body, and we, in that unity, are living cells. Of the celestial yet most mercifully human economy of that Church, and of the nature of the New Life much, too, has been said, and that in it nothing of human and physical even was neglected, but that all co-operated.

Well, then, after this period of earth's experience, we pass into the world where the results of all that are made manifest.

Now, all the consequences of natural soul-success are, in the Christian revelation, retained, yet supernaturalized. Vastly clear has it been made that Grace does not stultify Nature, nor annul it. All of these unifications then, of which we have spoken, will survive, but immeasurably better. Recall, for example, what was said of the affinity of the human soul with *matter itself*. That survives. Shall we then quarrel with a dogma which asserts that the soul in heaven is, at the consummation, to *have its body*? That we are to be truly *men*; that as we now know ourselves for human, exactly that so we shall ever be? *How* soul shall be reunited with matter, to form as now a unity, why ask? How that is, even now, we know not. And of the state, precisely, of that "matter," we can say little. In fact, in violent paradox, the Church, with St. Paul, speaks of a *spiritual body*. But not of a fleshly soul, nor yet, just *soul*. Truly *ourselves* shall we then for ever be, soul-body, in perfect supernaturalized unity, neither this nor that discarded.

But before we speak of the seried planes on which the supernaturally saved achieves its union, we must first remind ourselves of what we hinted at above. Plato spoke of the "incurable" soul; Aristotle, of souls "maimed for virtue": men πεπηρωνέναι εἰς ἀρετήν: they had thrust themselves out of manhood. Alas, Faith teaches us that spirits do exist, and souls may exist, that have exhausted their whole self in their willed act of separation. I *am* my will: I am what I choose to be. Such a soul, then, at that last moment when it rejects God's grace, makes itself isolated, cleaves its own chasm, "fixes" the "great gulf." It utters its own judgment, its κρίσις, separation.

Walled within its lonely individuality; introverted, consummated in its egoism, it has share in the unities neither of world, nor of self, nor of Christ, nor of God. As near as may be the Indestructible has destroyed itself; all its greater selves it *has* destroyed; self-conscious, yet in all that counts, annihilated; pressed fiercely on by all that is, yet not unioned with it; knowing nature as its chosen enemy; linked, it too, with that matter to which it has affinity, embodied in that fire; dissociated, alas, from life and life's one Source, for which too it is thirsting—"its sin remaineth."

We know not how many thus drive themselves into the dark fire and the silence. Most of us feel, though, that we have in us some egoism; we are not willing yet for the real self-subordination to the greater union. We pass from this world, and what, then, is our fate? The soul sees God, sees what He is, and what it is. And then what happens? Look at a lover. He sees his ideal. He is in ecstasy, enskied. Perhaps in a flash his history of squandered passion is forgotten, his past falls from him, he could not think of it, he is another man with all his personality set towards his worshipped and the future. Perhaps (and better for him, maybe, it should be so) his past survives, in memory, even in instinct. But every thought of her, hope for her, makes that past hateful: what he has been, has made of himself, *is*, becomes a pain to him, but a cleansing pain, and an exultant pain just because so cleansing; in agony he draws his spiritual self up and through and out of that morass, till he becomes pure flame and mingles with her flame, and each within the other shines and is a light to the world.

That is a partial illustration of our doctrine about purgatory. The soul's vision of God's loveliness has meant a vision too of self: the actual unlikeness, the possible likeness; the present separateness, the destined union. Agony is that; but exultant cleansing agony. And let none think it a light suffering. Study yourself, and you may grow appalled to find how intertwined with the inmost fibres of life is man's self-worship; how purity of will is almost, in us, unrealizable, and, should it for a flash exist, how all-but quite impermanent. Purgatory has no days; the sun and earth measure no more years for souls there: but to our time-entangled fancy, how long, how long we feel it must be, before the taint, before the enduring aroma of the taint, have altogether passed, before the heavenward pain have altogether separated us from what alone made separation! But all the while the soul is being helped, co-operated with, by its fellow-souls, ourselves even yet on earth, in whom exists or should exist the self-same summoning grace of super-natural Life.

But the soul "in heaven," which has achieved its union, knows itself first (by "first" I mean nothing to do with time; I am trying to write upwards by logical ascents) an integral, living part of Christ's Body, which is the Church. Each within that is a living cell. Therefore not alone it *knows* the vital link which connects it with all souls on earth in whom that same life circulates, so that it can with all of this co-operate with "sympathy" as yet undreamt of, but, with all souls of every age of the world's history which now exist in that same immortal unity. With the lives of all its heroes and its saints it is now in organic touch; and with that element, indeed, within them whereby the vital contact had been however weakly established when it had knowledge of them only by "the hearing of the ear." On earth the Church exultantly celebrates "All Saints." Already with them she forms one Body. But "in heaven" the unity is revealed. "We are called 'God's sons,' and *are*: what we shall be, not yet hath been made manifest." Heaven is the making manifest of that one Eternal Life, in them and us. Our name-saints, our chosen saints, Francis, Stanislaus, Martin, Agnes and Augustine; the beggar-saints, the nun-saints; the learned men and bishops, the peasants and the princes who in Christ have triumphed; Magdalen, John and Peter; Joseph; Mary. We know, even now, Mary is our Mother; then shall the soul directly, from within itself, be conscious, too, of Motherhood. No vital tie more close: imperishably Mother of that Humanity whereinto we, its living members, are vitally made one. Incomparable interchange of life! From her, the flesh and blood; for her, His Spirit. And He in us, as He from her; we all, one perfect family.

Interchange of Life! Link up two passages of St. John's Apocalypse. To the victorious soul is given a white tessera, a badge to be worn; and on it is graven a "New Name," that no one knows save He who gives it, and he who shall receive it. In much of that time's mystical thought, the *name* went closely with the *self*; to the inner self belonged a secret name; he who had control over that name could rule the whole essence of its owner. To the Christian, Christ gives a new self, a super-nature self, participation in His own self; His Life is communicated to him. But later on, Christ speaks of His faithful as pillars in-builded into that Temple which is Himself, that New Jerusalem made of living stones, His ransomed, alive through Him;

and on each pillar is inscribed the Name of God, for full of God's life indeed that Temple is; and the Name of God's new City, that is, the consummated world, and the world's crown, the Church; and last, "My own New Name." Profound and terrible truth! As we, without Him, were nothing, so He is meaningless, without ourselves; we give Him a new extension in His Humanity; Christ is yet, through us, to be "formed"; St. Paul dares to say he fills up, in his own body, what was lacking in Christ's sufferings. . . . We *give* to Him . . . communion is reciprocal: *we* spread the feast. He knocks, He enters; "and I will eat with him, and he with Me." "I live, no longer I, but Christ *lives* in me." "Master, where dwellest Thou?" "In thee, beloved; and thou in Me."

I would not dare to write more about that union with God, Source of eternal life, which makes the essence of our heaven—for it is because of that, that we have the rest—were it not that our Lord Himself, in the tenderest and most human chapters of the Fourth Gospel, *wills* us to think upon that Mystery. Catholic Theology has ever written with humble daring upon the Beatific Vision, by which we see God no more "as in a mirror, dimly, but face to face," when "I shall know even as I am known."[1] No substantial absorption nor transformation into God in this: the soul remains distinct: yet is that Vision immediate, intuitive; we know God, though even so we do not comprehend Him. Yet ever remains that truth, that in the richest unity there are differences. All but begging for forgiveness from the God we scrutinize, we remind ourselves that His Unity, whereof all lower unities are shadows, is also Trinity. Therefore, though utterly ourselves shall we for ever be, yet shall we not fear to acknowledge, as the Church bids us to, and as Christ prayed for us, we shall be "in one" with God. "Believe for my works' sake," said Christ, "that I am in the Father, and the Father in Me." But, "The works that I do, he too shall do, who in Me believeth."

[1] "We all, beholding the glory of the Lord with open face, are transformed into the same image from glory to glory, as by the spirit of the Lord" (2 Cor. ii. 18).

"We now see as in a mirror, dimly; but then, face to face: now I know in part; but then I shall know even as I am known" (1 Cor. xiii. 12).

"We shall be co-heirs with Christ, receiving the consummation of our supernatural adoption as His sons" (cf. Gal. iv. 7; Eph. ii. 19).

"To him who conquers, I will grant to sit upon My throne, even as I have conquered and did sit down with My Father upon His throne" (Apoc. iii. 17).

"Beloved, we are now (already) sons of God, and it hath not yet appeared what we shall be. We know that when it shall have appeared, we shall be like unto Him, because we shall see Him as He is" (1 John iii. 2).

"All that is Mine is Thine, and Thine is Mine, and in *them* have I found my glory . . . and I ask that all they may be One, as Thou Father art in Me, and I in Thee, so they may be in Us . . . and the Glory Thou hast given Me, I have given them, that they may be one even as We are one, Thou in Me and I in Thee that they may be perfected into One . . . that the Love wherewith Thou hast loved Me, be in them, and I in them."

Dulcis hospes animæ: better than soul's dearest Guest is that Spirit who is God's Love: for ever He resides in the soul, *inhabits* it: the Water that "goes softly" forth from New Jerusalem, making God's city glad; the River that steals out from the throne of God and of the Lamb, and causes to spring up along its banks that Grove of Life whose very leaves are for the healing of the nations, and its fruits are living souls—that Water of Life is not only poured into man's spirit, but springs up thereform into a fountain, giving refreshment to all on whom its spray shall fall, and in the spray God's rainbow.

To such a state, then, death admits us. Death is dawn; through it, we pass into new worlds. Expansion, full freedom, richest activity, true selfhood. One at last with nature; alive with super-nature; united through the Church, united into Christ; one Vine, one Bread, one Christ. And with God, through Christ, "in whom, O God, with Thee is all our nature."

To this heaven, then, the Catholic is bidden move, through Him who is both Goal and Way, and all the while is Life.

Per Tuas semitas
Duc nos quo tendimus
Ad Lucem quam inhabitas.

INDEX